William Shakespeare

The Tragedy of

ANTONY AND CLEOPATRA

WILLIAM SHAKESPEARE

The Tragedy of

ANTONY AND CLEOPATRA

Edited, with Introduction and Notes, by
JAN H. BLITS

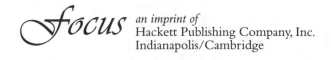
focus an imprint of
Hackett Publishing Company, Inc.
Indianapolis/Cambridge

A Focus book

Focus an imprint of
Hackett Publishing Company

Copyright © 2019 by Hackett Publishing Company, Inc.

22 21 20 19   1 2 3 4 5 6 7

For further information, please address
Hackett Publishing Company, Inc.
P.O. Box 44937
Indianapolis, Indiana 46244-0937

www.hackettpublishing.com

Cover design by Brian Rak
Interior design by Laura Clark
Composition by Aptara, Inc.

Cover painting: © Zsolt Horvath/Shutterstock

Library of Congress Cataloging-in-Publication Data

Names: Shakespeare, William, 1564–1616, author. | Blits, Jan H., editor,
  writer of introduction, writer of added commentary.
Title: The tragedy of Antony and Cleopatra / William Shakespeare ; edited,
  with introduction and notes, by Jan H. Blits.
Other titles: Antony and Cleopatra
Description: Indianapolis, Indiana : Focus, an imprint of Hackett Publishing
  Company, [2019] | Includes bibliographical references and index.
Identifiers: LCCN 2019010463 | ISBN 9781585109340 (paperback)
Subjects: LCSH: Cleopatra, Queen of Egypt, –30 B.C.—Drama. | Antonius,
  Marcus, 83 B.C.?–30 B.C.—Drama. | Generals—Rome—Drama. |
  Queens—Egypt—Drama. | Rome—History—Civil War, 43-31 B.C.—Drama. |
  Egypt—History—332-30 B.C.—Drama.
Classification: LCC PR2802.A2 B56 2019 | DDC 822.3/3—dc23
LC record available at https://lccn.loc.gov/2019010463

∞

In memory of
Mera J. Flaumenhaft

CONTENTS

PREFACE

This volume is the second in the Hackett series of editions of Shakespeare's Roman plays that provide extensive historical annotations and explanations. Other editions of the plays minimize or tacitly deny Shakespeare's interest in or understanding of ancient Rome. Shakespeare, in their view, borrowed materials—plots, characters, and subject matters—from ancient sources, particularly from Plutarch's *Lives*, but understood the source material in the light of the concerns and values of Elizabethan-Jacobean England. Although nominally about Rome, the plays reflect not Rome or the Roman world but the moral attitudes, cultural values, social circumstances, intellectual environment, and political conditions of Shakespeare's own world. According to these editions, they are, in effect, Renaissance plays, not Roman plays.

Some editors (as well as critics) suppose that Shakespeare was too busy as a man of the theater and productive playwright to have had the time to read widely or to think deeply on the subject of his Roman plays. He therefore drew his understanding of Rome from traditions widely held in Elizabethan London.[1] Other editors (and critics), embracing the principles of "historicism," assume that Shakespeare was essentially the product of his time, embedded in the moment in which he lived. Even had he tried, he could not have understood the Romans as the Romans understood themselves. Like all other writers of the time, he could understand them only through a Renaissance perspective. Where the first group of editors assumes that Shakespeare could not escape the workaday demands of his profession, the second takes for granted that he could not escape the intellectual spirit or social context of his time. Shakespeare's Roman plays, consequently, can teach us nothing significant about ancient Rome.[2]

Blinded by their own parochial professional presuppositions, Shakespeareans commonly blind their readers to the sum and substance of Shakespeare's Roman plays. They avoid analyzing the plays in the context of Rome's political history and culture, because they consider such material irrelevant. Instead, they impose what is professionally familiar

---

1. See, for example, T. S. Eliot's general criticism, Introduction to G. W. Knight's *Wheel of Fire* (London: Methuen, 1930), xiv.

2. For a fuller discussion of these approaches, see the Preface to my edition of *Julius Caesar*.

to them—Elizabethan-Jacobean England—on the unfamiliar world of ancient Rome. Historicism drives out history.

The editors' reliance on Plutarch is no exception. Editors, to be sure, frequently turn to Plutarch's *Lives*. But they limit their attention to Thomas North's Elizabethan translation (1579) and confine their focus to the similarities and possible sources of Shakespeare's language, as they do, as well, with Elizabethan writers other than North on the subject. This is especially true of editions of *Antony and Cleopatra*, which is rich in the language of North's translation of the *Life of Antony*. The editors concentrate on Shakespeare's manner of dramatizing or poeticizing Plutarch's prose narrative, such as in Enobarbus' wonderful description of Cleopatra on her extraordinary barge. While seeking the influence of Shakespeare's contemporaries, they pay no attention to the significance of what he actually wrote. Like students of Michelangelo who focus on the marble quarries in Carrara and Pietrasanta but ignore his completed statues, they are interested in the materials of his workshop, not in the fully realized thoughts of his mind.

This editorial approach results in misdirection or sheer omission on nearly every important point. One small example is illustrative of the problem. When Antony dies, Cleopatra laments, "The soldier's pole is fallen" (4.15.67). Editors struggle to find a plausible meaning of this line. The New Cambridge editor, David Bevington, for instance, suggests that Shakespeare was thinking of the festivities of a medieval or early modern village in which children dance around a pole decked with garlands of flowers.[3] Far from being obscure, however, "The soldier's pole" clearly refers to Roman military ensigns or standards (*signa militaria*), which regulated every movement of every body of troops. As Shakespeare himself emphasizes in *Julius Caesar* (5.3.3–4), an ensign is at once a long pole, suspending a banner, with an eagle at the top, and the brave warrior who holds it and leads his cohort in battle. Originally devised by Romulus (Plutarch, *Romulus*, 8.6), the soldier's pole was sacrosanct and revered in Rome (Dio Cassius, *Roman History*, 40.18).[4] Romans fought wars to recoup captured standards. Antony, in fact, began his Parthian campaign in 36 BC[5] by demanding the return of the standards that Crassus had

---

3. David Bevington, ed., *Antony and Cleopatra* (Cambridge: Cambridge University Press, 2005), 241, citing K. Deighton. See also Barbara A. Mowat and Paul Werstine, eds., *Antony and Cleopatra*, Folger Shakespeare Library (New York: Simon and Schuster, 1999), 284; A. R. Braunmuller, ed., *Antony and Cleopatra*, The Pelican Shakespeare (New York: Penguin Books, 2017), 119.

4. Hereafter cited as Dio.

5. All dates are BC unless otherwise noted.

lost seventeen years earlier (Plutarch, *Antony*, 37.2), and Augustus Caesar finally gains their return in 20 (Suetonius, *Augustus*, 21.3). Anyone who knows Roman history, particularly the history of Rome during the events of *Antony and Cleopatra*, would recognize what Cleopatra means. To confuse the celebrated sign of Rome's martial activity with boys and girls dancing around a maypole seems both risible and a caution to readers.

The complicated dramatic action in *Antony and Cleopatra* heightens the value of guidance on Rome's political and cultural history. The play depicts the epoch-making transition from the aftermath of the Roman Republic to the establishment of Imperial Rome and, more broadly, from the end of the ancient pagan world to the rise of Christianity. To understand the transition, a reader must be aware of what Rome has been, what it no longer is, and what it is becoming. Past, present, and future are essential to Shakespeare's drama. The transition, furthermore, occurs on various levels—personal, political, social, and others—at the same time. The play's plot, characters, settings, structure, allusions, tensions, puzzles, and more depend crucially on the context in which history has set them. Neither the vices of Mark Antony nor the virtues of Octavius Caesar, for example, would be found among Rome's early leaders. Readers must therefore have access to the pertinent political and cultural history if they are to understand the play.

Most generally, readers should at least be open to the possibility that Shakespeare has an understanding from which they may learn. They should reject the historicist reduction of Shakespeare's thought to the conventional understanding of his day. And putting aside any presumption of the superior wisdom of our own day, they should avoid the imposition of any post-structural or postmodern literary theory on his play. They should try, instead, to get out of the play the substance that Shakespeare deliberately put into it. Respectful receptivity is needed.

This edition is written for both general readers and Shakespeare scholars. It is meant to be helpful to both. With a handful of exceptions, I have omitted references to secondary works, including my own, in order to focus on Shakespeare's sources. Since events in the play span the world from Europe to the Euphrates, I have included maps to assist the reader. And since the play includes or alludes to events covering much of the first century BC, I have also included a timeline of relevant dates.[6]

---

6. For an act-by-act, scene-by-scene, and sometimes line-by-line interpretation of the play, from which some of these annotations, explanations, and references are drawn, see my *New Heaven, New Earth: Shakespeare's "Antony and Cleopatra"* (Lanham: Lexington Books, 2009).

INTRODUCTION

Shakespeare presents the tragic love story of Antony and Cleopatra within the historical context of passage from the pagan to the Christian world—from the aftermath of the collapse of the Roman Republic and the decline of the pagan gods to the emergence of the Roman Empire and the conditions giving rise to Christianity. Under the Republic, Rome conquered nearly the entire known world. Its empire ranged from Britain, Spain, and Gaul to North Africa, Asia, and the Middle East. At the start of the play, only the Parthians remain a serious foreign threat to Rome, and Ventidius soon crushes them (3.1.34–35). With the Parthians' defeat, Rome's centuries of foreign wars come to a triumphant conclusion. But in conquering the world, Rome has also destroyed its republican regime and its distinctive way of life. By the time of *Antony and Cleopatra*, Rome's greatness has destroyed what made Rome great.

Life in republican Rome had been rooted in the soil of its territory, the traditions of its people, and the worship of its gods. Rome's conquests, however, have extended Rome's boundaries to the boundaries of the world—"from edge to edge / O'th' world" (2.2.122–23). "All other lands have certain limits given," the Roman poet Ovid writes. "Our Rome with all the world's wide room is even" (Ovid, *Fasti*, 2.683–84).[1] The early Romans built the city's walls wider than they needed in order "to provide . . . for a future multitude in time to come" (Livy, *History of Rome*, 1.8.4).[2] Now its walls encompass virtually all the enemies that Rome has conquered. With its enormous expansion, Rome's republican traditions, although often persisting in name, have fallen into utter disuse. Sextus Pompey, the only character in the play claiming to champion the republican cause, addresses Antony, Caesar, and Lepidus as "[t]he senators alone of this great world" (2.6.9). He greets "the triumvirate" (3.6.29) with the title of members of the office which they have displaced.

---

1. Ovid, *Ovid's Festivals or Roman Calendar*, trans. John Gower (London: University of Cambridge, 1640), 41. "[T]he greatest glory of all glories in [Pompey the Great] was . . . that whereas Asia when he received it was the utmost frontier province and limit of the Roman Empire, he left the same in the very heart and mids thereof" (Pliny the Elder, *Natural History*, 7.99; trans. Philemon Holland [London: Adam Islip, 1601], 169). Where needed, the spelling and punctuation of early translations have been modernized, including some titles.

2. Livy, *The Roman History*, trans. Philemon Holland (1600) (London: Gabriel Bedell, 1659), 6.

Because Rome is now a worldwide empire, the gods, which for centuries were thought to protect the city as a separate political community and which inspired its martial way of life, lose their significance and strength. "[T]he god Hercules, whom Antony loved, / Now leaves him" (4.3.21–22). After Cleopatra wishfully and woefully invokes Juno, Mercury, and Jove as Antony lies dying (4.15.35–37), only two pagan gods are named. Cleopatra in her next breath rails against Fortune for Antony's death (4.15.45–47), and Charmian, bidding the dead Cleopatra farewell, sees her death as dimming Phoebus' visible splendor (5.2.315–17). A world in which one man has become "[t]he universal landlord," "[s]ole sir o'th' world" (3.13.76, 5.2.119), has no need for gods who support political freedom, warlike action, or earthly glory. A world of "universal peace" (4.6.5) needs a universal god of peace—a god supporting the habits of humility, submission, and patience, not of pride, strength, and action.

The Roman Republic had engaged its citizens in every aspect of their lives. The city's activities and concerns were those of its citizens. Rome's republican regime thus rested on the subordination of private goods to the public good. As Shakespeare shows in *Coriolanus*, Rome's early republicans thought a citizen's highest private good is attached to the city's public good. "If my son were my husband," Volumnia declares, "I should freelier rejoice in that absence wherein he won honor, than in the embracements of his bed, where he would show most love" (*Cor.*, 1.3.2–5).[3] Cominius goes further. "I do love / My country's good," he affirms,

> with a respect more tender,
> More holy and profound, than mine own life,
> My dear wife's estimate, her womb's increase
> And treasure of my loins.
> (*Cor.*, 3.3.110–14)

Where the Roman mother finds the city's honor superior to a lover's embrace, the one-time consul places no private good whatever above the city's good. The public good is superior to even the most precious private goods.

Rome's vast empire, however, has liberated private interests in Rome. The more spacious Rome's empire has grown, the more narrow the Romans' concerns have become. Universalism frees the private. Unlike in *Coriolanus* and even in *Julius Caesar*, in *Antony and Cleopatra* the word "Rome" always refers simply to a location, never to a political

---

3. All references to *Coriolanus* are to the Arden Shakespeare, ed. Peter Holland (London: Bloomsbury, 2013).

regime or a way of life.[4] It lacks political or moral connotations.[5] Reversing the superiority of the public to the private, patriotism is replaced by private interests and personal honor. Romans now think most of all of their own advantage and seldom, if at all, of Rome's.

The absence of public spirit is perhaps nowhere more salient or significant than in the army. During the Republic, Rome's soldiers were its citizens who served their country. They had a country to love, property to protect, and a share of political power to preserve. But with Rome's continual expansion, military campaigns became more prolonged and more remote from Rome. Rome's citizen army could no longer maintain or extend its empire. Noncitizens and even freed slaves needed to be recruited in the most distant provinces. Rome's soldiers thus ceased to be Romans.[6] Nor could Rome's commanders be rotated annually, one consul succeeding another, as had previously been done. Fighting far from home, the generals commanded their armies for extended periods of time—Julius Caesar for ten years in Gaul, for example, and Pompey the Great for six years in Spain and another five in the East. The commanders consequently conquered their own armies as well as their foreign enemies. Recruited and rewarded directly by their commanders, the armies ceased being the armies of Rome and became the private armies of their generals.[7] Rather than conscripted citizens fighting for their country, the soldiers were now mercenaries fighting for plunder and pay, recognizing no authority but that of their commander (see 3.1.31–35). "[N]o man [is] rich," Crassus famously boasted, "that [can] not maintain a whole army with his own proper goods" (Plutarch, *Crassus*, 2.7–8).[8] And just as the soldiers' ties to their commanders became purely private, so did the com-

---

4. Twenty-four of the thirty times the word appears in the play, "Rome" is preceded by prepositions expressing a local relation ("in," "to," "from," "at," "of"). Although the word "city" appears five times, it never refers to Rome. Enobarbus tells of "[t]he city" (Tarsus) casting its people out to see Cleopatra on her barge (2.2.223), Antony thrice refers to Alexandria as "the city" (4.8.8, 36; 4.10.5), and, looking back ruefully on his life, he boasts that he had once "made cities" (4.14.60).

5. The adjective "Roman," on the other hand, retains traditional significance (see 1.2.88; 1.3.85; 1.5.45; 2.6.16; 4.15.59 [twice], 91).

6. See, for example, Cicero, *For Balbus*, 24; Sallust, *Jugurthine War*, 86.2; Plutarch, *Marius*, 9.1; Suetonius, *Augustus*, 16.1; Gellius, *Attic Nights*, 16.10.10–15. On the earlier practice, see Polybius, *Histories*, 6.19.

7. See, for example, Cicero, *Philippics*, 10.12; Appian, *Civil Wars*, 4.93, 98. It was from Gaul that Caesar set out to cross the Rubicon (Caesar, *The Civil War*, 1.7–8).

8. *Plutarch's Lives*, The Tudor Translations, trans. Thomas North, 8 vols. (1579; rpt. London: David Nutt, 1895), 4:46, cited as Tudor. References to North's translations

manders' own aims. The generals now fought "for Rome" only in a quib-
bling sense. Instead of fighting to protect or to augment Rome, they now
fought to obtain it. Rome itself became the prize of civil wars rather than
the beneficiary of foreign wars.

Desertions are quite common in *Antony and Cleopatra*. Among others,
Menas deserts Pompey; Canidius, Enobarbus, Alexas, and Dercetus desert
Antony, as do his sailors, foot soldiers, and cavalry. Romans behave not like
fellow citizens, but like foreigners pursuing their own interests: "To Caesar
will I render / My legions and my horse. Six kings already / Show me the
way of yielding" (3.10.33–35). With all command now purely personal
and the only links between a commander and his troops ones of personal
interest, loyalty has become a matter of the soldier's own choice. Just as
men are no longer obliged to be soldiers, soldiers can switch their loyalties
as they choose.[9] Because all causes are alike and everyone is fighting only
for himself and only for the sake of his commander's private inducements,
the moral difference between loyalty and desertion largely disappears.
Rather than abandoning friend for foe, desertion now amounts to changing like for like. Indeed, where desertion was formerly unpardonable in
Rome, it not only has lost its deep opprobrium but is now handsomely
rewarded.[10]

The structure of *Antony and Cleopatra* reflects the joint ascendancy
of the universal and the private. Scenes are set not just in Italy and Egypt
but in Greece and Syria, and the play's most famous speech describes
Cleopatra in Asia Minor (2.2.201–36). In almost every scene, messengers
arrive or leave, crisscrossing "all the world," "the whole world," "this great
world."[11] On the other hand, none of the scenes in Rome occurs in public. In sharp contrast to *Coriolanus* and *Julius Caesar*, both of which begin
with scenes of civil strife in the streets of Rome,[12] the Roman scenes take
place indoors and in private rather than in the streets, the Capitol, or any

---

of the life of Antony are to T. J. B. Spencer, ed., *Shakespeare's Plutarch* (Penguin
Books, 1968), cited as Spencer.

9. See, for example, Caesar, *Gallic War*, 1.39–41; Plutarch, *Sulla*, 25.1, 28.1–3,
Lucullus, 7.1–2, 33–35; Appian, 1.85, 89–90, 112; 2.47; Dio, 36.14–16, 47.2, 41.26.1.

10. Appian, 5.17. Cp., for example, Polybius, 11.25–30; Livy, 28.24–29; also Veget-
ius, *Epitome of Military Science*, 3.4.

11. 2.6.9; 2.7.62, 63, 66; 4.14.87; 5.1.40; 5.2.133. The word "world" occurs forty-
four times in the play, far more often than in any other Shakespeare play.

12. Likewise, in *The Rape of Lucrece* Brutus carries Lucrece's body through the
streets of Rome to replace the kings with consuls (*Lucrece*, 1828–55).

other public setting.[13] With a single exception (which confirms the rule), the only streets mentioned are in Egypt.[14] The Capitol, the only public building in Rome named, is spoken of only in the context of Rome's historic past (2.6.18).

The common people, whose participation in Rome's political life was central to the Republic, are, likewise, mostly missing from *Antony and Cleopatra*. They are mentioned but never seen or directly heard. Only Pompey counts on them for support (2.1.9), and he is disappointed. All the leaders, including Pompey himself, have nothing but contempt for or bitter indignation at the people's fickleness. And all but Pompey seem more concerned about avoiding their opposition or directing it against others than gaining their backing. The people have lost their great political importance, not because they are fickle—they have always been a "many-headed multitude" (*Cor.*, 2.3.15–16)—but because Rome's centuries-old clash between plebeians and patricians is now over, succeeded by armed conflict among its victorious generals. Paradoxically, the people lost their political power with their victory over their centuries-old enemy. Once the people defeated the nobles, their champions—the party of Caesar—no longer needed them and consequently dispensed with them.

As the people are missing, so, too, is political oratory. Political oratory, critical to events in *Coriolanus* and *Julius Caesar*,[15] comes to an end in Rome with the end of the Republic. Where there is no political freedom or public deliberations, there is no use for political oratory. It surely is no accident that Shakespeare makes Antony's funeral oration, which leads directly to the ouster of the republicans from Rome, the final political oration in Rome. With the end of the Republic, "a hush fell upon

---

13. The one Roman scene set (presumably) out of doors (2.4) is a private meeting. The scene's stage-designation, "*a street*," which can be found in this and some other editions, comes not from the Folio, but from Edward Capell, *Comedies, Histories, & Tragedies*, 10 vols. (London: J. and R. Tonson, 1768; rpt. New York: AMS Press, 1968), 8:35.

14. 1.1.54, 1.4.20, 2.2.239, 4.3.3. The exception, whose location is universal or indefinite, is that Caesar, hearing of Antony's death, speaks of the failure of "[t]he round world" to shake lions "into civil streets / And citizens to their dens" (5.1.15–17). That is also the play's sole mention of "citizen." Although Caesar's complaint about Octavia's unobtrusive return to Rome (3.6.43–51), and Antony's and Cleopatra's warnings of Caesar's triumph in Rome, clearly allude to Rome's streets (4.12.33–37; 5.2.54–56, 208–14), they do not mention them.

15. For its role in founding the Republic, see *Lucrece*, Argument 31–36, 1818–55.

[political] eloquence" (Tacitus, *Dialogue on Orators*, 38).[16] While the leaders are fighting over who should be the people's master, the people, if
engaged at all, are now fighting over whose slaves they should be.[17]

The reduction of the public to the private deprives political action
of its noble character. Actions are only as noble as the cause they serve.
Courage alone does not make a deed noble. When an action serves no
good higher than one's own private good, it can be considered noble
only in a sharply diminished sense. This seems especially true in Rome.
While for the Greeks "the noble" (*to kalon*) implies the beautiful, the fine,
the admirable, for the Romans it has always signified the decorous. "[The
noble] may be named decorum in Latin, for in Greek it is called *prepon*
[seemliness]" (Cicero, *On Duties*, 1.93).[18] Where the Greek understanding
of the noble points to what is higher than or beyond the political realm,
the Roman understanding is inseparable from the supremacy and com-
pleteness of political life. It presupposes a way of life in which the city sets
a roof on the noble.[19]

But just as the word "decorum" is spoken in the play only by
Egyptians and only in un-Roman contexts (1.2.75–76, 5.2.17–18), the
word "noble" is used mostly in an un-Roman fashion. While characters
are frequently described or addressed as "noble," often by servants, subordinates, and the obsequious Lepidus, few deeds are called "noble." Antony
defiantly describes his and Cleopatra's loving embrace as "[t]he nobleness
of life" (1.1.37–38). Lepidus fawningly characterizes Antony's apology to
Caesar as "noble spoken" (2.2.104). And Thidias, reducing the noble to the
expedient, cynically advises Cleopatra that surrendering to Caesar would
be her "noblest course" (3.13.82). Apart from these instances of eros, servility, and surrender, nearly the only deeds that anyone calls "noble" are

---

16. Political speech is replaced by personal encomium, delivered in private (for
example, *JC*, 5.3.98–103, 5.5.69–76; *A&C*, 1.4.56–72, 2.2.200–250, 5.2.75–99).
All references to *Julius Caesar* are to *The Tragedy of Julius Caesar*, ed. Jan H. Blits
(Indianapolis: Hackett Publishing, 2018).

17. Dio, 46.34.4.

18. Cicero, *Marcus Tullius Cicero's Three Books of Duties*, trans. Nicholas Grimald
(1556; rpt. Washington: Folger Books, 1990), 86.

19. The fine arts come very late to Rome, around the turn of the second century
BC. The first poets in Rome, Livius Andronicus and Ennius, are "half-Greeks"
(Suetonius, *On Teachers of Grammar and Rhetoric*, 1) and arrive there more than half
a millennium after Romulus. Where the Greeks are largely formed by Homer,
Roman education consists of prose and, emphasizing precepts, teaches Roman
virtues and traditions chiefly through historical examples. The one idealizes, the
other reifies.

suicides.[20] Pointing up the problem of performing noble actions in post-republican Rome, Enobarbus and Menas jokingly acknowledge that while one of them is "a great thief by sea," the other is a great thief "by land." The men are indistinguishably "two thieves" (2.6.93–98). In the absence of a public good, the moral difference between a Roman officer and a notorious pirate vanishes.

The decline of noble deeds goes together with the rise of Fortune. Throughout the play, we hear of Fortune rather than virtue ruling human affairs.[21] As Caesar and Antony win victories through their subordinates (3.1.16–17), their subordinates, in turn, win advancement through flattery and favor.[22] Fortune's supremacy lessens even the greatest political achievement. "'Tis paltry to be Caesar," Cleopatra contemptuously declares. "Not being Fortune, he's but Fortune's knave, / A minister of her will" (5.2.2–4). Even supreme political glory deserves to be despised, for it depends not on the victor but on his good fortune.[23] Owing to the increased role of Fortune and the reduced possibility of noble action, some Romans surrender themselves to luxury and sensual pleasure, while others (as we see in *Julius Caesar*) seek refuge in Stoic and Epicurean

---

20. 4.14.61, 96–100; 4.15.90; 5.2.191, 236, 284, 343. Once Antony, the "[n]oblest of men" (4.15.61), dies, "noble," in effect unmanned, is spoken all but once to, by, or about women. See, further, 5.2.191n. Caesar and his subordinates seldom mention "noble" or its derivatives, and almost always disingenuously. Apart from his oxymoronic exclamation "O noble weakness!" at the suicides of Cleopatra and Charmian (5.2.343), Caesar mentions "noble" only in saying farewell to Antony when he leaves with Octavia (3.2.27); Agrippa, sarcastically, describing Lepidus (3.2.6); and Thidias and Proculeius, each trying to convince Cleopatra to surrender (3.13.82, 5.2.44). Octavia, on the other hand, lovingly calls Caesar "My noble brother" (3.2.42), and Dolabella similarly calls Cleopatra "Most noble empress" (5.2.70).

21. "Fortune" is mentioned in *Antony and Cleopatra* far more than in any other Shakespeare play.

22. "*Antony and Cleopatra* is the only one of Shakespeare's three principal Roman plays where the battles are narrated, not represented. Shakespeare confines battles to reports of action, and thus intensifies the feeling that the Roman concept of Antony's *virtus* belongs to the past, while in the present he subverts the Roman concept of *virtus* by his behaviour" (Krystyna Kujawinska-Courtney, *"Th' Interpretation of the Time": The Dramatury of Shakespeare's Roman Plays* [Victoria: English Literary Studies, 1993], 73).

23. Caesar himself will "ascrib[e] the making of himself as great as he was unto Fortune" (Plutarch, *Fortune of the Romans*, 7 [319e–f]; in *The Philosophy, commonly called, the Morals*, trans. Philemon Holland [London: A. Hatfield, 1603], 632). See, further, 5.2.2–4n.

philosophy. Eastern debauchery and Hellenistic philosophies take deep root in late- and post-republican Rome. The one turns men to pleasures of the body; the other, to the tranquility of the mind. While neither necessarily precludes a political life, as Antony on the one hand and Brutus and Cassius on the other show, both new pursuits, by placing happiness in the private sphere, tend to detach a man from the activities and outcomes of political life. Notwithstanding his claims of devotion to Rome's public good, when Brutus dies he is silent about Rome and expresses no lament for its passing. Instead, his last thoughts center on himself, and he judges himself and his life by a standard wholly separate from and even in conflict with the good of Rome: "I shall have glory by this losing day / More than Octavius and Mark Antony / By this vile conquest shall attain unto" (*JC*, 5.5.36–38). Brutus' triumphant "glory" is in no way diminished by his country's "losing day."

Yet, the self-satisfaction of private life soon turns against itself. Again and again, characters in *Antony and Cleopatra* express their deep dissatisfaction at gaining what they had long sought. "And what they undid did" applies not only to the pretty dimpled boys fanning Cleopatra's checks (2.2.215) but to nearly everyone in the play. Actions continually undermine and defeat themselves. Caesar complains that the people love the man they do not have until they have him and then no longer want him. "[H]e which is," he says, "was wished until he were, / And the ebbed man, ne'er loved till ne'er worth love, / Comes deared by being lacked" (1.4.42–44). Ventidius chooses not to pursue the Parthians back to Mesopotamia for fear of offending Antony, in whose name he would win the great victory. "[A]mbition, / The soldier's virtue," he explains,

> rather makes choice of loss
> Than gain which darkens him.
> I could do more to do Antonius good,
> But 'twould offend him. And in his offence
> Should my performance perish.
>
> (3.1.22–27)

For Ventidius to accomplish more in order to do his commander good would be to harm his own good and destroy his action. His doing would be his undoing. And Antony, who, much like Caesar, claims that the people's "love is never linked to the deserver / Till his deserts are past" (1.2.193–94), says the same about his own love: "What our contempts doth often hurl from us, / We wish it ours again" (1.2.130–31). Hence, Fulvia, whose death he "did . . . desire," is "good, being gone. / The hand could pluck her back that shoved her on" (1.2.129, 133–34). We desire what we do not have until we have it, and reject what we have until we no longer have it. Our desires resist satisfaction: "What willingly he did confound he wailed"; "And strange it is / That nature must compel us to lament / Our most persisted deeds" (3.2.58, 5.1.28–30). Accordingly, Antony, although declaring that "not a minute of our lives should stretch / Without some pleasure now" (1.1.47–48), finds that constant pleasure turns into displeasure. "The present pleasure, / By revolution lowering, does become / The opposite of itself" (1.2.131–33). A constant pleasure, by cloying or palling, becomes its own opposite. Turning unpleasant and causing us to desire something else, it is lowered in our estimation and replaced in our desire. Satisfaction, canceling itself, becomes dissatisfaction.

The prospects regarding death are even more disturbing. Citizens of the Republic thought of themselves, first and foremost, as Romans. The city was primary, and they as individuals were secondary. Identifying themselves with their city, Romans were born, lived, and died as Romans, not simply as human beings. Related to the city as parts to whole, they depended on the city for their being, while the city depended on them and their conduct for its continued existence and excellence. A Roman's desire for immortality could therefore find satisfaction in the continuation of Rome, for Rome bore the traces of his deeds and would retain his memory as long as it existed: "our renown Rome, whose gratitude / Towards her deserved children is enroll'd / In Jove's own book" (*Cor.*, 3.1.292–94). In dying for his country, a Roman gained his immortality. Seeing himself fundamentally as a member of the city's community, he needed no immortality other than his city's continued existence.[24]

Worldwide empire puts an end to this hope. Rome has ceased to be a city or a community. As Shakespeare shows, Romans now include men with such non-Roman names as Demetrius, Philo, Alexas, Eros, and Dercetus. "Roman," no longer a term of distinction, has become a term of inclusion. If men are still parts of a whole, that whole is now the entire world or even the cosmos itself. Men are therefore forced to think differently of death. As the supremacy of the public gives way to the ubiquity of the private, men become unable to think of themselves as living on through their city. Their concern for immortality remains. If anything, it becomes more troubling. But men are now compelled to seek their immortality as individuals rather than as citizens. Having become atomized subjects of a universal empire, they must find their immortality within themselves. Immortality, like everything else, becomes radically private. If formerly a Roman's immortality lay in the immortality of his country, it now comes to lie in that of his soul. Reversing the classical relation of a man and his country, the purely personal supplants the political.

---

24. See, for example, Cicero, *On Old Age*, 6.18–19.

The salvation of one's soul replaces the salvation of one's country. The next world replaces this one.

Antony concludes his initial exchange with Cleopatra by saying that she would need to find "new heaven, new earth" to contain his love (1.1.17). His remark is the first of the play's numerous allusions to the New Testament and, particularly, to the Book of Revelation: "And I saw a new heaven and a new earth: for the first heaven and the first earth were passed away" (Rev. 21:1).[25] Rome's universal empire brings forth a new heaven as it establishes a new earth.[26] While the empire does away with the need for gods who work through the city and provide for men by providing for their city, Christianity, speaking to all men everywhere, teaches that God has a direct, immediate relation with every person in the world individually. Related to private individuals rather than to political communities, the new religion is at once particular and universal. Its new heaven mirrors the new earth.[27]

By conquering the world, Rome's principle of war produces a religion of peace. The principle of war teaches men to love their fellow citizens and hate their country's enemies. But now that all of Rome's enemies have become Romans, there are no enemies left to hate, and so all of mankind must be loved.

> God . . . requires and rewards a benevolence that makes no distinctions between persons. . . . For to wish evil, to do evil, to speak evil, to think evil of any—are all equally forbidden to us.
>
> (Tertullian, *Apology*, 36.3–4)

Dolabella, a Roman officer, will thus speak of swearing by a "command," which his "love makes religion to obey" (5.2.197–98). An empire won by arms, paradoxically, ushers in a religion based on peace, whose "first and great commandment" is love (Matt. 22:37–39).

---

25. All quotations from the Bible are from *The Geneva Bible* (Geneva: Rovland Hall, 1560; rpt.: Madison: University of Wisconsin Press, 1969). See Ethel Seaton, "*Antony and Cleopatra* and the Book of Revelation," *Review of English Studies*, 22 (1946), 219–24.

26. "But (now), two great Powers sprung fully up, as (it were) out of one stream; and they gave peace to all, and brought all together to a state of friendship: (namely) the Roman Empire, which, from that time, appeared (as) one kingdom; and, the Power of the Saviour of all, whose aid was at once extended to, and established with, every one" (Eusebius, *Theophania*, 3.2). Also Augustine, *The City of God*, 5.12.15ff.; Orosius, *Seven Books of History against the Pagans*, 3.8, 6.22; Dante, *Convivio*, 4.5.

27. 1 Corinthians 15:22; 1 Timothy 2:4–6.

Antony, bored with Roman life, is drawn to the East: "I'th' East my pleasure lies" (2.3.39). Egypt is an exotic world of extravagance and sensuality. It is the opposite of what austere republican Rome had been. The East is also the source of Christianity: "Let me have a child . . . to whom Herod of Jewry may do homage" (1.2.29–30; cp. Matt. 2:8). The East represents both sensuality and spirituality. Charmian hails the dying Cleopatra, "O eastern star!" (5.2.307). The eastern star is, at once, Venus, the morning star, named for the goddess of love, and the star signifying the birth of Jesus:

> When Jesus then was born at Bethlehem in Judea in the days of Herod the King, behold, there came Wisemen from the East to Jerusalem, saying, "Where is the King of the Jews that is born? For we have seen his star in the East and are come to worship him."
>
> (Matt. 2:1–2)

Cleopatra, the "eastern star," gives up her voluptuary pleasures (5.2.281) and faces death filled with "[i]mmortal longings" (5.2.280), believing that she will find "[a] better life" in death (5.2.2). And both she and Antony imagine having a transcendent marriage in death reminiscent of the New Testament's apocalyptic marriage. Where John saw "the holy city, new Jerusalem, come . . . out of heaven, prepared as a bride trimmed for her husband" (Rev. 21:2), Antony and Cleopatra echo John's vision in envisioning their own deaths, he as the groom ("I will be / A bridegroom in my death and run into't / As to a lover's bed" [4.14.100–102]), she as the bride or the holy city itself ("Husband, I come!" [5.2.286]).[28]

Shakespeare brings out the significance of this transformation. Both Antony and Cleopatra abandon sensuality and seek proud Roman deaths. He in his last breath insists that he dies "a Roman by a Roman / Valiantly vanquished" (4.15.59–60), and she then aims to do "what's brave, what's noble," and kill herself "after the high Roman fashion" (4.15.90–91). But as death seems to offer a better life, Roman spiritedness turns against itself and becomes spiritualized. "I am fire and air; my other elements / I give to baser life," Cleopatra announces, renouncing all worldly life as base (5.2.288–89). Spiritedness, which has always animated and shaped republican Romans and Roman actions, rests on a fundamental distinction between the high and the low, the noble and the base. But with the victory of Augustus Caesar and Imperial Rome, nothing can any longer distinguish the splendid from the obscure, the excellent from the ordinary.

---

28. Jesus is born during the rule of Octavius Caesar (later named Augustus). See 4.6.5n.

"The odds is gone / And there is nothing left remarkable / Beneath the visiting moon" (4.15.68–70). By fulfilling itself, Rome destroys itself. And so, even as the West conquers the East politically, the East conquers the West spiritually. Replacing pride, honor, and victory with humility, abjectness and suffering as the highest good, pagan spirit, finally directed inward and against man's worldly nature, becomes Christian spirituality.

NOTE ON THE TEXT

The text for this edition is the First Folio (1623), which has no serious problems and is the play's only authoritative text. Following the same principles that I used in my edition of *Julius Caesar*, I have modernized the Folio's spellings and punctuation, and corrected the misspellings of some proper names: for example, Ventidius for the Folio's Ventigus, Canidius for the Folio's Camidius, and Sicyon for the Folio's Scicion. Where the Folio differs from North's Plutarch (for example, Enobarbus for North's Aenobarbus, Thidias for North's Thyreus), I have retained the Folio's spelling. General familiarity rather than historical accuracy dictates that choice. Where helpful, I have pointed out spelling changes. In one important instance (5.2.86), I have retained the Folio's reading, contrary to other modern editions. Throughout, I have avoided substantive emendations as unnecessary (and often misleading) editorial conjectures.

I have followed the line numbering of the Arden Edition (third series), edited by John Wilders, and have bracketed stage directions that have been added to the Folio's text.

Note on the Notes

Classical writings have standard numbers identifying various parts (books, chapters, sections, pages, lines, and so on). These numbers remain the same in all editions of the work, whether in the original language or in translation. For example, Plutarch, *Antony*, 65.2, refers to chapter 65, section 2, of Plutarch's life of Antony; Ovid, *Metamorphoses*, 15.832, refers to book 15, line 832 of Ovid's *Metamorphoses*. I follow this traditional numbering. Apart from Elizabethan translations, I have relied largely on Loeb Classical Library, Hackett Classics, and Penguin Classics editions for translations, with occasional modifications for greater accuracy.

TIMELINE

323	Death of Alexander the Great; Ptolemy I takes control of Egypt.
146	Rome conquers Carthage and Greece.
106	Pompey born.
104–100	Marius consul, for five successive terms.
100	Julius Caesar born.
87–82	Civil war between Sulla and Marius.
83	Mark Antony born.
69	Cleopatra born.
67	Pompey drives pirates from the Mediterranean.
63	Octavius Caesar born.
59	First Triumvirate (Julius Caesar, Pompey the Great, Crassus) formed.
55	Ptolemy Auletes (Cleopatra's father) restored to Egyptian throne.
53	Crassus defeated and killed by Parthians at Carrhae.
51	Ptolemy Auletes dies. Cleopatra succeeds him.
50	Cleopatra is forced to accept her brother, Ptolemy XIII, as joint ruler of Egypt.
49–45	Caesar at war with Pompey and his sons.
49	Caesar crosses the Rubicon. Gnaeus Pompey visits Alexandria.
49/48	Cleopatra flees from Egypt and raises an army.
48	Caesar defeats Pompey at the battle of Pharsalus. Pompey murdered in Egypt. Cleopatra becomes sole queen of Egypt.
48–47	Alexandrine War. Caesar and Cleopatra cruise the Nile. Birth of Caesarion.
46	Antony marries Fulvia.
45	Caesar wins war against Pompey's sons in Spain at Munda. Celebrates triumph in Rome.

44	Caesar assassinated. Antony rallies the crowd against the conspirators at Caesar's funeral. Octavius arrives in Rome.
43	Battle of Mutina (Modena). Antony defeated and retreats over the Alps.
43	Second Triumvirate (Antony, Octavius Caesar, Lepidus); start of proscriptions.
42	Antony and Octavius defeat Brutus and Cassius at the battle of Philippi. Brutus and Cassius kill themselves. Antony takes over eastern provinces. Julius Caesar declared a god.
41	Antony meets Cleopatra at Tarsus. They spend winter together in Alexandria. Perusine War, with Lucius Antonius (Antony's brother) and Fulvia against Octavius Caesar.
40	Labienus and Parthians invade and occupy Syria and Asia Minor. Fulvia dies. Antony marries Octavia.
39	Sextus Pompey blockades Italy. The triumvirs make pact with him at Misenum.
38	Ventidius defeats Parthians. Octavius renews conflict with Sextus Pompey.
37	Herod becomes king of Judea.
36	Octavius and Lepidus defeat Sextus Pompey. Pompey flees to Asia, where he is killed by Antony's general. Caesar strips Lepidus of power.
34	Antony conquers Armenia and grants Cleopatra titles and territories.
32	Caesar reads out Antony's will, declares war on Cleopatra.
31	Battle of Actium.
30	Deaths of Antony and Cleopatra. Caesarion executed.
29	Caesar closes doors of the Temple of Janus.
27	Octavius takes the name of Augustus.
c. 5 BC	Jesus born.

The World of *Antony and Cleopatra*

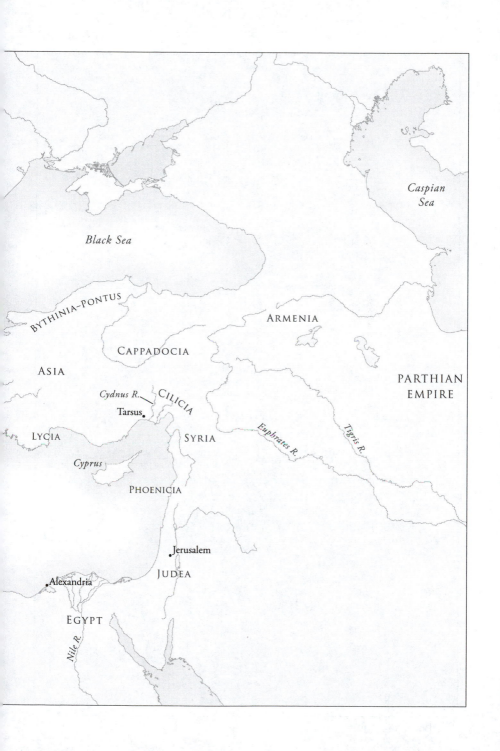

EPIRUS

Toryne

Caesar's camp

Nicopolis

Antony's smaller camp

Gulf of Ambracia

TAURUS

Actium

Antony's camp

ANTONY

AGRIPPA

CLEOPATRA

Anactorium

CAESAR

CANIDIUS

Ionian Sea

ACARNANIA

LEUCAS

The Battle of Actium

LIST OF CHARACTERS

Mark Antony	(Marcus Antonius)	
Octavius Caesar	(Caius Octavius Caesar, later Augustus)	*triumvirs*
Lepidus	(Marcus Aemilius Lepidus)	
Cleopatra	(Cleopatra VII)	*Queen of Egypt*
Charmian		*women attending on Cleopatra*
Iras		
Alexas	(Alexas Laodician)	*Cleopatra's minister*
Mardian		*a eunuch, attending on Cleopatra*
Diomedes	(unknown)	*Cleopatra's servant*
Seleucus		*Cleopatra's treasurer*
Enobarbus	(Gnaeus Domitius Ahenobarbus)	
Ventidius	(Publius Ventidius Bassus)	
Canidius	(Lucius Canidius Crassus)	*Antony's friends and followers*
Scarus	(Marcus Aemilius Scaurus)	
Dercetus	(Dercetaeus)	
Silius		
Eros		
Demetrius		
Philo		
Captain		
Schoolmaster	(Euphronius)	*Antony's ambassador to Caesar*
Agrippa	(Marcus Vipsanius Agrippa)	
Maecenas	(Gaius Maecenas)	
Dolabella	(Publius Cornelius Dolabella)	*Caesar's friends and followers*
Proculeius	(Gaius Proculeius)	
Taurus	(Statilius Taurus)	
Thidias	(or Thyreus)	
Gallus	(Gaius Cornelius Gallus)	
Octavia		*Caesar's sister; later, Antony's wife*
Sextus Pompey	(Sextus Pompeius)	*leading opponent of triumvirs*
Menas	(or Menodorus)	
Menecrates		*Pompey's friends*
Varrius	(uncertain)	
A Soothsayer		
A Clown		

Officers, Soldiers, Messengers, Attendants

ACT ONE, SCENE ONE

[Alexandria, a room in Cleopatra's palace.]

Enter Demetrius and Philo.

Philo: Nay, but this dotage of our general's
O'erflows the measure. Those his goodly eyes,
That o'er the files and musters of the war
Have glowed like plated Mars, now bend, now turn
The office and devotion of their view   5
Upon a tawny front. His captain's heart,
Which in the scuffles of great fights hath burst

S.D. 1. Neither Demetrius nor Philo is a Roman name. Like Cleopatra (literally, "glory of the fatherland" in Greek), both are Greek names with strong Egyptian associations. Philo is the name of the Hellenistic philosopher and political leader of Alexandria's large Jewish community (Eusebius, *Ecclesiastical History*, 2.18). Demetrius is the name of the Macedonian king with whom Plutarch compares Antony's life and against whom Ptolemy I Soter (see 1.1.10n) fought for possession of Egypt (Plutarch, *Demetrius*, 5ff.). Demetrius is also the name of the Peripatetic philosopher, Demetrius Phalereus, who was ousted as ruler of Athens by the former Demetrius and fled to Egypt, where he founded the Library of Alexandria under Ptolemy I (Cicero, *On Ends*, 5.54; Plutarch, *Demetrius*, 8.3–9.2).

1. "dotage": (1) infatuation, (2) folly.

1. "our general's": Antony's (a double genitive).

2. "O'erflows the measure": exceeds the proper limit. Shakespeare shows that virtually everything associated with Egypt "o'erflows the measure," both literally and figuratively. The land in which life depends on "the o'erflowing Nilus" (1.2.51) is a land of excess—of extravagance, exorbitance, luxuriance, prurience, indolence, and magnificence. On the early introduction of luxury and extravagance to Egypt, see Diodorus Siculus, *Library*, 1.45.1; on Egypt's unrivaled wealth, magnificence, and lavishness, see Diodorus, 1.45.4–49.6, 50.1.5–6, 57.45–8.3, 63.2–9, 71.5; on Alexandria, in particular, see Diodorus, 17.52.

3. "files and musters of the war": assembled ranks of troops (nearly synonymous words).

4. "glowed like plated Mars": shined like armored Mars, the Roman god of war. According to legend, Mars is the father of Romulus, the founder and first king of Rome, and was the lover of Venus, the goddess of love (Plutarch, *Romulus*, 4.2; Homer, *Odyssey*, 8.266–369).

5. "office and devotion": devoted service (a hendiadys).

6. "tawny": dark.

6. "front": face.

The buckles on his breast, reneges all temper
And is become the bellows and the fan
To cool a gypsy's lust.

*Flourish. Enter Antony, Cleopatra, her Ladies, the Train,
with Eunuchs fanning her.*

Look where they come.   **10**
Take but good note, and you shall see in him

---

8. "reneges all temper": (1) abandons all temperance or restraint, (2) loses the hardness and resiliency of tempered steel.

10. "To cool": to satisfy (after initially arousing). A bellows heats (a fire) and a fan cools.

10. "gypsy": (1) an Egyptian (gypsies were mistakenly believed to have come from Egypt; their name is a shortened form of "Egyptian"), (2) a slut.

Shakespeare later identifies Cleopatra as a Ptolemy and hence of pure Macedonian blood (1.4.6, 17; 2.7.34; 3.6.15; 3.12.18). The first Ptolemy to rule Egypt, Ptolemy I Soter, was a Macedonian general, who, after the death of Alexander the Great, whose childhood friend and general he had been, seized power in Egypt, in 323 (Pausanias, *Description of Greece*, 1.6.2–4). Ten generations of Ptolemies ruled Egypt before Cleopatra (Strabo, *Geography*, 17.1.11). They have kept their bloodline pure, while at the same time legitimating themselves as Pharaohs, by adopting the ancient Egyptian royal practice of incest (Pausanias, 1.7.1). Cleopatra is in fact the first Ptolemy to speak the Egyptian language (Plutarch, *Antony*, 27.4). Yet to Philo and other Romans, not least of all Antony, Cleopatra is emphatically Egyptian. Even as Rome has conquered the world and made many foreigners Romans—"Rome received [men of all nations] as slaves and sent them out as Romans" (Montesquieu, *Considerations on . . . the Romans*, 13)—Romans, whether in fascination or disgust, often emphasize and sometimes exaggerate the exoticness of foreigners.

S.D. 10. "*Flourish*": a trumpet fanfare announcing the entrance of royalty; "*Train*": retinue.

S.D. 10. "*Eunuchs fanning her*": Egypt is characterized by effeminacy and emasculation as well as by licentiousness. Its extraordinarily long history is one of continual enslavement. In addition to having been subservient to foreign monarchs for most of the last three-quarters of a millennium—Ethiopian (c.715–663), Persian (525–332), Macedonian (332–present)—Egyptians have lived since time immemorial under the absolute rule of divine kings and queens, incarnations of the gods' majesty (Herodotus, *Histories*, 2.142; Diodorus, 1.44.1–4). As a result, they not only pay no attention to political matters, but risk criminal punishment if they attempt to meddle in politics (Diodorus, 1.74.7). They are political eunuchs. Where Roman freedom has always rested on the Romans' sense of their manliness (see, for example, *JC*, 1.3.80–84), Egyptian submission and passivity are at once a cause and a consequence of Egyptian emasculation. While the only Egyptians she listens to are women, Cleopatra surrounds herself with eunuchs as well as with a female court. The eunuchs, viewed by Romans with horror or disgust, represent

The triple pillar of the world transformed
Into a strumpet's fool. Behold and see.

Cleopatra: If it be love indeed, tell me how much.

Antony: There's beggary in the love that can be reckoned.   **15**

Cleopatra: I'll set a bourn how far to be beloved.

Antony: Then must thou needs find out new heaven, new earth.

---

the effeminacy, docility, servility, and impotence of the Egyptian way of life (see, for example, Seneca, *Benefits*, 5.16.6).

12. "triple pillar . . . world": one of the three triumvirs—Antony, Octavius, and Lepidus—who, in 43, divided the rule of the Roman Empire "as if it had been their own inheritance" (Plutarch, *Antony*, 19.1; Spencer 194). Following the defeat of the republicans at Philippi in 42, Antony and Octavius Caesar divided Rome's military and political functions. Antony kept for himself the wealthy and more promising East, to which he was to restore order, while Octavius was given the West and the opprobrious task of settling the veterans in Italy (Appian, 5.3; Dio, 48.1–2; Suetonius, *Augustus*, 13.3). Lepidus, who did not fight at Philippi and was much weaker than either of the other triumvirs, was given a share of power because Octavius feared that he might lead senatorial opposition to him (Appian, 5.12; Dio, 48.3.6). The triumvirs' agreement gave each a portion of the world in which he is to have consular power as well as the power to make or annul laws without consulting the senate or the people, to exercise judicial authority with no right of appeal, and to nominate public officials (Appian, 4.7).

13. "fool": dupe, plaything.

1–13. Although criticizing his excessiveness, Philo adopts Antony's un-Roman, Asiatic style of speech, which, Plutarch says, "was like to his manners and life" (Plutarch, *Antony*, 2.5; Spencer, 175). Asiatic speech is characterized by long, florid sentences amplifying thoughts and words, including the use of redundancy, expansiveness, ornateness, histrionics, listings, and periphrasis for what might have been said directly, and various rhetorical or poetic tropes (Quintilian, *Institutes*, 12.10.16–19).

14. "If it . . . how much": Unless Antony can tell her how much he loves her, he loves her not "indeed," but only in words (cp. 1.5.15–17). Cleopatra begins her first exchange with Antony with the conditional "If." She will often use conditional words and phrases to tease, challenge, contrive, threaten, or promise those she deals with. In this instance, she makes it impossible for Antony to fulfill the stated condition, for he cannot tell her how much he loves her without limiting his love and suggesting that he could love her still more.

15. "There's beggary . . . reckoned": there is extreme poverty in a love that can be measured.

16. "bourn": boundary, limit.

17. "new heaven, new earth": "And I saw a new heaven and a new earth: for the first heaven and the first earth were passed away" (Rev. 21:1). Antony's allusion

Enter a Messenger.

Messenger: News, my good lord, from Rome.

Antony: Grates me, the sum.

Cleopatra: Nay, hear them, Antony.   **20**
Fulvia perchance is angry. Or who knows
If the scarce-bearded Caesar have not sent
His powerful mandate to you: "Do this, or this;
Take in that kingdom, and enfranchise that.
Perform't, or else we damn thee."

Antony: How, my love?   **25**

---

points to the imminent rise of Christianity and to Christianity's immeasurable
spiritual heaven beyond the natural heavens of fixed proportions and the fixed
stars. "[T]he pure in heart . . . [will] ascend to the region of the air, until he
reaches the kingdom of the heavens, passing through the series of those 'abiding
places,'. . . which the Greeks have termed spheres but which the divine scripture
calls heavens" (Origen, *On First Principles*, 2.11.6). Cp. Aristotle, *On the Heavens*,
286b10–11; Cicero, *Republic*, 6.17, with Matt. 25:31–33; 2 Cor. 4:17–5:10; and
Rev. 7, 14, 21.

19. "Grates me, the sum": irritates me, be brief.

20. "them": the news (sometimes singular, sometimes plural in Shakespeare).

21. Fulvia is Antony's wife. Notorious for her licentiousness, she married Antony
in 44. When he left Rome to administer the East in 41, she was the real authority in Rome and became the first woman to command a Roman army when
Octavius made war on her and Antony's brother, Lucius (Dio, 48.4.1–4, 10.1–14.6;
see, further, 1.2.93–99n). She was, Plutarch writes, "not so basely minded to spend
her time in spinning and housewifery, and was not contented to master her husband at home, but would also rule him in his office abroad, and command him"
(Plutarch, *Antony*, 10.3; Spencer, 184). "She had nothing of the woman about her
except her body" (Velleius Paterculus, *Roman History*, 2.74.3).

21. "Fulvia . . . angry": Cleopatra scorns Antony for being hen-pecked by Fulvia.

22. "scarce-bearded": young and unmanly. Octavius Caesar is twenty-three years
old, two decades younger than Antony. Antony frequently disparages his young age.

24. "Take in": conquer, occupy.

24. "enfranchise": set free.

25. "we damn thee": condemn, doom to death. Cleopatra quotes Caesar using the
royal pronoun "we," addressing Antony as "thee," generally the pronoun used by a
master to a servant, and threatening to condemn him to death if he fails to obey.

25. "How": an exclamation.

Cleopatra: Perchance? Nay, and most like.
    You must not stay here longer; your dismission
    Is come from Caesar. Therefore hear it, Antony.
    Where's Fulvia's process? Caesar's, I would say. Both?
    Call in the messengers. As I am Egypt's queen,   **30**
    Thou blushest, Antony, and that blood of thine
    Is Caesar's homager; else so thy cheek pays shame
    When shrill-tongued Fulvia scolds. The messengers!

Antony: Let Rome in Tiber melt and the wide arch
    Of the ranged empire fall. Here is my space.   **35**
    Kingdoms are clay. Our dungy earth alike

---

26. "like": likely.

27. "dismission": dismissal, order to leave.

28. "Is": has.

29. "process": a summons to appear in court (the first step of a legal action).

32. "homager": an inferior who shows reverence to a superior (Antony's blush confesses that he must obey Caesar).

32. "else so": or else.

30–33. "thy cheek . . . scolds": the only other possible explanation of your blush is that it owns up to the shame you feel when Fulvia scolds you and you think you deserve her reproach. Shame, which often shows on the face—in a blush, an averted gaze, lowered eyes, a lowered head (see, for example, 3.11.47, 51–54; 4.14.74–77)—involves a sense of having been seen uncovered and therefore prompts a strong desire not to be seen. Cleopatra, compounding Antony's shame, adds to his loss of face by drawing attention to his face.

34. Tiber is the river which flows past Rome (and into which the infants Romulus and Remus were ordered to be thrown; see Plutarch, *Romulus*, 3–4).

35. "ranged": well-ordered, wide-ranging.

34–35. "wide . . . empire": (1) a synecdoche for the triumphal arches honoring Rome's victorious generals, (2) a metaphor for the reach across the vast empire Rome has conquered.

35. "space": all the empire I seek. Antony reverses the sense of Aeneas' words arriving on Italian shores at the mouth of the Tiber, "Here is our home, here is our country" (Virgil, *Aeneid*, 7.121). Where Aeneas gives up the love of Dido to found Rome, Antony would let Rome be destroyed for the love of Cleopatra.

36. "dungy": full of dung.

36. "alike": equally.

Feeds beast as man. The nobleness of life
Is to do thus; when such a mutual pair
And such a twain can do't, in which I bind,
On pain of punishment, the world to weet   **40**
We stand up peerless.

Cleopatra: Excellent falsehood!
Why did he marry Fulvia and not love her?
I'll seem the fool I am not. Antony
Will be himself.

---

37. "as": as it does.

38. "do thus": Beginning with Alexander Pope (1723), the second editor of Shakespeare, some editors insert the stage-direction "*embracing*." Others find it too limiting and at odds with Cleopatra's present mood.

38. "mutual pair": equal in love for each other.

39. "twain": two, pair.

39. "bind": command.

40. "On pain of punishment": the language of an official proclamation, for not fulfilling a command.

40. "weet": recognize, know.

37–41. "The nobleness . . . peerless": From the Republic's earliest days, Romans vied with one another for the highest public honors. Hungry for glory, they strove to surpass one another in public achievements in order to win the city's highest renown. The ambition for unrivaled distinction still governs Antony, but its object has changed. The "nobleness of life," he declares, lies not in public deeds but in private pursuits, not in political but in amorous activity. Yet Antony wants public recognition for himself and Cleopatra as unrivaled lovers. Antony, accordingly, uses traditional Roman locution. Rome may "melt" and the empire may "fall," but he and Cleopatra will "stand up" unequaled for their love. The high stands up and stands out; the low loses shape and falls. See Blits, *Julius Caesar*, xix.

41. "Excellent falsehood": Cleopatra twice calls something excellent: "Excellent falsehood," here; "excellent dissembling," later (1.3.80). Both times, "excellent" describes something that pleases or gratifies her in love, though untrue.

42. "and not": if he did not. Cleopatra overlooks that Antony's marriage to Fulvia might have been a loveless political marriage, which, as we shall see, is common in Rome, or that he could love a later love more than an earlier one, as she will protest is true of herself (1.5.76–78). Despite enjoying Antony's superlative claim for their love, Cleopatra speaks jealously and tauntingly of Fulvia, as she will do even after Fulvia dies.

43–44. "I'll seem . . . himself": Cleopatra will fool Antony by playing the fool. She will pretend to be fooled by his excessive professions of love, and, in doing so, will fool Antony, who, being himself, will be deceived.

Antony: But stirred by Cleopatra.
Now for the love of Love and her soft hours,   **45**
Let's not confound the time with conference harsh.
There's not a minute of our lives should stretch
Without some pleasure now. What sport tonight?

Cleopatra: Hear the ambassadors.

Antony: Fie, wrangling queen,
Whom everything becomes—to chide, to laugh,   **50**
To weep; whose every passion fully strives
To make itself, in thee, fair and admired!
No messenger but thine, and all alone
Tonight we'll wander through the streets and note

---

44. "But stirred by Cleopatra": Antony will be himself if (1) inspired, (2) sexually aroused, by Cleopatra. Antony shifts the sense of Cleopatra's "himself" from deceived (and failed deceiver) to noble lover and turns her derisive description of him into his flattery of her.

45. "Love": Venus, the Roman goddess of love. In speaking of "the love of Love," Antony makes Love the object of love. While tending to beautify the beloved (see, for example, 1.1.49–52; 1.3.34–38; 1.5.20–28, 56–64; 5.2.75–99), love also flatters itself. The lover's belief that love itself is beautiful seems to point to an element of self-love which, though manifest in jealousy, is often hidden in love.

46. "confound": waste.

46. "conference": conversation.

47–48. "stretch . . . pleasure now": pass without some present pleasure (see 1.2.133n).

48. "sport": amusement, entertainment.

49. "Fie": an exclamation of impatience.

49. "wrangling": quarreling.

50. "becomes": adorns, graces.

50. "chide": scold.

51. "passion": emotional mood.

53. "No messenger but thine": I will listen to no messenger but one that comes from you.

54. "note": observe.

The qualities of people. Come, my queen,   **55**
Last night you did desire it. [*To the Messenger*] Speak not to us.
Exeunt [Antony and Cleopatra] with the Train.

Demetrius: Is Caesar with Antonius prized so slight?

Philo: Sir, sometimes when he is not Antony
He comes too short of that great property
Which still should go with Antony.

Demetrius   I am full sorry   **60**
That he approves the common liar who
Thus speaks of him at Rome; but I will hope
Of better deeds tomorrow. Rest you happy!   *Exeunt.*

---

55. "qualities": characteristics, activities.

54–55. "And sometime also, when [Antony] would go up and down the city disguised like a slave in the night, and would peer into poor men's windows and their shops, and scold and brawl with them within the house, Cleopatra would be also in a chambermaid's array, and amble up and down the streets with him, so that oftentimes Antonius bare away both mocks and blows" (Plutarch, *Antony*, 29.1; Spencer, 205–6).

56. Cleopatra "[always] devised sundry new delights" for Antony (Plutarch, *Antony*, 29.1; Spencer, 205–6).

S.D. 56. "*Exeunt*": the plural form of "exit."

57. "prized so slight": valued so little.

58–60. "sometimes . . . with Antony": Philo separates Antony from Antony himself. When Antony behaves in an infatuated fashion, he is not Antony. He is Antony only when he measures up to the great quality proper to him. What is always ("still") proper to him—"that great property" which makes Antony, Antony—is somehow separable from him. By alienating Antony when he is "not Antony," Philo is able to identify only the noble Antony as Antony—the only Antony he identifies (twice) by name—and thus to shield him from blame. Scarus will similarly divorce Antony from Antony himself at Actium (3.10.26–27), and Antony and Enobarbus will divide themselves in the same way in order to preserve their noble selves (3.10.35–37, 3.11.7–20, 3.13.42; see also 1.2.123, 3.4.22–24).

60. "full": very.

61. "approves . . . liar": proves the common gossip (which is usually malicious) true in this case.

63. "Of": for.

63. "Rest you happy": may the gods keep you fortunate (a good wish in parting).

ACT ONE, SCENE TWO

[Alexandria, another room in Cleopatra's palace]

Enter Enobarbus, [other Roman officers], a Soothsayer, Charmian, Iras,
Mardian the Eunuch, Alexas, and Servants.

Charmian: Lord Alexas, sweet Alexas, most anything
Alexas, almost most absolute Alexas, where's the
soothsayer that you praised so to th' Queen? O, that
I knew this husband which you say must charge his
horns with garlands! 5

Alexas: Soothsayer!

Soothsayer: Your will?

Charmian: Is this the man? Is't you, sir, that know
things?

Soothsayer: In nature's infinite book of secrecy 10

S.D. 1. Enobarbus (Gn. Domitius Ahenobarbus, 80–31) was a strong opponent of
Julius Caesar. He fought against him at Pharsalus in 48 and was subsequently pardoned by him in 46. From 44–42, he commanded the Adriatic fleet of Brutus and
Cassius, who were his near relatives. Following the republicans' defeat at Philippi
in 42, he retained the fleet and fought successfully against the triumvirs. In 40,
he reconciled with Antony, against Octavius' opposition. For a summary of his
political life, see Suetonius, *Nero*, 3. Nero was his great-grandson.

S.D. 1. *"other Roman officers"*: The Folio names Lamprius, Rannius, and Lucillius,
who do not speak in this scene and are not mentioned later in the play.

2. "absolute": perfect.

4. The Folio reads "change."

4–5. "this husband . . . garlands": Whether "change" (as "changing clothing") or
"charge" (as "loading up"), Charmian seems to mean that she will cuckold her
future husband, whose horns on his forehead (a symbol of a cuckold) will be fes-
tively dressed or dressed up with garlands. Her husband, so thoroughly beguiled
by her, will proudly celebrate her frequent infidelities. Romans decorated with
garlands and gilded the horns of an ox brought to sacrifice (Ovid, *Metamorphoses*,
15.130–35).

6. "Soothsayer": fortune-teller.

7. "Your will": what do you wish.

A little I can read.

Alexas: Show him your hand.

Enobarbus: [*To servants*] Bring in the banquet quickly, wine enough
    Cleopatra's health to drink.

Charmian: [*Giving her hand to the Soothsayer*] Good
    sir, give me good fortune.   **15**

Soothsayer: I make not, but foresee.

Charmian: Pray then, foresee me one.

Soothsayer: You shall be yet far fairer than you are.

Charmian: He means in flesh.

Iras: No, you shall paint when you are old.   **20**

Charmian: Wrinkles forbid!

Alexas: Vex not his prescience. Be attentive.

Charmian: Hush!

10–11. "In nature's . . . can read": "And while they are often successful in predict-
ing to men the events which are going to befall them in the course of their lives,
[Egyptian soothsayers or astrologists] have prior knowledge . . . of all things which
the ordinary man looks upon as beyond all finding out" (Diodorus, 1.81.5).

11. "your hand": your palm (to be read). Palm reading tells a person's fortune by
looking at the lines on the person's palm.

13. "banquet": dessert with fruit and wine (not a sumptuous feast).

15. "give me . . . good fortune": Powerless and passive, the Egyptians characteristically place their trust in fortune rather than in themselves. See, further, S.D.
2.3.10n.

16. "but": only.

18. "fairer": more fortunate.

19. "in flesh": "fair in flesh" means plump, complete, in good condition.

20. "paint": use cosmetics (another quibble on "fair," which can also mean beautiful). Cosmetics, particularly eye and face paints, oils and ointments, trace back to
early Egypt and were used lavishly by Cleopatra and those under her rule. For
Cleopatra's use, see, for example, Lucan, *Pharsalia*, 10.137. After her death, some
ancient writers (erroneously) credited Cleopatra as the author of a book on cosmetics (see, for example, Aetius, *Sixteen Books on Medicine*, 6.56.27).

22. "prescience": foreknowledge, ability to see the future.

Soothsayer: You shall be more beloving than beloved.

Charmian: I had rather heat my liver with drinking.   **25**

Alexas: Nay, hear him.

Charmian: Good now, some excellent fortune! Let me
   be married to three kings in a forenoon and widow
   them all. Let me have a child at fifty to whom Herod
   of Jewry may do homage. Find me to marry me with   **30**
   Octavius Caesar, and companion me with my mistress.

Soothsayer: You shall outlive the lady whom you serve.

Charmian: O, excellent! I love long life better than
   figs.

Soothsayer: You have seen and proved a fairer former fortune   **35**
   Than that which is to approach.

---

25. "heat my liver": arouse her sexual desire (the liver was seen as the source of sexual desire).

27. "Good now": come now (an expression of encouragement).

28. "forenoon": a morning (before noon).

28. "widow": become the widow of.

30. "Find . . . me with": discover (in my palm) that I will marry.

31. "companion me": become the companion or equal.

29–31. "Let me . . . my mistress": Charmian alludes irreverently to the birth of Jesus. "[T]hree kings" is a traditional synonym for the three wise men, the Magi, whom Herod the Great "sent . . . to Bethlehem, saying, 'Go and search diligently for the babe . . . that I may come also, and worship him'" (Matt. 2:8). Instead of worshipping the newborn child, Herod, a cruel tyrant, infamously searched for the child so he could kill him, and, unable to find him, slew all the male children in Bethlehem and the region under the age of two (Matt. 2:13–18). By wishing to "have a child at fifty to whom Herod . . . may do homage," Charmian imagines herself the mother of Jesus. For if Charmian is eighteen or twenty when the play opens (in 40), she will be fifty in the year Jesus is born. Charmian wishes also to be the wife of Octavius Caesar and hence the equal of Cleopatra (via Caesar's fellow triumvir, Antony). Her wishes combine the new heaven and new earth—the religion of Christianity and the politics of triumviral Rome.

34. "figs": a bawdy allusion to female genitalia, whose shape figs were supposed to resemble (Plutarch, *On Isis and Osiris*, 36 [365B]).

35. "proved": experienced.

Charmian: Then belike my children shall have no
   names. Prithee, how many boys and wenches must I
   have?

Soothsayer: If every of your wishes had a womb,   **40**
   And fertile every wish, a million.

Charmian: Out, fool! I forgive thee for a witch.

Alexas: You think none but your sheets are privy to
   your wishes.

Charmian: Nay, come. Tell Iras hers.   **45**

Alexas: We'll know all our fortunes.

Enobarbus: Mine, and most of our fortunes tonight,
   shall be drunk to bed.

Iras: [*Giving her hand to the Soothsayer*] There's a palm presages
   chastity, if nothing else.   **50**

Charmian: E'en as the o'erflowing Nilus presageth
   famine.

Iras: Go, you wild bedfellow, you cannot soothsay!

---

37. "belike": perhaps.

37–38. "have no names": be bastards.

38. "Prithee": I pray you ("please").

38. "wenches": girls.

40. "every": every one.

41. "fertile every wish": every wish were fertile.

42. "Out": exclamation of pretended reproach.

42. "forgive . . . a witch": either (1) I forgive you, because you are a witch, or (2) you are no witch, if this is the best you can do.]

43–44. "privy . . . wishes": share knowledge of your secret wishes.

46. "We'll know all": we all wish to know.

48. "drunk to bed": go to bed drunk.

49–50. "In the palm of the hand is placed the sign of the bodily desires" (A. R. Craig, *The Book of the Hand* [London: Sampson, Low, Son, and Marston, 1867], 23).

51. "Nilus": the name for the deified Nile, the offspring of Oceanus and Tethys (Hesiod, *Theogony*, 337–38).

51. "the o'erflowing Nilus": the Nile irrigates the Egyptian soil and its overflowing predicts abundant fertility (ironical, but see 2.7.20–21n.).

Charmian: Nay, if an oily palm be not a fruitful
prognostication, I cannot scratch mine ear. Prithee,   **55**
tell her but a workaday fortune.

Soothsayer: Your fortunes are alike.

Iras: But how, but how? Give me particulars.

Soothsayer: I have said.

Iras: Am I not an inch of fortune better than she?   **60**

Charmian: Well, if you were but an inch of fortune
better than I, where would you choose it?

Iras: Not in my husband's nose.

Charmian: Our worser thoughts heavens mend!
Alexas—come, his fortune, his fortune! O, let him   **65**
marry a woman that cannot go, sweet Isis, I beseech
thee, and let her die, too, and give him a worse, and
let worse follow worse, till the worst of all follow him
laughing to his grave, fiftyfold a cuckold! Good Isis,
hear me this prayer, though thou deny me a matter   **70**
of more weight, good Isis, I beseech thee!

54–55. "an oily palm . . . prognostication": As the hand corresponds to the heart,
an oily palm signifies a lecherous disposition.

55. "scratch mine ear": do the simplest thing.

56. "workaday": ordinary, commonplace.

59. "I have said": I have spoken, I have nothing more to say (an ominous echo of
the Latin rhetorical formula for closure, *dixi* ["I have spoken"]). While the women
understand them in a lewd sense, the Soothsayer's prophecies will turn out to be
true in an untoward sense with Cleopatra's death.

63. "Not . . . husband's nose": by implication, she would prefer it to be in his penis.

64. "Our worser . . . mend": may heavens improve our indecent thoughts (mock
moral shock).

66. "a woman . . . go": a woman he cannot sexually satisfy.

66. Isis is the principal Egyptian deity. The sister and wife of Osirus, she is "the
female principle of nature" (Plutarch, *On Isis and Osiris*, 51 [372e]), a protector of
women and marriage, the goddess of fertility and maternity.

69. "fiftyfold": fifty times over.

70. "hear me": hear.

70–71. "though . . . more weight": even if you deny me the lovers I crave (for the
bawdy play on "weight," see 1.5.22n).

Iras: Amen, dear goddess, hear that prayer of the
   people! For, as it is a heartbreaking to see a handsome
   man loose-wived, so it is a deadly sorrow to behold
   a foul knave uncuckolded. Therefore, dear Isis, keep   **75**
   decorum and fortune him accordingly!

Charmian: Amen.

Alexas: Lo now, if it lay in their hands to make me a
   cuckold, they would make themselves whores but
   they'd do't.   **80**

                        Enter Cleopatra.

Enobarbus: Hush, here comes Antony.

Charmian: Not he. The Queen.

Cleopatra: Saw you my lord?

Enobarbus: No, lady.

Cleopatra: Was he not here?   **85**

Charmian: No, madam.

Cleopatra: He was disposed to mirth, but on the sudden
   A Roman thought hath struck him. Enobarbus!

Enobarbus: Madam?

72–73. "that prayer . . . people": Iras imagines that Charmian's prayer comes from
the whole nation.

74. "loose-wived": married to an unfaithful wife.

75. "a foul knave uncuckolded": an ugly man with a faithful wife.

75–76. "keep decorum": preserve propriety (see Introduction, xvi).

76. "fortune him": reward him.

78–79. "make . . . whores": they would make themselves whores just to cuckold
me.

81–82. "Hush, . . . The Queen": Whether intentionally or not, Enobarbus identifies
Cleopatra as Antony. His identification seems to reflect not only Antony's boast of
themselves as an unparalleled couple, but the strong criticism in Rome that they
can scarcely be told apart. So much under her influence, Antony is not merely seen
with Cleopatra, but seen as her (cp. 1.4.5–7).

87. "disposed to": in the mood for.

88. "A Roman thought": (1) a thought about Rome, or (2) a thought in the serious character of Rome.

Cleopatra: Seek him and bring him hither.   [*Exit Enobarbus.*]

                        Where's Alexas?   **90**

Alexas: Here at your service. My lord approaches.

Enter Antony with a Messenger.

Cleopatra: We will not look upon him: go with us.

Exeunt [all but Antony and the Messenger].

Messenger: Fulvia thy wife first came into the field.

Antony: Against my brother Lucius?

Messenger: Ay.   **95**

    But soon that war had end, and the time's state

    Made friends of them, jointing their force 'gainst Caesar,

    Whose better issue in the war from Italy

    Upon the first encounter drave them.

Antony: Well, what worst?   **100**

Messenger: The nature of bad news infects the teller.

---

92. "We," "us": the royal "we."

93. "came into the field": began military operations.

94. On Lucius Antonius and his war on Caesar, see lines 93–99n.

96. "time's state": circumstances at that time.

97. "jointing their force": combining their armies.

98. "better issue": better success.

99. "drave": drove.

93–99. Fulvia looked after Antony's interests in Rome when he was in the East. At first, she and Antony's younger brother Lucius, who was consul, quarreled over the distribution of land for the triumvirs' veterans and went to war against each other. But circumstances changed and forced them to join together and fight against Octavius, who defeated them in the first battle and drove them out of Italy (Plutarch, *Antony*, 30.1; Appian, 5.19, 32–50; Dio, 48.5–14.). The so-called Perusine War (41–40) was a bloody prelude to the civil war that followed.

101. "The nature ... teller": Anger seeks satisfaction as well as retribution or justice. It therefore needs an object to punish, and so, if it cannot punish its true object, it will find another that it can punish instead. Moreover, anger seeks to punish an animate object, for it wishes to punish (or think it is punishing) what caused or intended the harm. Thus, making no distinction between a messenger and his news, it is apt to punish the former for the latter (see 2.5.60–106).

Antony: When it concerns the fool or coward. On.
Things that are past are done with me. 'Tis thus:
Who tells me true, though in his tale lie death,
I hear him as he flattered.

Messenger: Labienus—   **105**
This is stiff news—hath with his Parthian force
Extended Asia: from Euphrates
His conquering banner shook, from Syria
To Lydia and to Ionia,
Whilst—

Antony: "Antony," thou wouldst say—

Messenger: O, my lord!   **110**

Antony: Speak to me home; mince not the general tongue.
Name Cleopatra as she is called in Rome;

---

102. "On": go on, continue.

105. "as": as if.

106. "stiff": hard.

107. "Extended": seized.

107. The Euphrates River, running from (present-day) eastern Turkey through Syria and Iraq, and joining the Tigris near the Persian Gulf, is the border between Rome's dominions in the East and the western boundary of the Parthian Empire.

109. Syria, Lydia, and Ionia are Roman territories or dominions in the East. Syria, which Pompey the Great captured and made a Roman province in 64, lies between the Euphrates in the east, the Aegean in the west, the foothills of the Taurus Mountains in the north, and Judea and the Arabian Desert in the south. Antioch is its major city. Lydia is a territory in western Asia Minor (modern Turkey). In 133, King Attalus of Pergamum left his entire kingdom, including Lydia, to Rome. Ionia lies on the western shore of Asia Minor, bordering on the Aegean. Its cities include Ephesus and Smyrna.

105–9. Quintus Labienus, who supported Brutus and Cassius in the civil war following Caesar's death, had been sent by Cassius in 43/42 to enlist the Parthians' aid against Antony and Octavius. After the republicans' defeat at Philippi, he was stranded in Parthia. Now, with an army of Parthian cavalry under Pacorus, the king's son, he is easily overrunning virtually all the Roman provinces in Asia as far west as the Aegean Sea (Plutarch, *Antony*, 30.1; Dio, 48.24.4–26.5). This is the first time the Parthians, a long-standing (if intermittent) dangerous enemy, have reached farther west than Syria.

111. "home": fully, frankly, without reserve.

111. "mince not . . . tongue": don't lessen or soften what everybody is saying.

Rail thou in Fulvia's phrase, and taunt my faults
With such full license as both truth and malice
Have power to utter. O, then we bring forth weeds　　**115**
When our quick minds lie still, and our ills told us
Is as our earing. Fare thee well awhile.

Messenger: At your noble pleasure.　　　　*Exit Messenger.*

Enter another Messenger.

Antony: From Sicyon how the news? Speak there.

Second Messenger: The man from Sicyon—

Antony:　　　　　　　　　Is there such a one?　　**120**

Second Messenger: He stays upon your will.

Antony:　　　　　　　　　Let him appear.

[*Exit Second Messenger.*]

These strong Egyptian fetters I must break,
Or lose myself in dotage.

---

113. "Rail . . . Fulvia's phrase": scold in the language Fulvia would use.

114. "full license": complete freedom.

116. "quick": living, active.

116. "minds": The Folio reads "winds." The phrase "quick winds lie still," continuing the agriculture metaphor, is sometimes understood to mean "soil not scoured by quick winds."

116. "still": inactive.

116. "told us": told to us.

115–17. "O, then . . . our earing": our minds produce vices rather than virtues when left idle, but when we are scolded for our vices we uproot them. "To ear" means both "to hear" and "to plow." In order to act, Antony must be shamed by others—or imagine that he is. As much as he loves honor and fame, he, like many other Romans, is moved more by the fear of ignominy than by the desire for praise. Shame is his paramount concern (see 3.11.49n). On the trait in general, see Cicero, *Of the Classification of Rhetoric*, 91.

119. Sicyon is a Greek city in the northern Peloponnesus, near Corinth, where Antony left Fulvia about a year ago (see, further, lines 124–26n).

121. "stays . . . will": awaits your orders.

122. "fetters": shackles.

123. "lose myself": On Antony's self-separation, see 1.1.58–60n.

123. "dotage": (1) infatuation, (2) folly.

Enter another Messenger with a letter.

What are you?

Third Messenger: Fulvia thy wife is dead.

Antony: Where died she?   **125**

Third Messenger: In Sicyon.
    Her length of sickness, with what else more serious
    Importeth thee to know, this bears.

                [*Gives Antony the letter.*]

Antony: Forbear me. **[*Exit Third Messenger*]**
    There's a great spirit gone! Thus did I desire it.
    What our contempts doth often hurl from us,   **130**
    We wish it ours again. The present pleasure,
    By revolution lowering, does become
    The opposite of itself. She's good, being gone.
    The hand could pluck her back that shoved her on.
    I must from this enchanting queen break off.   **135**

---

123. "What": who.

124–26. In Shakespeare's sources, Fulvia, having been driven out of Italy, went to Greece in 40, where Antony, who had come from the East, met her, reproached her for having caused the war with Octavius, and soon left for Italy to deal with Caesar. Fulvia then took ill in Sicyon and died (Plutarch, *Antony*, 30.1–2; Appian, 5.59). Shakespeare omits the episode.

128. "Importeth": concerns.

128. "Forbear me": please leave me.

130. "What our . . . from us": what often we throw away in contempt.

132. "By revolution lowering": being lowered in our estimation in the course of time (as if by the turn of a wheel).

133. "The opposite of itself": Antony, generalizing (as he often does), reflects on the inconstancy of human pleasure and desire. Earlier, he said that our lives should have constant pleasure. Now, he makes explicit that constant pleasure requires constantly changing pleasures. To avoid satiety or boredom, "some pleasure now" (1.1.48) means "some pleasure new." See Introduction, xviii–xix.

134. "could": would now like to.

135. "enchanting": bewitching (a strong term).

Ten thousand harms more than the ills I know
My idleness doth hatch. How now, Enobarbus!

Enter Enobarbus.

Enobarbus: What's your pleasure, sir?

Antony: I must with haste from hence.

Enobarbus: Why then we kill all our women. We see   **140**
how mortal an unkindness is to them. If they suffer
our departure, death's the word.

Antony: I must be gone.

Enobarbus: Under a compelling occasion, let women
die. It were pity to cast them away for nothing,   **145**
though between them and a great cause, they should
be esteemed nothing. Cleopatra, catching but the
least noise of this, dies instantly. I have seen her die
twenty times upon far poorer moment. I do think
there is mettle in death which commits some loving   **150**
act upon her, she hath such a celerity in dying.

Antony: She is cunning past man's thought.

Enobarbus: Alack, sir, no, her passions are made of
nothing but the finest part of pure love. We cannot

---

136. "ills": evils (in a general sense; the opposite of good).
137. "idleness": (1) folly, (2) inactivity, indolence.
140. "then": under such circumstances.
141. "mortal": deadly, fatal.
141. "suffer": undergo, experience.
142. "the word": the watchword (a word representing a rule of action).
148. "noise": rumor.
149. "far poorer moment": far less weighty circumstance or cause.
150. "mettle": vigor, ardent spirit.
150. "commits": performs.
151. "celerity": quickness.
144–51. Throughout the speech, Enobarbus plays on the sexual sense of "die" (to experience orgasm) and the related words "kill" and "death," as well as the ribald senses of "mettle" and "nothing."
152. "cunning": clever, crafty.

call her winds and waters sighs and tears; they are   **155**
greater storms and tempests than almanacs can report.
This cannot be cunning in her; if it be, she makes a
shower of rain as well as Jove.

Antony: Would I had never seen her!

Enobarbus: O, sir, you had then left unseen a wonderful   **160**
piece of work, which not to have been blest
withal would have discredited your travel.

Antony: Fulvia is dead.

Enobarbus: Sir?

Antony: Fulvia is dead.   **165**

Enobarbus: Fulvia?

Antony: Dead.

Enobarbus: Why, sir, give the gods a thankful sacrifice.
When it pleaseth their deities to take the wife of a
man from him, it shows to man the tailors of the   **170**
earth; comforting therein, that when old robes are
worn out, there are members to make new. If there
were no more women but Fulvia, then had you indeed
a cut, and the case to be lamented. This grief is

---

156. "almanacs": chronological accounts of recent events, including meteorologi-
cal information.

157. "cunning": deceitful (Antony's word with a different meaning).

158. For Jove as god of rain (Jupiter Pluvius), see Tibullus, *Elegies*, 1.7.26.

159. "Would": I wish.

161. "piece of work": (1) masterpiece, (2) difficult woman.

162. "withal": with.

162. "discredited your travel": injured your reputation as a traveler. Egypt—the
land of the Nile, pyramids, eunuchs, revels, serpents, crocodiles and Cleopatra—is
the land of exotic travel (Herodotus, 2.35; Strabo, 17.1).

171. "therein": in this respect.

172. "members": individuals (with wordplay on sexual organs).

171–72. "when old . . . new": new garments replace old ones.

174. "cut": blow (with wordplay on female genitals).

174. "case": situation (with wordplay on female genitals; a case sheathes a sword).

crowned with consolation; your old smock brings　　　**175**
forth a new petticoat, and indeed the tears live in an
onion that should water this sorrow.

Antony: The business she hath broached in the state
　　Cannot endure my absence.

Enobarbus: And the business you have broached here　　　**180**
　　cannot be without you, especially that of Cleopatra's,
　　which wholly depends on your abode.

Antony: No more light answers. Let our officers
　　Have notice what we purpose. I shall break
　　The cause of our expedience to the Queen　　　**185**
　　And get her leave to part. For not alone
　　The death of Fulvia, with more urgent touches
　　Do strongly speak to us, but the letters too
　　Of many our contriving friends in Rome
　　Petition us at home. Sextus Pompeius　　　**190**

175–76. "smock . . . petticoat": both undergarments worn by women.

176–77. "tears . . . onion": tears produced by an onion (feigned tears).

178. "broached": started.

180. "broached": pierced (with bawdy wordplay on Antony's use of the word).

182. "abode": staying.

183. "light answers": frivolous, indecent comments. Enobarbus demonstrates Plutarch's remark, repeated disapprovingly by Caesar (1.4.18–21), that Antony flattered himself by allowing his subordinates to be informal and forward as well as frank in speaking to him and making jokes about his love affairs (Plutarch, *Antony*, 4.2–3, 24.7–8).

183. "our": the royal "we" (which Antony uses nine times in this speech, setting formal distance between himself and Enobarbus).

184. "notice": notice of.

184. "purpose": intend.

184. "break": reveal.

185. "expedience": hasty departure.

186. "leave": consent. The Folio reads "love."

186. "part": depart.

187. "with . . . touches": together with matters more pressing.

188. "Do": does.

189. "our contriving friends": friends of mine who are making plans in my interest.

190. "Petition . . . home": beg me to come home.

Hath given the dare to Caesar and commands
The empire of the sea. Our slippery people,
Whose love is never linked to the deserver
Till his deserts are past, begin to throw
Pompey the Great and all his dignities   **195**
Upon his son, who—high in name and power,
Higher than both in blood and life—stands up
For the main soldier; whose quality, going on,
The sides o'th' world may danger. Much is breeding

---

191. "given the dare to": challenged.

191. "commands": controls.

190–92. Sextus Pompey (c. 67–35) is Pompey the Great's younger son. He and his brother Gnaeus continued Pompey's fight after his defeat and death. *Julius Caesar* begins with Caesar's celebration of his defeat of Gnaeus at Munda in southern Spain in 45 (*JC*, 1.1.1–60; Plutarch, *Caesar*, 56.1–3). Sextus subsequently gathered a considerable naval force, composed of all the vessels he could find in the ports of Spain and Gaul, allied himself with pirates, including former slaves, and is now threatening Rome with starvation. Having been proscribed by the Senate in 43 (see 1.3.50n), he has successfully challenged Octavius and now occupies Sicily, where he gives refuge to many proscribed by the triumvirs, and dominates the sea lanes, able to raid Italy and blockade Rome's grain supply (Dio, 48.17–19). On the freedmen and pirates, see, further, 1.4.49n.

192. "slippery": unstable, fickle.

193–94. Antony's indignation seems misplaced. Pompey the Great was especially well loved by the Roman people. "[N]ever any other Roman but Pompey had the people's earnest goodwills so soon, nor that in prosperity and adversity continued longer constant, than unto Pompey" (Plutarch, *Pompey*, 1.2; Tudor, 4:206). Antony might have said, instead, that the people's gratitude toward Pompey should have prevented their celebrating his sons' defeat, as the tribune Marullus says (*JC*, 1.1.36–52; see, further, Plutarch, *Caesar*, 56.4).

194–96. "throw . . . Upon his son": cast upon Sextus all the honor and veneration the Romans gave his father. Names, particularly family names, matter very much in Rome (see *JC*, 3.3.26–35). The name Caesar gave the young Octavius a significance he could not otherwise have had. "You who owe everything to a name—," Antony mocked him (Cicero, *Philippics*, 13.25).

197. "blood and life": courage and spirit.

197–98. "stands up . . . soldier": presents himself as the most important soldier in the world.

198–99. "Whose quality . . . danger": whose nature, if not checked, may endanger the triumvirs' worldwide empire.

Which, like the courser's hair, hath yet but life   **200**
And not a serpent's poison. Say our pleasure,
To such whose place is under us, requires
Our quick remove from hence.

Enobarbus: I shall do't.   [***Exeunt.***]

ACT ONE, SCENE THREE

[Alexandria, another room in Cleopatra's palace]

Enter Cleopatra, Charmian, Alexas, and Iras.

Cleopatra: Where is he?

Charmian: I did not see him since.

Cleopatra: [*to Alexas*]
See where he is, who's with him, what he does.
I did not send you. If you find him sad,
Say I am dancing; if in mirth, report   **5**
That I am sudden sick. Quick, and return.   ***Exit Alexas.***

Charmian: Madam, methinks, if you did love him dearly,
You do not hold the method to enforce
The like from him.

---

200. "courser's hair": horse hairs. "[I]t is believed . . . that an horse hair laid in a pail full of . . . [stagnant] water will in short time stir and become a living creature" (William Harrison, *Description of England*, in Raphael Holinshed's *Chronicles* [1586], 6 vols., [rpt. New York: AMS Press, 1976], 3.3, 1:376).

200. "yet but": still only.

204. "I shall": stronger than "I will." As the reply of an inferior to a superior, it combines "I am bound to" and "I am sure to" (see Abbott, §315).

2. "since": recently.

1–3. "Cleopatra . . . never once [let] him go out of her sight" (Plutarch, *Antony*, 29.1; Spencer, 205).

4. "I did . . . you": do not let on that I sent you.

4. "sad": grave, serious (not "sorrowful").

6. "sudden": suddenly.

7. "methinks": it seems to me.

8. "hold the method": pursue the right course.

7–9. Like Enobarbus with Antony, Charmian freely advises her queen on her private life.

Cleopatra:	What should I do I do not?

Charmian: In each thing give him way; cross him in nothing.	**10**

Cleopatra: Thou teachest like a fool: the way to lose him.

Charmian: Tempt him not so too far. I wish, forbear.
	In time we hate that which we often fear.

Enter Antony.

	But here comes Antony.

Cleopatra:	I am sick and sullen.

Antony: I am sorry to give breathing to my purpose—	**15**

Cleopatra: Help me away, dear Charmian! I shall fall.
	It cannot be thus long; the sides of nature
	Will not sustain it.

Antony:	Now, my dearest queen—

Cleopatra: Pray you stand farther from me!

Antony:	What's the matter?

Cleopatra: I know by that same eye there's some good news.	**20**
	What, says the married woman you may go?

---

9. "I": that I.

10. "way": his way.

10. "cross": oppose.

12. "Tempt": try, provoke.

12. "I wish, forbear": I wish that you would stop.

13. "we hate . . . fear": we come to hate what we fear because we fear it.

14. "sullen": melancholy, in low spirits.

15. "breathing": utterance.

15. "purpose": intention.

17. "It cannot . . . long": my condition cannot last long.

17–18. "the sides . . . sustain it": my bodily strength will not hold up under the strain.

21. "the married woman": your wife, Fulvia.

21. "What, says, . . . may go?" Throughout the play, Cleopatra frequently asks rhetorical questions, including almost whenever she speaks of Fulvia. Most notably, her words when Antony dies and her own dying words are rhetorical questions (4.15.61–64, 5.2.312). A declaration in the guise of an inquiry, a rhetorical question forcefully answers what it ostensibly asks. Calculated entirely for effect, it seeks confirmation or disaffirmation rather than information (Quintilian, 9.2.7–11).

Would she had never given you leave to come!
Let her not say 'tis I that keep you here.
I have no power upon you. Hers you are.

Antony: The gods best know—

Cleopatra: O, never was there queen   **25**
So mightily betrayed! Yet at the first
I saw the treasons planted.

Antony: Cleopatra—

Cleopatra: Why should I think you can be mine, and true—
Though you in swearing shake the throned gods—
Who have been false to Fulvia? Riotous madness,   **30**
To be entangled with those mouth-made vows
Which break themselves in swearing!

Antony: Most sweet queen—

Cleopatra: Nay, pray you seek no color for your going,

21–22. Cleopatra echoes Ovid's portrayal of Dido's letter to Aeneas when he deserts her: "But God doth force thee flee, / Would God had kept away" (Ovid, *Heroides*, 7.139–40, trans. George Turberville [London: Henry Denham, 1567]). Where the earlier North African queen blames the earlier Roman for his pious duty to his city, the later North African queen blames the later Roman for his henpecked obedience to his wife.

24. "upon": over.

20–24. Despite appearing to match or even to exaggerate Antony's mood, Cleopatra does not abandon her stated tactic of opposing it (lines 10–13). She doubly opposes it by attributing a cheerful mood to Antony and then countering it. She crosses Antony's mood by willfully misreading it and then opposing what, with bitter irony, she pretends it is.

26. "Yet": even.

29. "the throned gods": the gods enthroned on Mount Olympus.

30. "Who": you who.

28–30. As Dido accuses Aeneas of having forsaken and betrayed not only her but his Trojan wife (Ovid, *Heroides*, 7.81–84), Cleopatra accuses Antony of having forsaken and betrayed not only her but his Roman wife.

30. "Riotous madness": it was raving madness for me.

31. "with": by.

32. "break themselves in swearing": are broken even as they are being sworn.

33. "color": pretext (a rhetorical term for the skillful manipulation of facts; see Quintilian, 4.2.88).

But bid farewell and go. When you sued staying,
Then was the time for words. No going then!   35
Eternity was in our lips and eyes,
Bliss in our brows' bent; none our parts so poor
But was a race of heaven. They are so still,
Or thou, the greatest soldier of the world,
Art turned the greatest liar.

Antony: How now, lady?   40

Cleopatra: I would I had thy inches. Thou shouldst know
    There were a heart in Egypt.

Antony: Hear me, queen:
    The strong necessity of time commands
    Our services awhile, but my full heart
    Remains in use with you. Our Italy   45
    Shines o'er with civil swords; Sextus Pompeius
    Makes his approaches to the port of Rome;
    Equality of two domestic powers

---

34. "sued staying": pleaded to stay.

36. "our": Cleopatra is quoting Antony's past compliments back to him. "Our," here and in the next line, is therefore the royal "we."

37. "our brow's bent": my eyebrow's arch.

37. "none our parts": none of my qualities, features, conduct, was.

38. "race of heaven": of divine origin or kind.

36–40. Antony's quoted words exemplify love's tendency to speak in perpetual hyperbole and to make a certain kind of falsehood an essential part of love speech. A lover says things which both the lover and the beloved know are untrue, but which the beloved still welcomes, for the words express what the lover wishes were true. The indicative is really the optative.

41. "inches": (1) stature, (2) manliness (cp. 1.2.61–63).

42. "heart": a lover with the courage to fight for love.

42. "Egypt": (1) the country, (2) its queen.

44. "Our services . . . heart": Antony, by moving from the royal plural to the personal singular pronoun, emphasizes the distinction between himself as a triumvir and as Cleopatra's lover.

45. "in use with": possessed by.

46. "civil swords": swords of civil war.

47. "the port of Rome": the harbor of Rome, Ostia, at the mouth of the Tiber; see 1.2.190–92n.

Breed scrupulous faction; the hated grown to strength
Are newly grown to love; the condemned Pompey,   **50**
Rich in his father's honor, creeps apace
Into the hearts of such as have not thrived
Upon the present state, whose numbers threaten;
And quietness, grown sick of rest, would purge
By any desperate change. My more particular,   **55**
And that which most with you should safe my going,
Is Fulvia's death.

Cleopatra: Though age from folly could not give me freedom,
   It does from childishness. Can Fulvia die?

Antony: She's dead, my queen.   **[*Gives her the letters.*]**   **60**
   Look here, and at thy sovereign leisure read

48–49. "Equality . . . faction": the equality of power between Sextus and the triumvirs has produced sharp divisions among the Romans on even small matters.

49–50. "the hated . . . love": those who were hated, having become powerful, are now loved.

50. "condemned": Falsely labeled as one of the conspirators against Julius Caesar, Sextus was outlawed and proscribed by the Senate at Octavius' behest, fled Italy, and made ready for war (Dio, 46.48.3–4).

51. "creeps": insinuates himself quietly and stealthily (so as to elude observation; no sense of slowness).

51. "apace": quickly.

53. "Upon the present state": under the triumvirs, the present government.

53. "threaten": are threatening.

54–55. "quietness, . . . change": peace has made the body politic sick, which would heal or clear itself of the illness by war or violence. Antony alludes to the Hippocratic doctrine of the four humors. According to that doctrine, a sick body contains an excess of one or more of the body's fluids or humors (yellow bile, black bile, blood, and phlegm) and must be purged of that excess through medicinal bloodletting (or other means) to achieve a balance of the four humors (Hippocrates, *On the Nature of Man*).

   Antony says nothing about Labienus and his Parthian forces. He mentions the dangers that draw him back to Rome, but not the one that might keep him in the East.

55. "more particular": more personal (reason for going).

56. "safe": make safe.

58. "folly": the madness of love.

59. "childishness": the gullibility of childhood.

The garboils she awaked; at the last, best,
See when and where she died.

Cleopatra: O, most false love!
Where be the sacred vials thou shouldst fill
With sorrowful water? Now I see, I see,   **65**
In Fulvia's death, how mine received shall be.

Antony: Quarrel no more, but be prepared to know
The purposes I bear, which are or cease
As you shall give th'advice. By the fire
That quickens Nilus' slime, I go from hence   **70**
Thy soldier, servant, making peace or war
As thou affects.

Cleopatra: Cut my lace, Charmian, come!
But let it be; I am quickly ill and well;
So Antony loves.

Antony: My precious queen, forbear,
And give true evidence to his love, which stands   **75**
An honorable trial.

Cleopatra: So Fulvia told me.

---

62. "garboils": disturbances, tumult, commotions.

62. "at the last, best": the last item is the best.

64. "sacred vials": small bottles of tears which a Roman mourner placed in the urn of a friend.

68. "are or cease": shall be either carried out or abandoned.

69. "advice": instruction.

69–70. "By the fire . . . slime": by the sun which produces life in the Nile's mud (an Egyptian oath invoking what the Egyptians believe gives life to Egypt; see 2.7.26–27n).

72. "affects": prefers, chooses.

72. "lace": the lace tightening Cleopatra's bodice (cut to make breathing easier).

73. "well": well again (Cleopatra feigns fainting and a rapid recovery).

74. "So": (1) since, (2) in the same (inconstant) way. The former would express her love; the latter, her accusation.

74. "forbear": stop this kind of talk.

75–76. "give true . . . trial": bear true witness to the love of one who is ready to submit to any honorable test.

76. "So Fulvia told me": so your betrayal of Fulvia has taught me.

I prithee turn aside and weep for her,
Then bid adieu to me, and say the tears
Belong to Egypt. Good now, play one scene
Of excellent dissembling, and let it look   **80**
Like perfect honor.

Antony: You'll heat my blood. No more!

Cleopatra: You can do better yet, but this is meetly.

Antony: Now by my sword—

Cleopatra: And target. Still he mends.
But this is not the best. Look, prithee, Charmian,
How this Herculean Roman does become   **85**
The carriage of his chafe.

_____

77–79. "I prithee . . . to Egypt": turn away and weep for Fulvia, but then say good-bye to me and pretend the tears are for me.

79. "Good now": please (an expression of entreaty).

80. "excellent dissembling": excellent playacting (see 1.1.41n).

81. "perfect honor": a gallant gesture.

81. "heat my blood": inflame my anger.

82. "meetly": not bad (she taunts his anger as playacting, which she says he performs moderately well).

83. "my sword": a solemn Roman oath (metonymy for heroic masculinity).

83. "target": small shield (reduces Antony's angry oath to a braggart's bluster).

83–84. "Still . . . not the best": he keeps improving, but a good actor would do better. Cleopatra further crosses Antony's angry mood by speaking of him in the third person, as though she were a disinterested spectator judging his theatrical performance.

85. Hercules, whom Antony claims as his ancestor (4.12.44), is the greatest of Greek heroes. "It had been a speech of old time, that the family of the Antonii were descended from one Anton, the son of Hercules, whereof the family took name. This opinion did Antonius seek to confirm in all his doings: not only resembling him in the likeness of his body, . . . but also in the wearing of his garments. For when he would openly show himself abroad before many people, he would always wear his cassock girt down low upon his hips, with a great sword hanging by his side, and upon that, some ill-favored cloak" (Plutarch, *Antony*, 4.1–2; Spencer, 177).

85–86. "become . . . his chafe": acts out very well the bearing ("carriage") of his fury ("chafe"). Cleopatra characterized Fulvia as a shrill-tongued scold dominating Antony (1.1.33). Yet, ironically, Fulvia's domination prepared Antony for Cleopatra's. "Cleopatra was to give Fulvia thanks for that she had taught Antonius

Antony: I'll leave you, lady.

Cleopatra: Courteous lord, one word.
    Sir, you and I must part, but that's not it;
    Sir, you and I have loved, but there's not it;   **90**
    That you know well. Something it is I would—
    O, my oblivion is a very Antony,
    And I am all forgotten!

Antony: But that your royalty
    Holds idleness your subject, I should take you
    For idleness itself.

Cleopatra: 'Tis sweating labor   **95**
    To bear such idleness so near the heart
    As Cleopatra this. But, sir, forgive me,
    Since my becomings kill me when they do not
    Eye well to you. Your honor calls you hence;
    Therefore be deaf to my unpitied folly,   **100**
    And all the gods go with you. Upon your sword
    Sit laurel victory, and smooth success
    Be strewed before your feet!

---

this obedience to women, [who] learned so well to be at their commandment"
(Plutarch, *Antony*, 10.3; Spencer, 184).

92–93. "O, my oblivion . . . forgotten": Cleopatra, equating Antony with oblivion, plays on the active and the passive, the subjective and the objective, senses of "oblivion" and "forgotten": she forgets entirely and is entirely forgotten. Her memory abandons her just as—or because—Antony does. On "very" placed before a noun to indicate that the noun must be understood in its full and unrestricted meaning, see Schmidt, s.v. "very."

94. "idleness": (1) folly, (2) feigning.

93–95. "But that . . . idleness itself": if I did not know that you are entirely in command of your appearance of foolishness, I would take you for the personification of foolishness itself.

95. "sweating labor": as painful as childbirth.

97. "As Cleopatra this": as Cleopatra bears the love and sorrow that Antony calls her "idleness."

98. "becomings": (1) graces, (2) changes.

99. "Eye well": look good.

102–3. "Sit . . . before your feet": Cleopatra alludes to two important features of a Roman triumph, of which "[t]here was no more magnificent distinction in Rome" (Livy, 30.15.12). Standing on a chariot drawn by four horses, the triumphing general enters the city via the Triumphal Gate (*Porta Triumphalis*)—a gate

Antony: Let us go. Come.
Our separation so abides and flies
That thou, residing here, goes yet with me,   **105**
And I, hence fleeting, here remain with thee.
Away!   *Exeunt.*

ACT ONE, SCENE FOUR

[Rome. Caesar's House]

Enter Octavius [Caesar] reading a letter, Lepidus, and their Train.

Caesar: You may see, Lepidus, and henceforth know,
It is not Caesar's natural vice to hate

---

opened only for such occasions—amid shouts of joy from huge, jostling crowds, who, dressed in holiday attire and strewing flowers or sprays of laurel in the path of the general, have climbed atop public buildings and erected scaffoldings to get a better view of the spectacle (see *JC*, 1.1.33–52). The triumphant general, dressed in a gold-embroidered robe and a flowered tunic, wears a wreath of Delphic laurel, while holding a laurel bough in his right hand and a scepter in his left (Dionysius of Halicarnassus, *Roman Antiquities*, 5.47; Pliny, 15.39; Plutarch, *Aemilius Paulus*, 34.3–4); see, further, 5.2.207–20.

104. "abides and flies": in our separation we remain together and travel swiftly away (a deliberate paradox).

103–5. "Let us . . . with me": Antony shifts from the royal plural to the personal singular pronoun.

104–6. These are Antony's last words to Cleopatra until just before the battle of Actium (3.7.23).

S.D. 1. Lepidus, a man of modest abilities and minor achievements, has been most notable for his loyalty and reliability to Julius Caesar, his political patron. He proposed Caesar's first dictatorship in 49 (Caesar, *Civil Wars*, 2.21.5), was appointed by Caesar governor of Nearer Spain in 48 (Appian, 2.48; Dio, 43.1.1), was Caesar's co-consul in 46 (Plutarch, *Antony*, 10.1; Dio, 43.1–2), and his master of the horse (the dictator's deputy) until 44 (Appian, 2.107; Dio, 43.33.1, 43, 49.1). Upon his return from Spain, Caesar honored him with a triumph. But, contrary to time-honored Roman practice, he gained the triumph without winning a victory or even fighting an enemy, but for preserving the peace in Further Spain and collecting needed money (Dio, 43.1.1–3; cp. Valerius Maximus, *Memorable Deeds and Sayings*, 2.8.1).

2. "natural vice": unprovoked fault.

Our great competitor. From Alexandria
This is the news: he fishes, drinks, and wastes
The lamps of night in revel, is not more manlike   5
Than Cleopatra, nor the queen of Ptolemy
More womanly than he; hardly gave audience, or
Vouchsafed to think he had partners. You shall find there
A man who is the abstract of all faults
That all men follow.

Lepidus: I must not think there are   **10**
Evils enow to darken all his goodness.
His faults in him seem as the spots of heaven,
More fiery by night's blackness, hereditary

---

3. "competitor": (1) partner, associate, (2) rival.

1–3. Caesar's first words are about himself (to whom he refers in the third person and by the royal "we"), negative (telling what is not natural to him), meant as an edifying lesson ("You may see . . . and henceforth know"), and a self-justification. A defense of himself for criticizing Antony, the words seem meant to disclaim his own pettiness and defend his dignity, which Caesar is always eager to protect (Suetonius, *Augustus*, 25.1).

5. "revel": partying.

6. "queen of Ptolemy": Cleopatra, who became queen at the age of eighteen, was required by her father's will to share the throne with her ten-year-old brother, Ptolemy XIII, and marry him in due time, following ancient Egyptian royal tradition (see 1.1.10n). Before long, the co-rulers fell out and went to war against each other. Ptolemy, stirred up by his regent, the eunuch Pothinus, drove Cleopatra out of Egypt. Julius Caesar, who had pursued Pompey the Great to Egypt after defeating him at Pharsalus, mediated the dispute. He reestablished joint rule and required Cleopatra to marry her young brother, as their father had wished. Led again by his advisors, Ptolemy made war on Caesar and Cleopatra and died in battle. Cleopatra is now his widow (Plutarch, *Caesar*, 48.3, 49.2–5).

7. "gave audience": received messengers from Rome.

8. "Vouchsafed": deigned, condescended.

8. "there": in the letter.

9–10. "the abstract . . . men follow": the epitome of every fault that any man possesses.

10. "must": can.

11. "Evils enow": faults enough.

12. "the spots of heaven": stars.

13. "More fiery . . . blackness": appear more fiery against the dark sky.

Rather than purchased, what he cannot change
Than what he chooses.   **15**

Caesar: You are too indulgent. Let's grant it is not
Amiss to tumble on the bed of Ptolemy,
To give a kingdom for a mirth, to sit
And keep the turn of tippling with a slave,
To reel the streets at noon and stand the buffet   **20**
With knaves that smells of sweat. Say this becomes him—
As his composure must be rare indeed
Whom these things cannot blemish—yet must Antony
No way excuse his foils when we do bear
So great weight in his lightness. If he filled   **25**
His vacancy with his voluptuousness,
Full surfeits and the dryness of his bones
Call on him for't. But to confound such time

---

14. "purchased": acquired.

15. "Than": rather than.

14–15. "what he . . . chooses": since Antony's faults are innate rather than chosen, he cannot change them and so ought not to be blamed for them. Necessity excuses (see Aristotle, *Nicomachean Ethics*, 1109b30–32; Cicero, *On Invention*, 2.98ff).

18. "for a mirth": as a reward for a novel amusement.

19. "keep . . . tippling": keep up with, drink for drink.

20. "reel": stagger drunkenly.

20. "stand the buffet": engage in fistfights.

21. "smells": smell.

18–21. On Antony's taste for low company, see Cicero, *Philippics*, 2.15, 67, 101; Plutarch, *Antony*, 4.2, 6.5, 43.3.

22. "composure": temperament, personal composition (that which composes him).

24. "foils": disgraces.

24–25. "we do . . . lightness": his triviality throws such a heavy burden on us (the metaphor of a scale in which one pan falls as the other rises).

26. "vacancy": free time, leisure.

27. "surfeits": sickness caused by excessive eating and drinking.

27. "dryness of his bones": a symptom of venereal disease.

28. "Call . . . for't": call him to account for it.

28. "confound": waste.

That drums him from his sport and speaks as loud
As his own state and ours, 'tis to be chid   **30**
As we rate boys who, being mature in knowledge,
Pawn their experience to their present pleasure
And so rebel to judgment.

Enter a Messenger.

Lepidus: Here's more news.

Messenger: Thy biddings have been done, and every hour,
Most noble Caesar, shalt thou have report   **35**
How 'tis abroad. Pompey is strong at sea,
And it appears he is beloved of those
That only have feared Caesar. To the ports
The discontents repair, and men's reports

---

29. "drums him": summons him (the metaphor of a military call to arms).

29. "sport": amusement and sexual enjoyment.

29–30. "speaks . . . and ours": makes itself felt and warns of danger to his and our positions as triumvirs.

30. "'tis to be chid": this needs to be rebuked.

31. "rate": berate, scold.

31. "mature in knowledge": old enough to know better.

32. "Pawn . . . pleasure": give up what they have learned to enjoy an immediate pleasure.

33. "to judgment": against good judgment.

37. "of": by.

38. "only have feared Caesar": supported Caesar only out of fear (not love). Caesar is feared because, needing to pay his veterans, he takes land from his political enemies and exacts high taxes in Italy (2.1.13–14; Plutarch, *Antony*, 58.1; Suetonius, *Augustus*, 13.3). When Roman soldiers were citizens obliged to serve, their meager pay was supplemented by plunder and by gifts on the occasion of a general's triumph (see *Cor.*, 1.5.1–8, 1.9.37–38). At the end of their term of military service, they returned to their civilian jobs (Polybius, 6.19). Beginning with Marius (in 107), however, men without property were enlisted into the army, and whenever a major war was finished, the veterans, who had no civilian jobs to return to, looked to their generals for gifts of land in Italy to settle on. The gifts served both to reward the troops and to punish the general's enemies—and contributed greatly to the soldiers' fighting for their commanders rather than for Rome (see Introduction, xiii–xiv).

38. "ports": harbors.

39. "discontents": discontented, malcontents.

Give him much wrongèd.

Caesar: I should have known no less.   **40**
It hath been taught us from the primal state
That he which is was wished until he were,
And the ebbed man, ne'er loved till ne'er worth love,
Comes deared by being lacked. This common body,
Like to a vagabond flag upon the stream,   **45**
Goes to and back, lackeying the varying tide
To rot itself with motion.

Enter a Second Messenger.

Messenger: Caesar, I bring thee word
Menecrates and Menas, famous pirates,

---

40. "Give him": declare him (Pompey) as.

40. "Give him much wrongèd": The discontented, feeling wronged themselves, see Pompey as having been wronged too. In their view, they share not only a common enemy, but a common cause. The discontented, moreover, include not only the dispossessed landowners whose land Caesar confiscated, but the veterans to whom he gave it. While the former complain that they were driven from their homes, the latter complain that they were not treated as well as their service had led them to hope (Suetonius, *Augustus*, 13.3; Appian, 5.3; Dio, 48.8.24).

41. "the primal state": the earliest political society.

42. "which is": who is in power.

42. "wished": wished for (by the people).

42. "he were": he had power.

43. "the ebbed man": the man whose power has receded.

43. "ne'er loved . . . love": never loved until no longer worthy of love (because no longer able to benefit them).

44. "Comes deared": becomes endeared, loved. The Folio reads "feared."

44. "common body": the common people.

45. "vagabond": ever shifting (literally, "wandering").

45. "flag": water iris (or any reed or rush).

46. "lackeying": like a lackey serving his master.

47. "rot itself": make itself putrid.

49. "famous": notorious.

49. Although his father, Pompey the Great, drove from the sea the pirates who had been threatening Rome (Plutarch, *Pompey*, 28.2; Appian, 2.1; Dio, 36.20–37), Sextus has joined forces with them to oppose the triumvirs (see 1.2.190–92n). Menas and Menecrates are Sextus' "foremost sea-captains" (Appian, 5.83). On

Makes the sea serve them, which they ear and wound   **50**
With keels of every kind. Many hot inroads
They make in Italy—the borders maritime
Lack blood to think on't—and flush youth revolt.
No vessel can peep forth but 'tis as soon
Taken as seen, for Pompey's name strikes more   **55**
Than could his war resisted.

Caesar: Antony,
Leave thy lascivious wassails. When thou once
Was beaten from Modena, where thou slew'st
Hirsius and Pansa, consuls, at thy heel

Menas and Menecrates as freedmen, see Appian, 5.76, 96; Dio, 48.30.4. On freedmen serving in Pompey's forces, see Appian, 5.72. Caesar will claim that his war against Pompey was a war against pirates and slaves; see Augustus, *Res Gestae*, 25.1; Horace, *Epodes*, 4.19, 9.7–10.

50. "Makes": make.

50. "ear": plow.

51. "keels": ships.

51. "hot inroads": fierce incursions.

52. "borders maritime": coastal areas.

53. "Lack blood": turn pale (with fear).

53. "flush": spirited.

53. "revolt": revolt to join the pirates

55. "Taken": captured.

55–56. "strikes . . . resisted": causes more trouble than if he attacked and we had to resist.

57. "wassails": revels.

58. "Modena": The Folio reads Medena. Ancient sources refer to the city as Mutina, which North translates as Modena, the city's modern name.

57–59. In 43, Cicero persuaded the Senate to declare Antony a public enemy and to send the consuls, Pansa and Hirtius, to drive him out of Italy. They defeated Antony at Modena (near Bologna) and forced him to retreat westward across the Alps, but both consuls were either killed or mortally wounded (Plutarch, *Antony*, 17.1; Suetonius, *Augustus*, 10.3). Vibius Pansa served under Caesar in Gaul, was tribune in 51, (probably) governor of Bithynia in 47 and Cisalpine Gaul in 45 (Cicero, *Letters to Friends*, 8.8.6, 12.14.4, *Letters to Atticus*, 2.14.4, *For Ligario*, 7). Aulus Hirtius was Caesar's deputy in Gaul before 52, his envoy to Pompey in 50, governor of Transalpine Gaul in 45 and of Belgic Gaul in 44, and Caesar's successor as consul in 43 (Cicero, *Letters to Friends*, 16.27.1–2, *Letters to Atticus*, 7.4.2,

Did famine follow, whom thou fought'st against,   **60**
Though daintily brought up, with patience more
Than savages could suffer. Thou didst drink
The stale of horses and the gilded puddle
Which beasts would cough at. Thy palate then did deign
The roughest berry on the rudest hedge.   **65**
Yea, like the stag when snow the pasture sheets,
The barks of trees thou browsed. On the Alps
It is reported thou didst eat strange flesh
Which some did die to look on. And all this—
It wounds thine honor that I speak it now—   **70**
Was borne so like a soldier that thy cheek
So much as lanked not.

14.9.3; Dio, 45.17.1). He was a student of Cicero and his interlocutor in *On Fate*. He is also the author of the final book (Book 8) of Caesar's *Gallic War* and completed his *Alexandrian War* (Caesar, *Gallic War*, 8 Pref.).

60. "whom": which.

61. "daintily": in great comfort, with a refined palate.

61. "patience more": greater composure.

62. "suffer": summon up.

63. "stale": urine.

63. "gilded": covered with yellow scum.

64. "deign": not disdain, not refuse.

65. "roughest berry . . . hedge": harshest-tasting berry on the wildest bush.

66. "sheets": covers.

67. "browsed": fed on.

68–69. "strange flesh . . . look on": kill anyone who looked at it (cp. looking at the Gorgons, Apollodorus, *Library*, 2.39–41).

71. "so like a soldier": Antony is often described as a heroic warrior, especially by Cleopatra. But, apart from the narrations of his shameful action at Actium (3.1) and of his (apparently avoidable) final defeat at Alexandria (4.7–12), and his own wild exaggeration of his fighting at Philippi (3.11.35–38), Caesar's depiction is the play's only extended description of Antony as a soldier, and it depicts not his noble display of courage in attack and victory, but his arduous endurance of hardship in defeat and retreat. See, further, Introduction, 22n.

72. "lanked not": did not grow thin. If Antony is at his weakest in the presence of pleasure, he is naturally at his best in adversity (Plutarch, *Antony*, 17.2).

Lepidus: 'Tis pity of him.

Caesar: Let his shames quickly
    Drive him to Rome. 'Tis time we twain
    Did show ourselves i'th' field, and to that end   **75**
    Assemble we immediate council. Pompey
    Thrives in our idleness.

Lepidus: Tomorrow, Caesar,
    I shall be furnished to inform you rightly
    Both what by sea and land I can be able
    To front this present time.

Caesar: Till which encounter,   **80**

    It is my business too. Farewell.

Lepidus: Farewell, my lord. What you shall know meantime
    Of stirs abroad, I shall beseech you, sir,
    To let me be partaker.

Caesar: Doubt not, sir.
    I knew it for my bond.   ***Exeunt.***   **85**

---

73. "pity of": regrettable about.
73–74. "Let his shames . . . Rome": On shame moving Antony, see 1.2.115–17n.
74. "twain": two.
75. "i'th' field": on the battlefield.
76. "immediate": an immediate.
78. "furnished": prepared.
79. "I can be able": I can muster.
80. "front": confront.
80. "time": situation, crisis.
82. "my lord": This is the only time a triumvir addresses another submissively as "my lord." Antony, lost in remorse, will use the term addressing no one present (3.11.35); Caesar, trying to bring the drinking party aboard Pompey's ship to an end, will address all the other guests as "Gentle lords" (2.7.121).
83. "stirs": stirrings, disturbances.
84. "partaker": a partaker.
85. "knew": already knew (admonishes Lepidus for asking).
85. "bond": duty, obligation.

ACT ONE, SCENE FIVE

[Alexandria, a room in Cleopatra's palace]

Enter Cleopatra, Charmian, Iras, and Mardian.

Cleopatra: Charmian!

Charmian: Madam?

Cleopatra: Ha, ha!
   Give me to drink mandragora.

Charmian: Why, madam?

Cleopatra: That I might sleep out this great gap of time   **5**
   My Antony is away.

Charmian: You think of him too much.

Cleopatra: O, 'tis treason!

Charmian: Madam, I trust not so.

Cleopatra: Thou, eunuch Mardian!

---

3. "Ha ha": usually understood as a yawn of boredom.

4. "mandragora": mandrake, a narcotic herb. Dioscorides Phacas, Cleopatra's physician, whose medical judgments remained well regarded until the modern era, is the author of a five-book study on the drugs used in medicine. In his chapter on mandrake, he says that the juice extracted from the plant can induce sleep and relieve melancholy (Dioscorides, *Materials of Medicine*, 4.76). See, further, 5.2.352–55.

   Under the Ptolemies, Alexandria, with its magnificent library and generous royal patronage, became the most important center for art and science, including medical science, in the Hellenistic world. Euclid, Archimedes, and Eratosthenes studied and wrote there at this time, Apollonius of Perga and Apollonius of Rhodes earlier, and Galen, Plotinus, Claudius Ptolemy, Clement of Alexandria, and Philo later. See P. M. Fraser, *Ptolemaic Alexandria*, 3 vols. (Oxford: Oxford University Press, 1998).

6. "My Antony": Cleopatra uses the affectionate "[m]y Antony" and "my brave Mark Antony" (line 40) only in this scene. When together, she usually uses the more formal "my lord"—a term she later uses for Caesar. While they quarrel in half of their ten scenes together, she reserves her strongest terms of endearment when Antony is away.

2–8. "Madam? . . . not so": When Cleopatra, here, issues a command, Charmian forces her queen to explain herself, then admonishes her, and finally contradicts her; cp. 1.3.7–9n.

Mardian: What's your Highness' pleasure?

Cleopatra: Not now to hear thee sing. I take no pleasure   **10**
In aught an eunuch has. 'Tis well for thee
That, being unseminared, thy freer thoughts
May not fly forth of Egypt. Hast thou affections?

Mardian: Yes, gracious madam.

Cleopatra: Indeed?   **15**

Mardian: Not in deed, madam, for I can do nothing
But what indeed is honest to be done.
Yet have I fierce affections, and think
What Venus did with Mars.

Cleopatra: O, Charmian,
Where think'st thou he is now? Stands he, or sits he?   **20**
Or does he walk? Or is he on his horse?

---

10. "to hear thee sing": Mardian is the court's official singer (see S.D. 2.5.2).

11. "aught": anything.

12. "unseminared": castrated.

12. "freer": unrestrained, lustful.

13. "of": from.

13. "affections": sexual desires, passions.

15–17. "Indeed? . . . indeed": Where Cleopatra means "Really?" Mardian twice puns on her expression of surprise. He first means "in action" ("in deed") and then uses the word as an adverb for emphasis ("really," "in truth").

17. "honest": chaste.

15–19. "Indeed? . . . Mars": Cleopatra and Mardian play bawdily on "do" (and its variants) and "deed" as euphemisms for sexual intercourse.

18. "have fierce affections": On the sexual desire of eunuchs, see Philostratus, *Life of Apollonius of Tyana*, 1.33, 36, 37.1.

19. Venus, the Roman goddess of love, and Mars, the Roman god of war, were lovers (Ovid, *Metamorphoses*, 4.171–89). Just as he is able only to sing, Mardian refers to a poetic representation of a sexual act rather than to the act itself. His acquaintance is mediated by literature. Moreover, Mardian thinks of the act from Venus' point of view—from a woman's perspective rather than a man's ("What Venus did with Mars").

20. "he": Antony.

O happy horse, to bear the weight of Antony!
Do bravely, horse, for wot'st thou whom thou mov'st?
The demi-Atlas of this earth, the arm
And burgonet of men. He's speaking now,   25
Or murmuring "Where's my serpent of old Nile?"
For so he calls me. Now I feed myself
With most delicious poison. Think on me
That am with Phoebus' amorous pinches black,
And wrinkled deep in time. Broad-fronted Caesar,   30
When thou wast here above the ground, I was
A morsel for a monarch. And great Pompey

---

22. "bear . . . Antony": Cleopatra is thinking of her own pleasure when bearing his weight. "Riding (or mounting) a horse" is a bawdy phrase for sexual intercourse.

23. "bravely": splendidly (display a proud spirit).

23. "wot'st thou": do you know.

24. "The demi-Atlas . . . earth": Antony supports half the world, as Atlas bore the globe on his shoulders. Cleopatra seems to disregard Lepidus as a member of the triumvirate.

24–25. "arm And burgonet": weapon (for offense) and light steel helmet (for defense).

26–27. "Where's my serpent . . . calls me": Antony turns the Egyptian reverence for serpents into his amorous name for Cleopatra. The Egyptians worship the serpent because it "does never age and wax old, but moves in all facility, ready ease and celerity, without the means of any instrument of motion" (Plutarch, *Isis and Osiris*, 74 [381a–b]; Holland, 1316); cp. 2.2.245–46.

28. "delicious poison": delicious, because she imagines Antony thinking of her; poison, because it reminds her that they are apart.

28–30. "Think . . . time": While exaggerating her age (barely thirty), Cleopatra invents a past, godly lover, turning her skin tanned by the sun into her skin darkened by the sun-god's (Phoebus') caresses. On Phoebus, see 5.2.316n.

30. "Broad-fronted Caesar": Julius Caesar had been her lover and the father of her son Caesarion. "Of stature [Caesar] is reported to have been tall, . . . with limbs well trussed and in good plight, [and] somewhat full faced" (Suetonius, *Caesar*, 45.1; in *History of Twelve Caesars*, trans. Philemon Holland [1606], 2 vols. [London: David Nutt, 1899], 1:48).

32. "morsel": sexual mouthful (eating will now become a frequent metaphor for sex).

32. "great Pompey": not Pompey the Great, but his son Gnaeus (79–45). The Ptolemies, for generations, have used their influence (and wealth) in Rome to secure their rule in Egypt. And ever since she was first on the throne, Cleopatra

Would stand and make his eyes grow in my brow;
There would he anchor his aspect, and die
With looking on his life.   35

Enter Alexas from Antony.

Alexas: Sovereign of Egypt, hail!

Cleopatra: How much unlike art thou Mark Antony!
Yet coming from him, that great medicine hath
With his tinct gilded thee.
How goes it with my brave Mark Antony?   40

Alexas: Last thing he did, dear queen,
He kissed—the last of many doubled kisses—
This orient pearl. His speech sticks in my heart.

Cleopatra: Mine ear must pluck it thence.

Alexas: "Good friend," quoth he,

---

has used love for her own political interests. While Caesar was conquering in Gaul,
Pompey the Great became Egypt's patron and protector. And when Pompey, in
return, appealed to her for help in his civil war with Caesar, Cleopatra received his
son Gnaeus, who became her lover, and sent Pompey the Great ships loaded with
grain. After Pompey's defeat at Pharsalus, Cleopatra, seducing the man she had
opposed, won the love and much-needed support of Caesar in her own civil war
with her brother. While Cleopatra's political fortunes have helped determine her
choice of lovers, her choice of lovers has helped determine her political fortunes
(Plutarch, *Antony*, 25.3; Appian, 2.87; see, further, 2.6.70n).

33. "make . . . brow": fix his eyes on my face.

34. "aspect": gaze.

34. "die": experience orgasm.

35. "With": from.

37. "thou": you to.

38–39. "Great medicine" and "tinct" ("tincture") are technical terms of alchemy
for the elixir thought to turn base or "sick" metals into gold. By virtue of his
mere presence, Cleopatra says, Antony has imparted some—but only some—of
his luster to a lesser man. He has not given Alexas the properties of gold, but has
covered him in gold. In Cleopatra's day, Alexandria was the center of Hellenistic
alchemy; see line 4n.

40. "brave": splendid.

43. "orient": brilliant, lustrous. Pearls from the East were thought to be the most
beautiful, and the special sheen of such a beautiful pearl is called its "orient."

"Say the firm Roman to great Egypt sends **45**
This treasure of an oyster; at whose foot,
To mend the petty present, I will piece
Her opulent throne with kingdoms. All the East,
Say thou, shall call her mistress." So he nodded
And soberly did mount an arm-gaunt steed, **50**
Who neighed so high that what I would have spoke
Was beastly dumbed by him.

Cleopatra: What, was he sad, or merry?

Alexas: Like to the time o'th' year between the extremes
Of hot and cold, he was nor sad nor merry. **55**

Cleopatra: O, well-divided disposition! Note him,
Note him, good Charmian, 'tis the man! But note him:
He was not sad, for he would shine on those
That make their looks by his; he was not merry,
Which seemed to tell them his remembrance lay **60**

---

45. "firm": constant, unwavering.

45. "Egypt": queen of Egypt, Cleopatra.

47. "To mend . . . present": to compensate for this trivial gift.

47. "piece": add to, enlarge.

47–49. "I will . . . mistress": Antony treats the lands which he has conquered or defends as a triumvir as belonging to him, not to Rome. They are his to give to whomever he wishes as personal gifts (see 1.1.12n).

50. "soberly": somberly.

50. "arm-gaunt steed": (probably) hard and trim from service in battle. "Gaunt" seems meant as praise.

51. "high": loudly, strongly.

52. "beastly dumbed": silenced or drowned out by the beast's noise.

53. "sad": serious.

55. "nor": neither.

56. "well-divided disposition": well-balanced temperament.

56. "Note": observe.

57. "'tis the man": that's exactly what he's like.

57. "But": only, just.

58. "would": wished to.

59. "make their looks by his": fashion their demeanor according to his.

60. "remembrance": memory.

In Egypt with his joy; but between both.
O, heavenly mingle! Be'st thou sad or merry,
The violence of either thee becomes,
So does it no man's else. Met'st thou my posts?

Alexas: Ay, madam, twenty several messengers.   65
Why do you send so thick?

Cleopatra: Who's born that day
When I forget to send to Antony
Shall die a beggar. Ink and paper, Charmian!
Welcome, my good Alexas! Did I, Charmian,
Ever love Caesar so?

Charmian: O, that brave Caesar!   70

Cleopatra: Be choked with such another emphasis!
Say "the brave Antony."

Charmian: The valiant Caesar!

Cleopatra: By Isis, I will give thee bloody teeth
If thou with Caesar paragon again

---

63. "The violence ... becomes": the vehement display of either looks well on him.
This is the only time Cleopatra praises Antony (or anyone else) for moderation.
Antony will later say that she does not know what moderation is (3.13.125–27).
Here, proving him right, she gets it wrong. Where Alexas, sounding like an old-
fashioned Roman, explicitly spoke of Antony's avoiding extremes, Cleopatra,
although initially claiming that he was "between both," quickly shifts and takes
him to mean that Antony mixed ("mingle") rather than avoided both. "[B]etween
both" comes to mean not holding a middle degree, but alternately subject to the
"violence" of opposite extremes.

64. "So": as.

64. "posts": messengers.

65. "several": separate.

66. "thick": often, in rapid succession.

66. "Who's": anyone who is.

66–68. "The Egyptians were also the first to assign each month and each day to a
particular deity, and to foretell by the date of a man's birth his character, his fortunes, and the date of his death" (Herodotus, 2.82); see also S.D. 2.3.10n.

70. "Caesar": Julius Caesar.

71. "emphasis": emphatic expression.

74. "paragon": compare, match.

My man of men!

Charmian: By your most gracious pardon,   **75**
I sing but after you.

Cleopatra: My salad days,
When I was green in judgment, cold in blood,
To say as I said then. But come, away,
Get me ink and paper.
He shall have every day a several greeting,   **80**
Or I'll unpeople Egypt.   ***Exeunt.***

---

75. "man of men": a superlative man, distinguished from all by his manly excellence.

76. "I sing . . . you": as a good servant follows her mistress, I simply repeat the tune you sang earlier.

76. "My salad days": when I was immature. "Caesar and [Gnaeus] Pompey knew her when she was but a young thing, and knew not then what the world meant" (Plutarch, *Antony*, 25.3; Spencer, 200).

77. "blood": desire.

80. "several": separate.

81. "Or I'll . . . Egypt": even if I have to empty my kingdom of people to deliver them.

ACT TWO, SCENE ONE

[Messina, Pompey's house.]

Enter Pompey, Menecrates, and Menas, in warlike manner.

Pompey: If the great gods be just, they shall assist
   The deeds of justest men.

Menecrates: Know, worthy Pompey,
   That what they do delay they not deny.

Pompey: Whiles we are suitors to their throne, decays
   The thing we sue for.

Menecrates: We, ignorant of ourselves,   5
   Beg often our own harms, which the wise powers
   Deny us for our good; so find we profit
   By losing of our prayers.

Pompey: I shall do well.
   The people love me, and the sea is mine;
   My powers are crescent, and my auguring hope   10

---

1. "shall": will surely.

1–2. "If the great gods . . . justest men": Pompey, priding himself on his piety, has taken the word "Pius" as his cognomen. He thinks that he represents the justest cause, for he champions his father's cause and has given refuge in Sicily to many who were proscribed or feared they would be (Appian, 5.25). A clear sign that he believes the gods assist the deeds of just men, after unseasonable storms ravaged Caesar's fleet near Sicily, Pompey celebrated Neptune's help as the god's just reward for his piety and vowed to call himself "son of Neptune" (Appian, 5.100).

4. "suitors": petitioners.

4–5. "Whiles . . . sue for": the thing we pray for steadily loses value while we continue to pray for it.

5–8. "We, ignorant . . . prayers": the gods protect us from ourselves; their wisdom corrects our ignorance; we wish for what is good for us, but the gods know what is good for us; their denial is their blessing in disguise (see Seneca, *Letters*, 60.1; Juvenal, *Satires*, 10.346–52).

9. "the sea is mine": Pompey's dominance of the sea is the crux of his power.

10. "powers": forces, strength.

10. "crescent": growing from day to day (waxing like the moon).

10. "auguring": prophesying.

Says it will come to th' full. Mark Antony
In Egypt sits at dinner, and will make
No wars without doors. Caesar gets money where
He loses hearts. Lepidus flatters both,
Of both is flattered; but he neither loves,   **15**
Nor either cares for him.

Menas: Caesar and Lepidus
Are in the field. A mighty strength they carry.

Pompey: Where have you this? 'Tis false.

Menas: From Silvius, sir.

Pompey: He dreams. I know they are in Rome together,
Looking for Antony. But all the charms of love,   **20**
Salt Cleopatra, soften thy waned lip!
Let witchcraft join with beauty, lust with both;
Tie up the libertine in a field of feasts;
Keep his brain fuming. Epicurean cooks
Sharpen with cloyless sauce his appetite,   **25**
That sleep and feeding may prorogue his honor
Even till a Lethe'd dullness—

---

11. "it": his fortunes, his hope of victory.

13. "without doors": out of doors, outside (as opposed to his bedroom warfare with Cleopatra).

15. "Of": by.

15. "neither loves": loves neither.

17. "in the field": ready for battle.

20. "Looking for Antony": on the lookout for Antony, hoping for his arrival.

21. "Salt": lecherous.

21. "waned": faded (or dark) and diminished (like the waning moon). The Folio reads "wand."

22–23. "Let witchcraft . . . up": let witchcraft, beauty and lust join together to tie up.

24. "Keep his brain fuming": keep him drunk from the fumes of wine in his brain.

24. "Epicurean": devoted to sensual pleasure.

25. "cloyless": never cloying.

26–27. "prorogue . . . Lethe's dullness": postpone all thoughts of his honor until he has sunk into oblivion. In the classical underworld, Lethe is a river which causes

Enter Varrius.

How now, Varrius?

Varrius: This is most certain that I shall deliver:
Mark Antony is every hour in Rome
Expected. Since he went from Egypt 'tis   **30**
A space for farther travel.

Pompey: I could have given less matter
A better ear. Menas, I did not think
This amorous surfeiter would have donned his helm
For such a petty war. His soldiership   **35**
Is twice the other twain. But let us rear
The higher our opinion, that our stirring
Can from the lap of Egypt's widow pluck
The ne'er lust-wearied Antony.

---

those who drink from it to forget completely this life. In Greek, *lēthē* means forgetfulness or oblivion.

28. "deliver": report.

29. "every": each.

30–31. "Since . . . farther travel": enough time has passed for him to have traveled even farther.

32. "less matter": news of less substance.

36. "twice . . . twain": double the other two. "Now there were divers hot skirmishes and encounters [against Pompey the Great at Dyrrhachium in 48], in the which Antonius fought so valiantly, that he carried the praise from them all: but specially at two several times, when [Julius] Caesar's men turned their backs and fled for life. For he stepped before them, and compelled them to return again to fight: so that the victory fell on Caesar's side. For this cause he had the second place in the camp among the soldiers, and they spake of no other man unto Caesar, but of him: who showed plainly what opinion he had of him, when at the last battle of Pharsalus (which indeed was the last trial of all, to give the conqueror the whole empire of the world) he himself did lead the right wing of his army, and gave Antonius the leading of the left wing, as the valiantest man and skilfullest soldier of all those he had about him" (Plutarch, *Antony*, 8.1–2; Spencer, 181–82).

36–37. "rear . . . our opinion": think better of ourselves. Pompey is highly susceptible to flattery, including self-flattery; see, further, 2.6.42–46n.

38. "lap": a sexual allusion.

38. "Egypt's widow": widow of brother, Ptolemy XIII; see 1.4.6n.

Menas: I cannot hope
Caesar and Antony shall well greet together.   **40**
His wife that's dead did trespasses to Caesar;
His brother warred upon him, although I think
Not moved by Antony.

Pompey: I know not, Menas,
How lesser enmities may give way to greater.
Were't not that we stand up against them all,   **45**
'Twere pregnant they should square between themselves,
For they have entertained cause enough
To draw their swords. But how the fear of us
May cement their divisions and bind up
The petty difference, we yet not know.   **50**
Be't as our gods will have't! It only stands
Our lives upon to use our strongest hands.
Come, Menas.   ***Exeunt.***

---

39. "cannot hope": do not expect.

40. "well greet together": (1) meet on friendly terms, (2) come to an amicable agreement.

41. "wife that's dead": Fulvia.

41. "trespasses": wrongs.

42. "His brother . . . him": on Lucius Antonius, see 1.2.93–99n.

43. "moved": instigated, encouraged.

44. "enmities": hostilities.

46. "pregnant": (1) to be expected, (2) obvious.

46. "square": square off, quarrel, fight.

47. "entertained": provided each other.

49. "cement their divisions": repair their disagreements.

50. "difference": quarrel.

51. "Be't . . . will have't": For Pompey's deference to the gods, see lines 1–2n.

51–52. "It only . . . strongest hands": our lives depend on nothing but our using our utmost strength.

ACT TWO, SCENE TWO

[Rome. Lepidus' house.]

Enter Enobarbus and Lepidus.

Lepidus: Good Enobarbus, 'tis a worthy deed,
    And shall become you well, to entreat your captain
    To soft and gentle speech.

Enobarbus: I shall entreat him
    To answer like himself. If Caesar move him,
    Let Antony look over Caesar's head   5
    And speak as loud as Mars. By Jupiter,
    Were I the wearer of Antonio's beard,
    I would not shave't today.

Lepidus: 'Tis not a time
    For private stomaching.

Enobarbus: Every time
    Serves for the matter that is then born in't.   **10**

Lepidus: But small to greater matters must give way.

Enobarbus: Not if the small come first.

Lepidus: Your speech is passion;

---

3. "gentle": gentlemanlike.

4. "like himself": as befits his greatness (namely, openly and strongly).

4. "move": provoke.

5. "look over Caesar's head": Antony was taller and more imposing. While Caesar wore elevated shoes so that he might seem taller than he was (Suetonius, *Augustus*, 73), Antony resembled pictures depicting Hercules (Plutarch, *Antony*, 4.2); see, further, 1.3.85n.

6. "as loud as Mars": "The brazen Ares [Mars] bellowed loud as nine thousand warriors or ten thousand cry in battle, when they join in the strife of the war god" (Homer, *Iliad*, 5.859–61).

8. "not shave't today": to answer like himself is for Antony to answer like a manly man.

9. "private stomaching": personal resentment.

3–12. In each reply, Enobarbus contradicts Lepidus by catching a key word and hurling it back at him with a contrary result. The rhetorical tactic is called *urbanitas* in Latin, *asteismus* in Greek.

But pray you stir no embers up. Here comes
The noble Antony.

Enter Antony and Ventidius.

Enobarbus: And yonder Caesar.

Enter Caesar, Maecenas, and Agrippa.

Antony: If we compose well here, to Parthia. **15**
Hark, Ventidius.

Caesar: I do not know, Maecenas. Ask Agrippa.

Lepidus: Noble friends,
That which combined us was most great, and let not
A leaner action rend us. What's amiss, **20**
May it be gently heard. When we debate
Our trivial difference loud, we do commit
Murder in healing wounds. Then, noble partners,
The rather for I earnestly beseech,
Touch you the sourest points with sweetest terms, **25**
Nor curstness grow to th' matter.

---

15. "compose": come to terms.

15. "Parthia": see 1.2.105–9n and lines 152–61n.

16. "Hark": pay close attention.

17. "I do not . . . Ask Agrippa": On Caesar's frequent deference to Agrippa's judgment, see, for example, Dio, 50.31.1–2.

18. "Noble": Lepidus, always praising what promises peace among the triumvirs, addresses or describes Antony, Antony and Caesar, and Antony's speech as "noble" five times in the scene (lines 14, 18, 23, 104, 180). Apart from pronouns, prepositions, articles, etc., the obsequious "noble" is his most frequent word. When encouraging or praising Antony's and Caesar's subordinates for peace-promoting speeches, he uses the less exalted but still flattering "worthy" (line 1) and "worthily" (line 108).

20. "leaner": slighter.

20. "What's": whatever is.

21. "gently": kindly.

22. "loud": loudly.

23. "in healing": in trying to heal.

24. "The rather . . . beseech": all the more because I earnestly beg you to do so.

25. "Touch": touch upon.

26. "Nor . . . th' matter": and do not let ill temper be added to the matter we discuss.

Antony: 'Tis spoken well.
Were we before our armies, and to fight,
I should do thus.   **Flourish.**

Caesar: Welcome to Rome.

Antony: Thank you.   **30**

Caesar: Sit.

Antony: Sit, sir.

Caesar: Nay, then.   **[*They sit.*]**

Antony: I learn you take things ill which are not so,
   Or, being, concern you not.

Caesar: I must be laughed at   **35**
   If, or for nothing or a little, I
   Should say myself offended, and with you
   Chiefly i'th' world; more laughed at, that I should
   Once name you derogately when to sound your name
   It not concerned me.

Antony: My being in Egypt, Caesar,   **40**
   What was't to you?   •

Caesar: No more than my residing here at Rome

----

27. "to fight": to be about to fight (the enemy).

28. "do thus": offering a gesture, such as shaking hands or embracing. The Flourish indicates some ceremonial action. Neither Antony nor Caesar, upon entering, acknowledged the other.

31–33. Each man jockeys to get the other to sit first. Honor goes with giving rather than receiving (see lines 229–32, 3.13.69–73), and a hospitable gesture, even in small matters, may be seen as a sign of superiority among spirited rivals. However, even though he is always guarding his status among the triumvirs, Caesar accepts the invitation and sits first. Although not wanting to appear subordinate, he needs Antony's support of arms and aid. On the hostility behind ritual competition in generosity, see, for example, Livy, 2.41.5–7.

35. "being": being so.

36. "or": either.

39. "derogately": derogatorily, disparagingly.

39. "sound": mention.

40–41. "My being . . . you": For their unvarnished exchange, see Suetonius, *Augustus*, 69.2.

Might be to you in Egypt. Yet if you there
Did practice on my state, your being in Egypt
Might be my question.

Antony: How intend you, "practiced"?   **45**

Caesar: You may be pleased to catch at mine intent
By what did here befall me. Your wife and brother
Made wars upon me, and their contestation
Was theme for you; you were the word of war.

Antony: You do mistake your business. My brother never   **50**
Did urge me in his act. I did inquire it,
And have my learning from some true reports
That drew their swords with you. Did he not rather
Discredit my authority with yours,
And make the wars alike against my stomach,   **55**
Having alike your cause? Of this my letters

---

44. "practice . . . my state": plot or scheme against my rule.

45. "my question": a cause of my concern.

45. "intend": mean.

46. "catch at": guess.

47. "befall": happen to.

48. "contestation": contention, contest.

49. "theme for you": an affair undertaken in your interest.

49. "you were . . . war": they made war in your name. Fulvia claimed to be working in Antony's behalf (Dio, 48.5.4).

50. "business": matter of concern.

51. "urge me": use my name (to justify his action).

51. "inquire": inquire into.

52. "learning": information.

52. "true reports": trustworthy reporters.

53. "with": along with.

54. "Discredit": bring into discredit.

54. "with": together with.

55. "stomach": desire, wishes.

56. "Having . . . cause": I having the same cause to be offended as you. Lucius Antonius (82–39) was consul in 41 and defended that office, the Republic's highest elective office, against the triumvirs, who, proceeding in the guise of legitimate, traditional authority, claimed its powers. Thus Antony, arguing that his brother's

Before did satisfy you. If you'll patch a quarrel,
As matter whole you have to make it with,
It must not be with this.

Caesar: You praise yourself
By laying defects of judgment to me; but   **60**
You patched up your excuses.

Antony: Not so, not so!
I know you could not lack—I am certain on't—
Very necessity of this thought, that I,
Your partner in the cause 'gainst which he fought,
Could not with graceful eyes attend those wars   **65**
Which fronted mine own peace. As for my wife,
I would you had her spirit in such another.
The third o'th' world is yours, which with a snaffle
You may pace easy, but not such a wife.

Enobarbus: Would we had all such wives, that the men   **70**
might go to wars with the women!

---

war was a rebellion against the authority of all the triumvirs, claims to have as
much reason as Caesar to be displeased with his brother. On the establishment
and legal authority of the triumvirate, see Plutarch, *Antony*, 19–20; Appian, 4.2–12;
Dio, 46.54–56; on Lucius Antonius, see Appian, 5.19ff.; Suetonius, *Augustus*, 14.1.

57. "did . . . you": fully informed you.

57. "patch a quarrel": piece together scraps to make up a cause to quarrel.

58. "As matter . . . with": as though you have a substantial matter on which to
make it.

62. "lack": fail to understand.

62. "on't": of it.

63. "Very necessity": the absolute unavoidableness.

65. "with . . . attend": with friendly eyes regard.

66. "fronted": confronted, opposed.

63–66. "I, . . . peace": self-interest alone should acquit me.

67. "I would . . . another": I wish you had such a wife (then you would know how
difficult she was to control); see 1.1.21n.

68. "snaffle": a bridle bit (with less retraining power than a bit with a curb).

69. "pace easy": train to pace easily (to ride with a snaffle is to guide with a light
hand).

71. "with": (1) on the same side, or (2) on the opposite side. For sex as erotic
warfare, see 2.1.12–13.

Antony: So much uncurbable, her garboils, Caesar,
Made out of her impatience—which not wanted
Shrewdness of policy too—I grieving grant
Did you too much disquiet. For that you must   **75**
But say I could not help it.

Caesar: I wrote to you
When rioting in Alexandria; you
Did pocket up my letters, and with taunts
Did gibe my missive out of audience.

Antony: Sir,
He fell upon me ere admitted, then.   **80**
Three kings I had newly feasted, and did want
Of what I was i'th' morning. But next day
I told him of myself, which was as much
As to have asked him pardon. Let this fellow

---

72. "So much uncurable": she being so unmanageable.

72. "garboils": disturbances.

73. "Made out of her impatience": "[Antony] was informed that his wife Fulvia was the only cause of this war, who, being of a peevish, crooked, and troublesome nature, had purposely raised this uproar in Italy, in hope thereby to withdraw him from Cleopatra" (Plutarch, *Antony*, 30.2; Spencer, 208).

73. "not wanted": did not lack.

74. "Shrewdness of policy": cunning as a scheme (to force Antony's return).

75. "Did": caused.

75. "For": as for.

75–76. "must But say": must at least admit.

77. "rioting": you were reveling.

79. "gibe": flout, express contempt for.

79. "missive": messenger.

79. "out of audience": without being heard.

80. "ere admitted": before permitted.

81. "Three kings . . . feasted": As a defensive step before the Parthian campaign, Antony will have reorganized client-kingdoms in the East, placing on the thrones reliable kings whose political sentiments serve his interests (see 3.6.69–77n). His feasting three Eastern kings may have been political preparation for the campaign, of which he may not want Caesar to know.

81–82. "did want . . . morning": was not as I had been earlier in the day.

83. "of myself": of my previous condition.

Be nothing of our strife; if we contend,   **85**
Out of our question wipe him.

Caesar: You have broken
The article of your oath, which you shall never
Have tongue to charge me with.

Lepidus: Soft, Caesar!

Antony: No, Lepidus, let him speak.   **90**
The honor is sacred which he talks on now,
Supposing that I lacked it. But on, Caesar:
"The article of my oath"?

Caesar: To lend me arms and aid when I required them,
The which you both denied.

Antony: Neglected, rather;   **95**
And then when poisoned hours had bound me up
From mine own knowledge. As nearly as I may
I'll play the penitent to you, but mine honesty
Shall not make poor my greatness, nor my power
Work without it. Truth is that Fulvia,   **100**

85–86. "if we contend . . . him": if we are to quarrel, leave him out of it.

87. "The article . . . oath": the terms of our sworn agreement.

88. "Have tongue . . . with": be able to reproach me for.

89. "Soft": be calm, be careful. The seriousness of Caesar's accusation is evident from Lepidus' caution, which is the closest he ever comes to a command or an injunction. To give one's oath is to give one's word of honor. It is to pledge one's honor as the guarantor of one's promise. To violate one's oath is to violate one's honor.

91. "talks on": talks of.

91. "The honor . . . now": "An oath was regarded and kept by the Romans as something inviolable and sacred" (Gellius, 6.18).

92. "on": go on, continue.

94. "arms": soldiers.

94. "required": requested.

96–97. "bound me . . . knowledge": I was too drunk to know what I was doing. On such a defense as a last resort, see Aristotle, *Rhetoric to Alexander*, 1429a15–19.

98. "play the penitent": apologize.

97–100. "As nearly . . . without it": Antony tries to reconcile the demands of his dignity ("greatness") and of his honor ("honesty"). His honor will prompt him to apologize, but only to the extent that it does not compromise his dignity, yet his

To have me out of Egypt, made wars here,
For which myself, the ignorant motive, do
So far ask pardon as befits mine honor ·
To stoop in such a case.

Lepidus: 'Tis noble spoken.

Maecenas: If it might please you to enforce no further   **105**
The griefs between you, to forget them quite
Were to remember that the present need
Speaks to atone you.

Lepidus: Worthily spoken, Maecenas.

Enobarbus: Or, if you borrow one another's love for
the instant, you may, when you hear no more words   **110**
of Pompey, return it again. You shall have time to
wrangle in when you have nothing else to do.

Antony: Thou art a soldier only. Speak no more.

Enobarbus: That truth should be silent I had almost
forgot.   **115**

---

dignity will not cause him to ignore his duty to act with honor. Where Caesar is always concerned about his dignity, Antony, although often careless of his dignity, particularly in front of subordinates, is always attentive to it in front of Caesar, his great rival.

102. "ignorant motive": unknowing moving cause.

104. "noble": nobly.

105. "enforce": emphasize, insist on.

106. "griefs": grievances.

108. "atone": reconcile (literally "at one").

105–8. On Maecenas' distinctive mincing diction, see Seneca, *Letters*, 114.4–8; Suetonius, *Augustus*, 86; Tacitus, *Dialogue on Oratory*, 26.1. Note also 4.1.7–11, 5.1.34–35.

109–12. "Or, if you . . . do": the reconciliation can last only as long as Pompey threatens (a shrewd if cynical restatement, in plain language, of Maecenas' affected speech).

113. "a soldier only": just a subordinate, not a triumvir.

114–15. "That truth . . . almost forgot": Enobarbus misunderstands Antony—or, pretending to, understands him correctly—as referring to the truth of what he said rather than to his inferior status. Diplomatic exchanges are apt to leave unstated or half-stated at least some of the truth (for example, lines 18–26), even when

Antony: You wrong this presence; therefore speak no more.

Enobarbus: Go to, then. Your considerate stone.

Caesar: I do not much dislike the matter, but
  The manner of his speech; for't cannot be
  We shall remain in friendship, our conditions   **120**
  So differing in their acts. Yet if I knew
  What hoop should hold us staunch, from edge to edge
  O'th' world I would pursue it.

Agrippa: .   Give me leave, Caesar.

Caesar: Speak, Agrippa.

Agrippa: Thou hast a sister by the mother's side,   **125**
  Admired Octavia. Great Mark Antony
  Is now a widower.

Caesar: Say not so, Agrippa.
  If Cleopatra heard you, your reproof
  Were well deserved of rashness.

Antony: I am not married, Caesar. Let me hear   **130**
  Agrippa further speak.

---

otherwise brutally blunt (for example, 5.2.127–32). This is one of the many times that Enobarbus speaks in an aphorism.

116. "presence": eminent company.

117. "Go to, then": all right then (a phrase of concession).

117. "Your": I am your.

117. "considerate stone": (1) I will be considerate of your wishes and therefore be as silent as a stone, but (2) I will continue to consider or to think.

120. "conditions": temperaments, dispositions, characters.

121. "acts": conduct.

122. "What hoop ... staunch": what fastener could hold us fast together (the metaphor of a hoop holding a barrel together to make it watertight).

123. "Give me leave": allow me to speak.

129. "of": for its.

127–29. "Say not ... rashness": Caesar covers his (presumably) carefully contrived course by accusing his spokesman of rashness, allowing Antony to end the discussion with no embarrassment to Caesar.

130. "I am not married": "For he denied not that he kept Cleopatra, but so did he not confess that he had her as his wife" (Plutarch, *Antony*, 31.1; Spencer, 210).

Agrippa: To hold you in perpetual amity,
    To make you brothers, and to knit your hearts
    With an unslipping knot, take Antony
    Octavia to his wife, whose beauty claims   **135**
    No worse a husband than the best of men;
    Whose virtue and whose general graces speak
    That which none else can utter. By this marriage
    All little jealousies, which now seem great,
    And all great fears, which now import their dangers, **140**
    Would then be nothing. Truths would be tales,
    Where now half-tales be truths. Her love to both
    Would each to other and all loves to both
    Draw after her. Pardon what I have spoke,
    For 'tis a studied, not a present thought,   **145**
    By duty ruminated.

Antony: Will Caesar speak?

Caesar: Not till he hears how Antony is touched
    With what is spoke already.

Antony: What power is in Agrippa,
    If I would say "Agrippa, be it so,"   **150**
    To make this good?

135–38. "whose beauty . . . utter": "Lady Octavia, having an excellent grace, wisdom, and honesty, joined unto so rare a beauty . . . " (Plutarch, *Antony*, 31.2; Spencer, 210).

139. "jealousies": suspicions.

140. "import": bring with them.

141–42. "Truths . . . be truths": disturbing truths would be dismissed as mere gossip, where vague rumors are now accepted as truths.

142–43. "Her love . . . other": her love for her husband and for her brother would inspire each of them to love each other.

143–44. "all loves . . . after her": and the love of everyone for both men would follow from their love for her.

145–46. "'tis a studied, . . . ruminated": it is a carefully considered, not a momentary, thought, which by duty I have turned over many times in my mind. Aprippa's curious apology seems meant to confirm to Antony that the proposal comes from Caesar.

147–48. "touched With": affected by.

148. "is spoke already": has already been said.

149–51. "What power . . . good": Neither man wants to accept what the other might withhold or reject.

Caesar: The power of Caesar, and
His power unto Octavia.

Antony: May I never
To this good purpose, that so fairly shows,
Dream of impediment! Let me have thy hand
Further this act of grace; and from this hour   **155**
The heart of brothers govern in our loves
And sway our great designs!

Caesar: There's my hand. [*They clasp hands.*]
A sister I bequeath you whom no brother
Did ever love so dearly. Let her live
To join our kingdoms and our hearts; and never   **160**
Fly off our loves again.

---

153. "so fairly shows": seems so promising.

155. "Further": to further.

154–55. "Let me . . . act of grace": give me your hand in furtherance of this act of
reconciliation. Although the Folio has none, some editors add a stop after "hand,"
which seems to disrupt the intended meaning.

157. "There's my hand": Since faith is thought to be held in the right hand, which
is sacred to Fides, the Roman god of fidelity, "pledges by right hands [are] the customary witness to good faith" (Cicero, *Philippics*, 11.5). Consequently, the clasping
of right hands is a solemn gesture of mutual fidelity (Livy, 1.21.4, 23.9.3).

158. "bequeath": bestow upon.

158. "you": Although Antony, offering his hand, suddenly shifts to the familiar
"thy" (line 154), Caesar, accepting it, retains the distant "you." Throughout the
play, Caesar addresses Antony with the familiar pronoun only when apostrophiz-
ing him, never to his face (1.4.56–72, 5.1.35–48).

159. "love so dearly": "It is reported that he dearly loved his sister Octavia, for
indeed she was a noble Lady" (Plutarch, *Antony*, 31.1; Spencer, 210).

161. "Fly off our loves": our amity desert us.

123–61. From its earliest days, Rome, a city of sovereign fathers (Livy, 1.8; Plutarch, *Romulus*, 13.1–4), regarded marriage as sacred (Dionysius of Halicarnassus,
2.25). According to Plutarch, the first divorce in Rome occurred 230 years after
the city's founding (because the wife was barren) (Plutarch, *Comparison of Theseus
and Romulus*, 6.3). Other historians say it was not until some five centuries after
the founding (Dionysius of Halicarnassus, 2.25.7; Gellus, 4.3, 17.21.44; Valerius
Maximus, 2.1.4). Yet, despite the traditional sanctity of marriage, political mar-
riages and divorces have become the rule rather than the rare exception in Rome.
In *Antony and Cleopatra*, Pompey's family, which will in fact end with his death,

Lepidus: Happily, amen!

Antony: I did not think to draw my sword 'gainst Pompey,
For he hath laid strange courtesies and great
Of late upon me. I must thank him only,
Lest my remembrance suffer ill report;   **165**
At heel of that, defy him.

Lepidus: Time calls upon's.
Of us must Pompey presently be sought,
Or else he seeks out us.

Antony: Where lies he?

Caesar: About the Mount Misena.   **170**

---

is the only traditional Roman family, apart from the one Antony regrets he never had (3.13.111–13). The sanctity of marriage has been reduced to a distant memory.

152–61. Why does Antony agree to the marriage? Caesar will, of course, exploit his (predictable) betrayal of Octavia to rally Roman opinion against him and use it as a justification for war (see 3.6.1–24). Antony's decision may nevertheless show the same political astuteness which he demonstrates in *Julius Caesar* and which had made him initially the dominating member of the triumvirate. Defeat of the Parthians promises Antony unrivaled power and glory. Victory would bring the entire East under Roman control, revenge Roman honor for Crassus' disgraceful defeat and death at Carrhae twenty years earlier (see 3.1.2–3n), prove Antony in the eyes of the Romans, especially the legionaries, and, earning him a massive triumph in Rome, eclipse the unpopular Caesar, leaving Antony the sole ruler of the world. A Parthian campaign, however, requires peace in the West—peace between Pompey and the triumvirs, on the one hand, and Antony and Caesar, on the other. And, for that, Antony needs the proposed marriage: "If we compose well here, to Parthia" (line 15; see also 2.3.30–31). Once Antony has his Roman triumph, he need not care about offending Caesar or playing into his hands.

163. "strange": rare, remarkable.

163–64. "hath laid . . . upon me": For the courtesies, see 2.6.44–46.

164. "only": simply (and nothing more).

165. "remembrance": gratitude, memory of favors.

164–66. "I must thank . . . him": Antony will thank Pompey in order to protect his reputation, but then attack him right afterwards. Gratitude, he suggests, requires acknowledgement, not forbearance.

167. "Of": by.

167. "presently": immediately.

170. Mount Misena is a headland at the northern end of the modern-day Bay of Naples. It should not be confused with Messana, Pompey's base in Sicily (Appian, 5.122).

Antony: What is his strength by land?

Caesar: Great and increasing, but by sea
He is an absolute master.

Antony: So is the fame.
Would we had spoke together. Haste we for it.
Yet, ere we put ourselves in arms, dispatch we   **175**
The business we have talked of.

Caesar: With most gladness,
And do invite you to my sister's view,
Whither straight I'll lead you.

Antony: Let us, Lepidus, not lack your company.

Lepidus: Noble Antony, not sickness should detain me.   **180**

---

171. "What . . . by land": Pompey's increasing power on land is a problem particularly for Caesar. While Caesar's power rests largely on his control of the Italian
mainland, his position is being politically undermined by growing hardship and
disaffection in Italy (see 1.4.38n).

172–73. For the connection between Pompey's sea power and Caesar's domestic
political problem, see Appian, 5.67.

173. "fame": rumor, report.

174. "Would": I wish.

174. "spoke together": a highly ambiguous phrase: "speak" may be a euphe-
mism for exchanging blows or fighting (see 2.6.25) or may mean conferring;
and "together" is indefinite. Consequently, Antony may mean he wishes that (1)
Caesar and Antony had joined battle against Pompey (instead of trying merely to
contain him), (2) Caesar and Antony had consulted each other (instead of quarreling), or (3) Caesar and Antony had conferred with Pompey (instead of allowing
his power to grow).

174. "for": toward (Mount Misena).

175. "dispatch": carry out, complete.

176. "most": the greatest.

177. "do": I do.

177. "my sister's view": see my sister.

178. "straight": straightaway.

180. "not sickness . . . me": a mixture of obligingness and valetudinarianism, as
though sickness might be the grandest thing that could stop him.

Flourish. Exeunt all except Enobarbus, Agrippa and Maecenas.

Maecenas: Welcome from Egypt, sir.

Enobarbus: Half the heart of Caesar, worthy Maecenas!
My honorable friend, Agrippa!

Agrippa: Good Enobarbus!

Maecenas: We have cause to be glad that matters are so   **185**
well digested. You stayed well by't in Egypt.

Enobarbus: Ay, sir, we did sleep day out of countenance
and made the night light with drinking.

Maecenas: Eight wild boars roasted whole at a breakfast,
and but twelve persons there. Is this true?   **190**

S.D. 180. Maecenas (68–8) and Agrippa (c. 63–12) are Caesar's "two chief friends" (Plutarch, *Antony*, 35.2; Spencer, 221). Both have been his intimate and trusted friends since childhood. Maecenas fought for him at Philippi, was his envoy to Antony when Octavius needed arms and aid against Pompey, and will act as his deputy in Italy in his absence. More interested in the arts than in politics, he is the author of prose dialogues and verse and will become a lavish patron of the arts. Horace dedicates his first ode, the place of honor, to him (Horace, *Odes*, 1.1.1), and Virgil dedicates the *Georgics* to him (Virgil, *Georgics*, 1.2). Agrippa, who will remain Caesar's closest and most trusted friend to the end of Agrippa's life, persuaded young Octavius to return to Rome after Caesar's assassination, helped him to raise a private army, and played a leading part in the war against Lucius Antonius. He will crush Pompey's fleet at Mylae and Naulochus, defeat Antony at Actium, organize the army, navy, and administration of the empire, marry Caesar's daughter Julia, beautify the city of Rome, including building the Pantheon, hold three consulships, and become Caesar's co-regent and presumptive successor.

186. "digested": settled (the quibble on the alimentary sense leads to the topic of Egyptian feasts).

186. "stayed well by't": stuck to your reveling.

186. Maecenas' interest in Egyptian pleasures is no surprise. He is a man who prominently displays his own taste for profligate pleasures, particularly those of soft luxury, indolence, food, and sex (see, for example, Seneca, *Letters*, 114.4–8).

187. "sleep day . . . countenance": unsettled day by sleeping through it (so we could revel all night).

188. "light": a pun: they made the night (1) delightful (from pleasure), (2) light-headed (from drink), (3) wanton (from debauchery), and (4) bright (from artificial illumination).

189–90. As a sign of his immoderate taste in food, "Maecenas was the first that at feasts made a dainty dish of young ass foles, and preferred their flesh in his time

Enobarbus: This was but as a fly by an eagle. We had
  much more monstrous matter of feast, which worthily
  deserved noting.

Maecenas: She's a most triumphant lady, if report be
  square to her.   **195**

Enobarbus: When she first met Mark Antony, she
  pursed up his heart upon the river of Cydnus.

Agrippa: There she appeared indeed! Or my reporter
  devised well for her.

Enobarbus: I will tell you.   **200**

---

before the venison of wild asses" (Pliny, 8.170). Note that where Plutarch speaks of
"supper" (Plutarch, *Antony*, 28.3–4; Spencer, 204), Maecenas exaggerates Plutarch's
already-extravagant description by speaking of breakfast, which Enobarbus plays
up further in the sequel.

Roman taste for luxuries, including exotic food, came from the East. "For verily
the foreign excess and strange superfluities [in Rome] took beginning from the
Asian army, who brought all with them into the city.... Then began the board to be
furnished and set out with more exquisite and dainty viands, and of great expense.
The cooks, who in old time were reputed the most contemptible of slaves, as well
for calling as estimation, as for use they were put to, came to be in great request,
and that which before was a mechanical kind of service grew now to be accounted
a science of deep skill and understanding" (Livy, 39.6.7–9; Holland, 823).

191. "by": in comparison to.

192–93. "worthily deserved noting": Enobarbus adopts the language of an exotic
travel tale (cp. 1.2.160–62).

194. "triumphant": splendid, magnificent.

195. "square": just, true.

197. "pursed up": took possession, put in her purse (also a bawdy pun).

197. The Cydnus River, known today as the Tarsus or Berdan River, is in south-
eastern present-day Turkey. The city of Tarsus (Latin: *Cydnus*) is on the river.

198. "appeared indeed": made a truly magnificent appearance.

198. "reporter": informant.

199. "devised": invented.

200. Although his speech is usually pithy and blunt, often aphoristic, his account
of Cleopatra on the Cydnus contains nothing but magnificent, lyrical hyperbole.
In both style and substance, it runs counter to Philo's and Caesar's seamy char-
acterizations of Cleopatra as well as Enobarbus' own unseemly disparagement of
her. Editors frequently point out how closely Shakespeare follows the details of
North's translation of Plutarch's account (Plutarch, *Antony*, 26; Spencer, 201–2).

The barge she sat in like a burnished throne
Burned on the water. The poop was beaten gold,
Purple the sails, and so perfumed that
The winds were lovesick with them. The oars were silver,
Which to the tune of flutes kept stroke, and made   **205**
The water which they beat to follow faster,
As amorous of their strokes. For her own person,
It beggared all description: she did lie
In her pavilion, cloth-of-gold of tissue,   .
O'erpicturing that Venus where we see   **210**
The fancy outwork nature. On each side her

---

201. "burnished": bright, shining.

202. "Burned": ablaze with light.

201–2. "barge, . . . burnished, . . . Burned": Note the assonance.

202. "poop": poop deck (highest deck, nearest to the stern).

202. "beaten gold": purest gold.

203. "Purple the sails": dyed royal purple (see Pliny, 19.22).

203. "so perfumed": Perfumes, "the most superfluous of all forms of luxury" (Pliny, 13.20), were produced and used in abundance in Egypt, whose perfumes were the most highly praised (Pliny, 12.4). On the splendors of Egyptian perfumes, see Hicesius, *On Materials*, 2. The Egyptians applied perfumes not only to humans but also to large inanimate objects and even to swaths of land.

207. "As": as if.

207. "amorous": desirous.

207. "strokes": (1) rhythmic beat of the oars, (2) sexual strokes or thrusts. The Ptolemies were famous for grandiose naval showpieces. Ptolemy IV Philopater (245/4–204), Cleopatra's ancestor, built a vast floating palace, more than 300 feet long and 45 feet at its widest point, and towering 60 feet above the water line, with a purple topsail. It contained numerous large and extravagantly designed bedrooms, several lavish dining rooms, a pair of covered walkways around three sides of the ship (one, above deck, 500 feet long), a vestibule with a colonnade of rare wood ornamented with gold and ivory, and rooms dedicated to Aphrodite and Dionysus (Athenaeus, *The Learned Banqueters*, 5, 204e–6d).

207. "For": as for.

208. "beggared": surpassed.

209. "pavilion, . . . of tissue": stately tent of colored silk interwoven with threads of gold.

210. Venus is the Roman goddess of love; see 1.5.19n.

210–11. "O'erpicturing . . . nature": surpassed a picture of Venus in which the artist's imagination surpassed nature itself.

211. "side her": side of her.

Stood pretty dimpled boys, like smiling Cupids,
With divers-colored fans, whose wind did seem
To glow the delicate cheeks which they did cool,
And what they undid did.

Agrippa: O, rare for Antony!   **215**

Enobarbus: Her gentlewomen, like the Nereides,
So many mermaids, tended her i'th' eyes,
And made their bends adornings. At the helm
A seeming mermaid steers. The silken tackle
Swell with the touches of those flower-soft hands   **220**
That yarely frame the office. From the barge
A strange invisible perfume hits the sense
Of the adjacent wharfs. The city cast
Her people out upon her; and Antony,

---

212. "like": in the guise of (not merely resembling).

212. Cupid (Eros) is the Roman god of sexual love. He is sometimes said to be the offspring of Venus and Mars (Cicero, *On the Nature of the Gods*, 3.60; see 1.5.19n). For his depiction as a young boy, see Apollonius of Rhodes, *Argonautica*, 3.111ff.

213. "divers-colored": many-colored.

214. "glow": make glow, heat.

215. "what they undid did": the fanning has simultaneous contrary effects (Enobarbus' deliberate paradox); see 1.1.9–10.

216. Nereides are sea nymphs, human in shape, "passingly lovely even among goddesses" (Hesiod, *Theogony*, 240); see, further, 3.7.60n.

217. "So many": as if they were so many.

217. "tended . . . eyes": attended to and obeyed her every glance.

218. "made . . . adornings": bowed with such grace as to add to their beauty.

219. "seeming mermaid": an attendant in the guise of a mermaid.

219. "tackle": sails as well as ropes and cables.

220. "Swell": billow (a sexual allusion).

219–20. Note the alliterations: "silken," "Swell," and "tackle," "touches."

221. "yarely . . . office": skillfully perform their nautical duties. Throughout his description, Enobarbus pairs stage performance and indeterminacy. While everyone is in costume and performing a part, key distinctions disappear—between the imitation and the imitated, the human and the divine, the human and sea creatures, the animate and the inanimate. Everything in Egypt, including its palaces and fleets, Plutarch notes, is stage acting and painted scenery (Plutarch, *Aratus*, 15.2). And where everything is pretense or simulation, anyone can be anything.

223. "wharfs": river banks.

Enthroned i'th' market-place, did sit alone,   **225**
Whistling to th'air, which but for vacancy
Had gone to gaze on Cleopatra too
And made a gap in nature.

Agrippa: Rare Egyptian!

Enobarbus: Upon her landing, Antony sent to her,
Invited her to supper. She replied   **230**
It should be better he became her guest,
Which she entreated. Our courteous Antony,
Whom ne'er the word of "No" woman heard speak,
Being barbered ten times o'er, goes to the feast,
And for his ordinary pays his heart   **235**
For what his eyes eat only.

Agrippa: Royal wench!
She made great Caesar lay his sword to bed;
He ploughed her, and she cropped.

Enobarbus: I saw her once
Hop forty paces through the public street,
And having lost her breath, she spoke and panted,   **240**
That she did make defect perfection,
And breathless pour breath forth.

---

227. "Had": would have.

226–28. "but for . . . nature": only because it would have created a vacuum ("gap") in nature, the city's air did not go to gaze upon Cleopatra. The naturally determinate finally set limits on the staged indeterminate (cp. Aristotle, *Physics*, 213a11ff).

231. "should": might.

235. "ordinary": meal.

236. "eat": ate.

236. "Royal wench": an oxymoron (a wench is a girl of low breeding, sometimes a whore); cp. Propertius, *Elegies*, 3.11.19.

237. "great Caesar": Julius Caesar.

238. "she cropped": bore fruit. Agrippa's army gossip is the play's first hint of Caesar and Cleopatra's son, Caesarion.

241. "That": in such a way that.

241. "defect": a deficiency (breathlessness).

242. "pour": The Folio reads "powre," which is a frequent Elizabethan way of printing the verb "pour." Some editors take the word to be "power."

242. "breathless pour breath forth": breathe forth charm.

Maecenas: Now Antony must leave her utterly.

Enobarbus: Never! He will not.
    Age cannot wither her, nor custom stale   **245**
    Her infinite variety. Other women cloy
    The appetites they feed, but she makes hungry
    Where most she satisfies. For vilest things
    Become themselves in her, that the holy priests
    Bless her when she is riggish.   **250**

Maecenas: If beauty, wisdom, modesty can settle
    The heart of Antony, Octavia is
    A blessed lottery to him.

Agrippa: Let us go.
    Good Enobarbus, make yourself my guest
    Whilst you abide here.

Enobarbus: Humbly, sir, I thank you.   ***Exeunt.***   **255**

ACT TWO, SCENE THREE

[Rome. Caesar's house.]

Enter Antony, Caesar; Octavia between them.

Antony: The world and my great office will sometimes
    Divide me from your bosom.

Octavia: All which time
    Before the gods my knee shall bow my prayers
    To them for you.

---

245. "stale": render stale.

249. "Become themselves": make themselves becoming.

249. "that": so that.

250. "riggish": licentious.

251. "beauty, . . . modesty": On Octavia's personal qualities, see lines 135–38n.

253. "lottery": prize, gift of fortune.

S.D. 1. The stage-direction captures the purpose of Octavia's marriage as the link between the two men, while pointing toward her dilemma of having to choose between them.

Antony: Good night, sir. My Octavia,
    Read not my blemishes in the world's report.   **5**
    I have not kept my square, but that to come
    Shall all be done by th' rule. Good night, dear lady.

Octavia: Good night, sir.

Caesar: Good night.   ***Exeunt [Caesar and Octavia].***

                              Enter Soothsayer.

Antony: Now, sirrah, you do wish yourself in Egypt?   **10**

Soothsayer: Would I had never come from thence, nor you thither.

Antony: If you can, your reason?

Soothsayer: I see it in my motion, have it not in my tongue.
    But yet hie you to Egypt again.

Antony: Say to me,
    Whose fortunes shall rise higher, Caesar's or mine?   **15**

Soothsayer: Caesar's.
    Therefore, O Antony, stay not by his side.

---

5. "Read": interpret.

5. "world's report": what people say.

6. "kept my square": kept to the rule, lived a well-ordered life (a carpentry metaphor: a square is a carpenter's or joiner's tool for setting out or measuring right
angles).

S.D. 10. The Soothsayer, the only Egyptian we see in Rome, is a sign of the growing substitution of Egyptian soothsaying for Roman augury and, more broadly,
of the orientalizing of Rome. From the start, nothing was undertaken in Rome,
either in peace or war, without first taking the auspices (Livy, 1.36.6). But where
Roman augury seeks signs of divine approval or disapproval of proposed courses of
action, Egyptian soothsaying tells what the future holds. The former tests decisions,
the latter tells fortunes. Thus, while Roman augury is entirely compatible with
freedom, action, and self-governance, Egyptian soothsaying is reciprocally cause
and effect of their submission, passivity, and royal despotism. Denying that men can
make their own future, it is entirely at home in Pharaonic Egypt.

10. "sirrah": a term of address to servants and social inferiors.

11. "Would I": I wish.

11. "nor you thither": nor you had gone there in the first place.

13. "I see . . . my tongue": I know it as an inward prompting which I cannot
articulate.

14. "hie": hurry.

Thy dæmon—that thy spirit which keeps thee—is
Noble, courageous, high, unmatchable,
Where Caesar's is not. But near him, thy angel   **20**
Becomes afeard, as being o'erpowered. Therefore
Make space enough between you.

Antony: Speak this no more.

Soothsayer: To none but thee; no more but when to thee.
    If thou dost play with him at any game,
    Thou art sure to lose; and of that natural luck   **25**
    He beats thee 'gainst the odds. Thy luster thickens
    When he shines by. I say again, thy spirit
    Is all afraid to govern thee near him;
    But, he away, 'tis noble.

Antony: Get thee gone.   *Exit [Soothsayer].*
    Say to Ventidius I would speak with him.   **30**
    He shall to Parthia. Be it art or hap,
    He hath spoken true. The very dice obey him,
    And in our sports my better cunning faints

---

18. "that": that is.

18. "Thy daemon . . . keeps thee": "'thy Demon,' said [the soothsayer], '(that is to say, the good angel and spirit that keepeth thee)'" (Plutarch, *Antony*, 33.2; Spencer, 215–16). Antony's daemon is not a demon, but a benign guardian spirit that protects ("keeps") him.

20. "Where . . . is not": when Caesar's daemon is not present.

21. "afeard": afraid.

21. "as": as if.

23. "no more . . . thee": only when I am talking directly to you.

25. "of that": as a result of.

25. "natural luck": The soothsayer seems to identify Antony's "daemon" with both "[his] spirit which keeps [him]" and "natural luck." On his lips, one's personal guardian is hardly distinguishable from chance or fortune.

26. "thickens": dims, becomes darkened.

27. "by": nearby.

31. "Be it . . . hap": whether it is by prophetic art or by chance.

32. "him": Caesar. On Caesar's abiding interest in gambling, especially dicing, see Suetonius, *Augustus*, 71.

33. "better cunning": greater skill.

Under his chance. If we draw lots, he speeds;
His cocks do win the battle still of mine   **35**
When it is all to naught, and his quails ever
Beat mine, inhooped, at odds. I will to Egypt.
And though I make this marriage for my peace,
I'th' East my pleasure lies.

Enter Ventidius.

O, come, Ventidius.
You must to Parthia; your commission's ready.   **40**
Follow me and receive't.   *Exeunt.*

ACT TWO, SCENE FOUR

[Rome. A Street.]

Enter Lepidus, Maecenas, and Agrippa.

Lepidus: Trouble yourselves no further. Pray you hasten
　　Your generals after.

Agrippa:　　　　　　Sir, Mark Antony
　　Will e'en but kiss Octavia, and we'll follow.

Lepidus: Till I shall see you in your soldiers' dress,
　　Which will become you both, farewell.

Maecenas:　　　　　　　　　We shall,   **5**

---

34. "chance": luck.
34. "speeds": wins.
35. "still": always.
35. "of mine": from mine (implication of depriving; see Abbott, §166).
36. "all to naught": everything to nothing in my favor.
37. "inhooped": confined to fight within a ring.
37. "at odds": against the odds.
S.D. 1. "*A street*": See Introduction, n13.
1–2. "Trouble yourselves . . . after": Lepidus courteously dismisses Maecenas and Agrippa, Caesar's lieutenants, who have been escorting him and urges them, instead, to hasten their departure for the triumvirs' conference with Pompey.
3. "ev'n": only.

As I conceive the journey, be at the Mount
Before you, Lepidus.

Lepidus: Your way is shorter;
My purposes do draw me much about.
You'll win two days upon me.

Maecenas and Agrippa: Sir, good success.   **10**

Lepidus: Farewell.   ***Exeunt.***

ACT TWO, SCENE FIVE

[Alexandria. Cleopatra's palace.]

Enter Cleopatra, Charmian, Iras, and Alexas.

Cleopatra: Give me some music—music, moody food
Of us that trade in love.

All: The music, ho!

Enter Mardian the Eunuch.

Cleopatra: Let it alone. Let's to billiards. Come, Charmian.

Charmian: My arm is sore. Best play with Mardian.

———————

6. "the Mount": Mount Misena, where Pompey's ships lie at anchor and the conference with him is to take place; see 2.2.169–70.

7. "way": route.

8. "much about": much out of the way.

7–9. Lepidus' undisclosed "purposes" might look ahead to the political situation following the meeting with Pompey. His roundabout route may take him to
Pompey, with the intention of secretly negotiating an alliance, or to Pompey's allies
and sympathizers, with the intention of promoting himself as his successor to lead
the anti-Caesarian faction after Pompey is weakened and finally eliminated. Notwithstanding—or entirely in keeping with—his earlier concern for peace among
the triumvirs, Lepidus, a mixture of obsequiousness, aggressiveness, and duplicity,
is perfectly capable of asserting himself when he thinks he sees an opportunity
(see 3.5.4–12).

1. "moody": melancholy

2. "trade in": occupy ourselves with (as if love were her life's sole occupation; no
suggestion of commerce).

Cleopatra: As well a woman with an eunuch played   **5**
    As with a woman. Come, you'll play with me, sir?

Mardian: As well as I can, madam.

Cleopatra: And when good will is showed, though't come too short,
    The actor may plead pardon. I'll none now.
    Give me mine angle; we'll to th'river. There,   **10**
    My music playing far off, I will betray
    Tawny-finned fishes. My bended hook shall pierce
    Their slimy jaws, and as I draw them up,
    I'll think them every one an Antony
    And say "Ah ha! You're caught!"

Charmian: 'Twas merry when   **15**
    You wagered on your angling; when your diver
    Did hang a salt fish on his hook, which he
    With fervency drew up.

Cleopatra: That time? O, times!
    I laughed him out of patience; and that night

3–6. Both "billiards" and "play" are sexual allusions.

8–9. "And when . . . pardon": Cleopatra's risqué reply captures the core of Eastern and post-republican Roman virtue. Good will replaces manly action. When noble action is not possible, morality becomes internalized and a morality of intention and pardon replaces one of action and praise.

9. "I'll none": I won't play.

10. "angle": fishing tackle.

11. "betray": catch, trap.

13–15. "as I draw . . . You're caught!'": Cleopatra's art of love is an art of angling, a wily art which employs hooks dressed as lures.

17. "a salt fish": a fish dried and pickled in salt.

18. "fervency": great excitement.

15–18. As Plutarch tells the story, Antony went fishing but caught nothing, and was embarrassed because Cleopatra was watching. So he ordered some divers to secretly attach live fish to his hook underwater, which he proceeded to pull up several times. Cleopatra soon discovered the trick. Pretending to admire his success, she invited her friends to come and watch. Then, she had her own diver attach a salted fish to his line. Antony, believing he had made a catch, pulled up his line, whereupon the whole company burst out laughing (Plutarch, *Antony*, 29.3–4). Shakespeare adds Cleopatra's wagering.

18. "times": the times.

I laughed him into patience; and next morn,   **20**
Ere the ninth hour, I drunk him to his bed,
Then put my tires and mantles on him, whilst
I wore his sword Philippan.

Enter a Messenger.

O, from Italy!
Ram thou thy fruitful tidings in mine ears,
That long time have been barren.

Messenger: Madam, madam—   **25**

Cleopatra: Antonio's dead! If thou say so, villain,
Thou kill'st thy mistress. But well and free,
If thou so yield him, there is gold, and here
My bluest veins to kiss, a hand that kings
Have lipped and trembled kissing.   **30**

Messenger: First, madam, he is well.

Cleopatra: Why, there's more gold.
But sirrah, mark, we use
To say the dead are well. Bring it to that,
The gold I give thee will I melt and pour

---

21. "drunk": drank.

22. "tires and mantles": headdresses and cloaks.

23. "Philippan": the sword Antony used at the battle of Philippi to defeat Brutus and Cassius and destroy the republic forces. Cleopatra recalls having enacted the story of Hercules and Omphale, Queen of Lydia, who commanded him, at once her lover and her slave, to lay aside his lion skin, and dress in woman's clothes and perform domestic chores, while she dressed herself in his lion skin and carried his warrior club (Ovid, *Heroides*, 9.53–118, *Fasti*, 2.317–26; Plutarch, *Comparison of Demetrius and Antony*, 3.3).

24. "Ram": thrust (with sexual suggestion).

27. "free": not Caesar's captive.

28. "yield": report.

32. "use": are accustomed.

33. "the dead are well": For a Christian the phrase might mean that the person is in heaven (see *Macbeth*, 4.3.176–79). For a pre-Christian it might mean that the person is beyond the reach of evils and misfortunes (see Aristotle, *Nicomachean Ethics*, 1100a15–17).

33. "Bring it to that": if it comes to that, if that is what you mean.

Down thy ill-uttering throat.

Messenger: Good madam, hear me.   **35**

Cleopatra: Well, go to, I will.
    But there's no goodness in thy face if Antony
    Be free and healthful, so tart a favor
    To trumpet such good tidings! If not well,
    Thou shouldst come like a Fury crowned with snakes,   **40**
    Not like a formal man.

Messenger: Will't please you hear me?

Cleopatra: I have a mind to strike thee ere thou speak'st
    Yet if thou say Antony lives, is well,
    Or friends with Caesar or not captive to him,
    I'll set thee in a shower of gold and hail   **45**
    Rich pearls upon thee.

Messenger: Madam, he's well.

Cleopatra: Well said.

Messenger: And friends with Caesar.

Cleopatra: Thou'rt an honest man!

Messenger: Caesar and he are greater friends than ever.

Cleopatra: Make thee a fortune from me.

Messenger: But yet, madam—

34–35. "The gold . . . throat": A death similar to the Parthians' treatment of Crassus (Plutarch, *Crassus*, 33.2–4; see, further, 3.1.2–3n).

36. "go to": all right then; see 2.2.117n.

38. "so tart a favor": so sour a look or face.

39. "trumpet": announce (allusion to a triumphal flourish).

40. "a Fury . . . snakes": In Greek mythology, the Furies (Erinyes) are deities of retribution for wrongs with snakes entwined in their hair (Aeschylus, *The Libation Bearers*, 1048–50; Virgil, *Georgics* 4.471).

41. "formal": normal (in the form of a man).

44. "Or": either.

44. "friends": on friendly terms.

47. "honest": honorable, worthy (also "truthful").

49. "Make thee": you will have.

Cleopatra: I do not like "But yet." It does allay   **50**
   The good precedence. Fie upon "But yet."
   "But yet" is as a jailer to bring forth
   Some monstrous malefactor. Prithee, friend,
   Pour out the pack of matter to mine ear,
   The good and bad together: he's friends with Caesar,   **55**
   In state of health, thou say'st, and, thou sayst, free.

Messenger: Free, madam, no. I made no such report.
   He's bound unto Octavia.

Cleopatra: For what good turn?

Messenger: For the best turn i'th' bed.

Cleopatra: I am pale, Charmian.

Messenger: Madam, he's married to Octavia.   **60**

Cleopatra: The most infectious pestilence upon thee!

                                   Strikes him down.

Messenger: Good madam, patience!

Cleopatra: What say you? **Strikes him.**
                      Hence,

50–51. "does allay . . . precedence": diminishes the value of the preceding good news by mixing it with something undesirable (as alloys reduce the purity of gold).

53. "friend": Cleopatra uses "friend" as a term of address only for subordinates or servants whose assistance she needs; see also 4.8.26; 4.15.14, 32.

54. "Pour out . . . ear": tell me everything (the metaphor of a peddler coming to sell his goods).

57. "free": Twice before, Cleopatra questioned whether Antony is "free" (lines 27, 38). She meant that he is not Caesar's captive (line 44). Both times the Messenger avoided answering. Now, no longer able to delay, he must finally say what he came to report.

58. "bound": married. Cleopatra understands him to mean "obligated to."

58. "turn": purpose, favor.

59. "For . . . i'th' bed": At a loss for how to break the news, the Messenger initially blurts it out as a crude joke. The joke allows him to answer truthfully without explicitly saying what he fears to say. Playing on words and employing a synecdoche, he remains at a remove or two from stating the matter.

62. "patience": keep calm.

Horrible villain, or I'll spurn thine eyes
Like balls before me! I'll unhair thy head!

She hales him up and down.

Thou shalt be whipped with wire and stewed in brine,   **65**
Smarting in ling'ring pickle.

Messenger: Gracious madam,
I that do bring the news made not the match.

Cleopatra: Say 'tis not so, a province I will give thee
And make thy fortunes proud. The blow thou hadst
Shall make thy peace for moving me to rage,   **70**
And I will boot thee with what gift beside
Thy modesty can beg.

Messenger: He's married, madam.

Cleopatra: Rogue, thou hast lived too long!   **Draw a knife.**

Messenger: Nay then, I'll run.
What mean you, madam? I have made no fault.   **Exit.**

Charmian: Good madam, keep yourself within yourself.   **75**
The man is innocent.

Cleopatra: Some innocents 'scape not the thunderbolt.
Melt Egypt into Nile, and kindly creatures

---

63. "spurn": kick (a strong term).

S.D. 65. "*hales*": drags, pulls (by the hair).

66. "Smarting . . . pickle": suffering in a slow, painful pickling solution (of salt or acid).

67. "I that . . . not the match": On making no distinction between the messenger and the message, see 1.2.101n.

69. "proud": splendid.

70. "make thy peace": atone, make up.

71. "boot": enrich, make amends.

71. "what": whatever.

72. "modesty": humble rank.

77. "Some innocents . . . thunderbolt": whether justly or unjustly, the gods punish offenses to their honor. "Even the gods are subject unto wrath" (Ovid, *Metamorphoses*, 8.284; trans. Arthur Golding [London: Willyam Seres, 1567]; rpt. *Shakespeare's Ovid* [New York: Norton, 1961], 8.370); see, further, 4.13.2–3n.

78. "kindly": natural (as nature produces them).

Turn all to serpents! Call the slave again.
Though I am mad, I will not bite him. Call!   **80**

Charmian: He is afeard to come.

Cleopatra: I will not hurt him. **[*Exit Charmian.*]**
These hands do lack nobility that they strike
A meaner than myself, since I myself
Have given myself the cause.

> **Enter the Messenger again [*with Charmian*].**

                              Come hither, sir.
Though it be honest, it is never good   **85**
To bring bad news. Give to a gracious message
An host of tongues, but let ill tidings tell
Themselves when they be felt.

Messenger: I have done my duty.

Cleopatra: Is he married?
I cannot hate thee worser than I do   **90**
If thou again say "yes."

Messenger: He's married, madam.

Cleopatra: The gods confound thee! Dost thou hold there still?

Messenger: Should I lie, madam?

Cleopatra: O, I would thou didst,
So half my Egypt were submerged and made

78–79. "Melt Egypt . . . serpents": "[I]t is impossible to tell whether we have an imperative with a vocative, or a subjunctive used optatively or conditionally" (Abbott, §364), that is, whether a command or a wish.

81. "afeard": afraid.

83. "meaner": someone of lower social status.

84. "given myself the cause": Cleopatra does not say what she had done to cause her anger. She leaves unclear whether it was her letting Antony return to Rome or her loving him in the first place.

86. "gracious": pleasing.

87–88. "but let . . . be felt": do not announce bad news, but let it tell itself by its effects.

92. "confound": destroy.

92. "hold there": stick to that story.

94. "So": even if.

A cistern for scaled snakes! Go, get thee hence!   **95**
Hadst thou Narcissus in thy face, to me
Thou wouldst appear most ugly. He is married?

Messenger: I crave your Highness' pardon.

Cleopatra: He is married?

Messenger: Take no offense that I would not offend you.
To punish me for what you make me do   **100**
Seems much unequal. He's married to Octavia.

Cleopatra: O, that his fault should make a knave of thee
That art not what th'art sure of! Get thee hence.
The merchandise which thou hast brought from Rome
Are all too dear for me. Lie they upon thy hand,   **105**
And be undone by 'em!   [*Exit Messenger.*]

Charmian: Good your Highness, patience.

Cleopatra: In praising Antony, I have dispraised Caesar.

Charmian: Many times, madam.

Cleopatra: I am paid for't now.
Lead me from hence;

---

95. "cistern": receptacle of water.

96. In mythology, Narcissus, a very beautiful youth, loved no one until he saw a reflection of his own face in water, fell in love with it, and drowned trying to embrace it (Ovid, *Metamorphoses*, 3.339–510).

98. "crave": beg.

99. "that": because.

99. "would not": do not wish to.

101. "much unequal": very unjust, unfair.

102. "O, that . . . thee": it's too bad that Antony's fault makes you look like a villain to me.

103. "That art . . . sure of": when you are not as bad as the news you are so sure of.

105–6. "Lie . . . by 'em": may you be unable to sell them and be ruined by them. Cleopatra returns to her metaphor of the Messenger as a peddler (line 54). "Merchandise," here, is a plural noun.

108. "I am paid for't now": Cleopatra seems to be thinking of her damaged political interests. Politically, she is back where she was following Pharsalus, when the triumvir she had opposed, Julius Caesar, defeated the triumvir who supported her, Pompey the Great. Once again, neither triumvir will now support or protect her (see, further, 1.5.32n).

I faint. O, Iras, Charmian! 'Tis no matter.   **110**
Go to the fellow, good Alexas. Bid him
Report the feature of Octavia, her years,
Her inclination; let him not leave out
The color of her hair. Bring me word quickly.   [*Exit Alexas.*]
Let him forever go! Let him not, Charmian.   **115**
Though he be painted one way like a Gorgon,
The other way's a Mars. [*To Iras.*] Bid you Alexas
Bring me word how tall she is. Pity me, Charmian,
But do not speak to me. Lead me to my chamber.   *Exeunt.*

ACT TWO, SCENE SIX

[Near Misenum]

Flourish. Enter Pompey and Menas at one door, with Drum and Trumpet; at another Caesar, Lepidus, Antony, Enobarbus, Maecenas, and Agrippa, with Soldiers marching.

Pompey: Your hostages I have, so have you mine,
    And we shall talk before we fight.

Caesar: Most meet
    That first we come to words, and therefore have we

---

112. "feature": physical appearance (her beauty).

113. "inclination": temperament, disposition.

116–17. "Though he . . . a Mars": Antony resembles a painting on a furrowed surface which changes into its opposite when viewed from the opposite side. "[T]hey are like those double or turning pictures; stand before which, you see a fair maid on the one side, an ape on the other, an owl; look upon them at the first sight, all is well; but further examine, you shall find them wise on the one side and fools on the other; in some few things praiseworthy, in the rest incomparably faulty" (Robert Burton, *The Anatomy of Melancholy*, Democritus to the Reader, ed. Thomas C. Faulkner, 6 vols. [Oxford: Clarendon Press, 1989], 1:105). Seen from one side, Antony appears like the hideous monster Gorgon, whose face, wreathed in snakes, turns whoever sees it to stone (Apollodorus, 2.4.2). But seen from the opposite side, he appears like Mars, the most manly of gods.

S.D. 1. "*Drum and Trumpet*": drummer and trumpeter.

2. "meet": appropriate, fitting.

Our written purposes before us sent,
Which if thou hast considered, let us know   **5**
If 'twill tie up thy discontented sword
And carry back to Sicily much tall youth
That else must perish here.

Pompey: To you all three,
The senators alone of this great world,
Chief factors for the gods: I do not know   **10**
Wherefore my father should revengers want,
Having a son and friends, since Julius Caesar,
Who at Philippi the good Brutus ghosted,
There saw you laboring for him. What was't

---

4. "purposes": proposals.

6. "If 'twill": if it will.

7. Sicily is the base of Pompey's operations; see 1.2.190–92n.

7. "much tall": many stout, brave.

8. "else": otherwise.

9. "The senators . . . world": The Senate was the Republic's authoritative political institution. "Our ancestors . . . established annual magistrates on the presumption of making the Senate the perpetual supreme council of the republic. . . . They intended that the magistrates should depend on the Senate's authority and to be the ministers, as it were, of this most weighty council" (Cicero, *For Sestius*, 137; see, further, Polybius, 6.13). After Julius Caesar arrogated to himself the Senate's authority (see *JC*, 3.1.31–32), the triumvirs (and later Augustus) retained the outward trappings of the Senate (and other republican institutions) but stripped it of its independence and authority. "The masters of the Roman world surrounded their throne with darkness, concealed their irresistible strength, and humbly professed themselves the accountable ministers of the senate, whose supreme decrees they dictated and obeyed" (Edward Gibbon, *Decline and Fall*, 3 vols. [New York: Modern Library, n.d.], 1:61).

10. "factors": agents.

11. "Wherefore": why.

11. "revengers want": lack avengers.

12. "since": seeing that, inasmuch as.

13. "ghosted": appeared to as a ghost (see *JC*, 4.3.273–86).

10–14. "I do not . . . for him": The first of two justifications for his rebellion against the triumvirs that Pompey offers is revenge for his father: Pompey the Great, having a son and friends, should not lack avengers, since Julius Caesar's ghost saw Octavius and Antony work for his revenge against Brutus at Philippi. Pompey, while considering nothing but the private relations of the people involved, overlooks the difference between military defeat and political murder. While Caesar was assassinated by Brutus in the Senate, Pompey was defeated by Caesar at

That moved pale Cassius to conspire? And what   **15**
Made the all-honored, honest, Roman Brutus,
With the armed rest, courtiers of beauteous freedom,
To drench the Capitol, but that they would
Have one man but a man? And that is it
Hath made me rig my navy, at whose burden   **20**
The angered Ocean foams, with which I meant
To scourge th'ingratitude that despiteful Rome
Cast on my noble father.

Pharsalus. Although defeated by him, he was killed not by Caesar or his forces, but by Caesar's (and Cleopatra's) enemies, who murdered Pompey in Egypt, where he had fled for safety (Plutarch, *Caesar*, 40–46, *Pompey*, 77–79). On Pompey's murder, see, further, 3.7.14n.

15. "pale Cassius": This description comes from Julius Caesar: "Caesar also had Cassius in great jealousy [suspicion] and suspected him much. Whereupon he said . . . to his friends: 'What will Cassius do, think ye? I like not his pale looks'" (Plutarch, *Caesar*, 62.5; Spencer, 85). "Pale," because Cassius led a sedentary, indoor life rather than a robust, outdoor life (see *JC*, 1.2.197ff.).

16. "honest": honorable.

17. "rest": others.

17. "courtiers . . . freedom": wooers or courters of beautiful freedom.

18. "drench": drown (in Caesar's blood).

15–19. "And what . . . a man": Pompey's second justification is the republican cause. Pompey, the only character in the play who claims to champion that cause, describes Caesar's assassins, particularly Brutus, in the most admiring terms. For the republican refusal to be ruled by only one man, lest he thereby become more than a man, see *JC*, 1.2.115–18, 151–56.

20. "rig": make ready.

20. "burden": load (the carrying capacity).

21. "The angered Ocean": The god Oceanus, god of the stream that encircles the world, had witnessed Pompey the Great victorious three times: "[T]he very ocean sea which environeth the world round about saw the same man thrice victor and conqueror: the Numidians in Africa he repressed and vanquished, even to the coasts of the south sea; he subdued Spain which revolted and rebelled with Sertorius, as far as to the Atlantic sea; the kings of the Albanians he pursued, & never left the chase until he had driven them to the Caspian sea" (Plutarch, *On the Fortune of the Romans*, 11 [324a]; Holland, 636). See, further, 2.1.1–2n.

22. "despiteful": spiteful (also scornful).

14–23. Senate supporters backed Pompey in his struggle with Julius Caesar as the lesser of two enemies. Both men coveted sole power, but Pompey, "moderate in all things except his thirst for power" (Sallust, *Histories*, 2.18), retained some respect for the republican regime (Suetonius, *Caesar*, 76–79). Unlike Caesar, rather than

Caesar: Take your time.

Antony: Thou canst not fear us, Pompey, with thy sails.
We'll speak with thee at sea. At land thou know'st   25
How much we do o'ercount thee.

Pompey: At land indeed
Thou dost o'ercount me of my father's house;
But since the cuckoo builds not for himself,
Remain in't as thou mayst.

Lepidus: Be pleased to tell us—
For this is from the present—how you take   30
The offers we have sent you.

Caesar: There's the point.

Antony: Which do not be entreated to, but weigh
What it is worth embraced.

Caesar: And what may follow
To try a larger fortune.

---

take sole power, he wished that it be granted to him by the votes of the people or
the good will of the Senate (Dio, 41.54.1).

24. "fear": frighten.

25. "speak": meet, encounter.

26–27. "At land . . . father's house": Pompey twists Antony's words "land" and
"o'ercount." Antony means that the triumvirs' land forces "outnumber" or "over-
number" Pompey's. Pompey, reminding Antony that he bought but failed to pay
for his father's splendid, confiscated house and land in Rome, means "cheat" or
"overreach." "Afterwards when Pompey's house was put to open sale, Antonius
bought it, but when they asked him money for it, he made it very strange, and was
offended with them" (Plutarch, *Antony*, 10.2; Spencer, 184). For the "criminal auc-
tion" of the house and Antony's scandalous use of it, see Cicero, *Philippics*, 2.64–68.
On the recovery of his family's property as Pompey's principal interest, see Sextus
Aurelius Victor, *On Distinguished Men*, 79.2.

28. "cuckoo . . . himself": A cuckoo lays its eggs in other birds' nests.

29. "as thou mayst": as long as you can (an implied threat).

30. "from the present": irrelevant to the present business.

32. "entreated to": persuaded to accept.

32–33. "but weigh . . . embraced": consider how the proposal would serve your
interests if you accepted it.

34. "To try . . . fortune": if you try to get more by rejecting our terms and choosing to fight.

Pompey: You have made me offer
Of Sicily, Sardinia; and I must   **35**
Rid all the sea of pirates; then to send
Measures of wheat to Rome. This 'greed upon,
To part with unhacked edges and bear back
Our targes undinted.

Caesar, Antony, Lepidus: That's our offer.

Pompey: Know then
I came before you here a man prepared   **40**
To take this offer. But Mark Antony
Put me to some impatience. Though I lose
The praise of it by telling, you must know
When Caesar and your brother were at blows,
Your mother came to Sicily and did find   **45**
Her welcome friendly.

Antony: I have heard it, Pompey,
And am well studied for a liberal thanks,
Which I do owe you.

Pompey: Let me have your hand. **[*They shake.*]**
I did not think, sir, to have met you here.

---

36. "to send": I am to send.

37. "Measures": quantities.

35–37. "Of Sicily, . . . to Rome": On the proposal's terms, see lines 82–83n.

37. "'greed": being agreed.

38. "part . . . edges": depart with swords unnotched by blows.

39. "targes undinted": shields undented.

43. "you must know": I would have you know, you must let me tell you.

44. "your brother": Antony's brother, Lucius.

42–46. "Though I lose . . . friendly": Pompey recognizes that his reminder may cost him praise. To tell of his hospitality is to praise himself, and self-praise amounts to offensive boasting. Still, he cannot resist. Like his famously vain father (as his ostentatious cognomen shows) (Plutarch, *Pompey*, 57.3–5, 67.4, *Caesar*, 29.5), Pompey praises or flatters himself at every chance.

47. "well studied for": prepared to offer.

49. "I did not . . . you here": Pompey, after initially dismissing the possibility, concluded that Antony would join Caesar and Lepidus, while Menas remained unconvinced (2.1.32–53). Now, reversing himself again, he reverts to Menas' opinion, while stating it as though he had never thought otherwise. Aside from demonstrating his general vacillation, Pompey's reversion to Menas' view as though

Antony: The beds i'th' East are soft; and thanks to you,   **50**
  That called me timelier than my purpose hither,
  For I have gained by't.

Caesar: Since I saw you last,
  There's a change upon you.

Pompey: Well, I know not
  What counts harsh Fortune casts upon my face,
  But in my bosom shall she never come   **55**
  To make my heart her vassal.

Lepidus: Well met here.

Pompey: I hope so, Lepidus. Thus we are agreed.
  I crave our composition may be written
  And sealed between us.

Caesar: That's the next to do.

Pompey: We'll feast each other ere we part, and let's   **60**
  Draw lots who shall begin.

---

it has been his all along seems to demonstrate the stinging reproach that he is "a freedman to his freedman, a slave to his slaves, envying those in high places only to obey those in the lowest" (Velleius Paterculus, 2.73.1).

50. "thanks": my thanks.

51. "timelier . . . purpose": sooner than I had intended.

54. "What counts . . . face": what wrinkles or scars harsh Fortune has cast upon my face (a metaphor from making notches or marks on a tally-stick to reckon accounts).

55–56. "But . . . vassal": harsh Fortune can never master my heart.

57. "we are agreed": Although his power is at its zenith and he has forced his enemies to make peace, Pompey makes no counterdemands and accepts their terms with nothing more than personal protests. While fortune has often handed him excellent opportunities, "he . . . never take[s] the advantage of his enemies; neglecting many occasions, he . . . lie[s] still" (Appian, 5.143; *An Ancient History and Exquisite Chronicle of the Roman Wars, Both Civil and Foreign,* trans. W. B. [London: Raulfe Newberrie and Henrie [B]ynniman, 1578], 369). Concerned above all with regaining the position and wealth that are due him as his father's son, he would "rather defend his own than invade others, till so he was overcome also" (Appian, 5.25; W. B., 318). On a similar trait in his father, see Plutarch, *Pompey,* 67.4, *Caesar,* 39.5. Lacking resolution, Pompey has no strength of purpose to match his naval strength, and his irresolution will cost him everything. He will be the first to fall.

58. "composition": agreement.

58–59. "written . . . between us": Pompey seems to trust that a written agreement carrying each cosigner's official seal will not be broken.

Antony: That will I, Pompey.

Pompey: No, Antony, take the lot.
   But, first or last, your fine Egyptian cookery
   Shall have the fame. I have heard that Julius Caesar
   Grew fat with feasting there.

Antony: You have heard much.   **65**

Pompey: I have fair meanings, sir.

Antony: And fair words to them.

Pompey: Then so much have I heard.
   And I have heard Apollodorus carried—

Enobarbus: No more of that. He did so.

Pompey: What, I pray you?

Enobarbus: A certain queen to Caesar in a mattress.   **70**

Pompey: I know thee now. How far'st thou, soldier?

---

62. "take the lot": agree to draw lots.

63. "first or last": whether you come in first or last.

64–65. "Julius Caesar . . . feasting there": This ostensible praise is apt to offend the two principal triumvirs—Antony, by suggesting that his lover is well known as a whore, and Caesar, by reminding him of his rival to the claim of being Julius Caesar's son and legitimate heir (see 3.6.6n).

66. "fair": unobjectionable.

66. Most editors change the Folio's "meaning" to "meanings," which Antony's reply seems to require.

70. "A certain queen . . . mattress": Pompey alludes to Cleopatra's famous seduction of Julius Caesar. After pursuing Pompey the Great to Egypt, Caesar wanted to resolve the dispute between Cleopatra and her brother. Caesar summoned her to Alexandria, but Cleopatra, who had been driven out of Egypt, knew that she could not cross the enemy's lines safely. Needing a stratagem, she and a friend, Apollodorus, boarded a small boat and landed near Caesar's headquarters at dusk. Needing a way to enter unobserved, she stretched herself out full length upon a mattress, which Apollodorus rolled up and fastened with a strap, and, carrying it on his back, brought it in through the doors to Caesar. Caesar, astonished at the sight of the Egyptian queen rolling out of the mattress and springing to her feet, was immediately taken by her cleverness, daring, and charm. "This was the first occasion . . . that made Caesar to love her" (Plutarch, *Caesar*, 49.1–2; Spencer, 69).

71. "How far'st thou": how are you, how are you getting on (with secondary suggestion of asking how one is being regaled with food).

Enobarbus: Well,
     And well am like to do, for I perceive
     Four feasts are toward.

Pompey: Let me shake thy hand.

                              [*They shake hands.*]
     I never hated thee. I have seen thee fight
     When I have envied thy behavior.

Enobarbus: Sir,   **75**
     I never loved you much, but I have praised ye
     When you have well deserved ten times as much
     As I have said you did.

Pompey: Enjoy thy plainness;
     It nothing ill becomes thee.
     Aboard my galley I invite you all.   **80**
     Will you lead, lords?

Caesar, Antony, Lepidus: Show's the way, sir.

Pompey: Come

          Exeunt all but Enobarbus and Menas.

Menas: [*aside*] Thy father, Pompey, would ne'er have
     made this treaty. [*to Enobarbus*] You and I have known,
     sir.

---

73. "toward": coming, in the offing.

75–78. "Sir, I never, . . . did": Enobarbus offers an oblique compliment in the guise
of a direct discourtesy.

78. "Enjoy thy plainness": continue to indulge your plain speaking.

79. "nothing": not at all.

82. "Thy": Menas always addresses his captain, whether present or absent, by the
familiar "thou" and never by the formal "you."

82–83. "Thy father . . . treaty": Despite his strength, Pompey settles for Sicily and
Sardinia, which are already his, promises to rid the sea of pirates, who are his allies,
and undertakes to send wheat to Rome, whose starvation is his most effective
tactic. The wheat will not only provide Caesar with much-needed food, but will
also spare him, and earn Pompey, the disfavor of those from whom he will have to
collect it. Pompey, in a word, gives away his advantages, strengthens his enemies,
particularly Caesar, and gets nothing in return (see 1.2.190–92n). On the so-called
Treaty of Misenum, see Appian, 5.72; Dio, 48.36.

83. "have known": have been acquainted.

Enobarbus: At sea, I think.   **85**

Menas: We have, sir.

Enobarbus: You have done well by water.

Menas: And you by land.

Enobarbus: I will praise any man that will praise me,
    though it cannot be denied what I have done by land.   **90**

Menas: Nor what I have done by water.

Enobarbus: Yes, something you can deny for your own
    safety: you have been a great thief by sea.

Menas: And you by land.

Enobarbus: There I deny my land service. But give   **95**
    me your hand, Menas. [*They shake hands.*] If our eyes
    had authority, here they might take two thieves
    kissing.

Menas: All men's faces are true, whatsome'er their
    hands are.   **100**

Enobarbus: But there is never a fair woman has a true
    face.

Menas: No slander. They steal hearts.

Enobarbus: We came hither to fight with you.

Menas: For my part, I am sorry it is turned to a   **105**
    drinking. Pompey doth this day laugh away his
    fortune.

Enobarbus: If he do, sure he cannot weep't back again.

---

87. "done well": (1) fought well, (2) prospered.
97. "authority": official power to apprehend criminals.
97. "take": arrest.
97–98. "two thieves kissing": two thieving hands clasping.
99. "true": honest, unfeigned.
99. "whatsome'er": whatever.
101. "true": without makeup.
103. "No slander": that is no slander.

Menas: You've said, sir. We looked not for Mark Antony
    here. Pray you, is he married to Cleopatra?   **110**

Enobarbus: Caesar's sister is called Octavia.

Menas: True, sir. She was the wife of Caius Marcellus.

Enobarbus: But she is now the wife of Marcus
    Antonius.

Menas: Pray you, sir?   **115**

Enobarbus: 'Tis true.

Menas: Then is Caesar and he forever knit together.

Enobarbus: If I were bound to divine of this unity, I
    would not prophesy so.

Menas: I think the policy of that purpose made more in   **120**
    the marriage than the love of the parties.

Enobarbus: I think so, too. But you shall find the band
    that seems to tie their friendship together will be the
    very strangler of their amity. Octavia is of a holy, cold,
    and still conversation.   **125**

Menas: Who would not have his wife so?

Enobarbus: Not he that himself is not so, which is

---

109. "You've said": what you've said is indisputable. For the phrase's sense of finality, see 1.2.59n.

112. Caius Marcellus (88–40) was consul in 50, a friend of Pompey the Great,
and staunch enemy of Julius Caesar. After the civil war broke out, he stayed out
of politics and was pardoned by Caesar. He died five months before Octavia married Antony (Cicero, *Letters to Atticus*, 10.15.2; Plutarch, *Antony*, 31.2, *Pompey*,
58.1–59.1).

115. "Pray you": do you really mean what you just said (an expression of surprise
and disbelief).

117. "is": are.

118. "divine of": foretell, guess at.

120. "the policy . . . more in": the political expediency of the proposal counted
for more.

124. "is of": possesses.

125. "still": calm, quiet.

125. "conversation": behavior, manner of life.

Mark Antony. He will to his Egyptian dish again.
Then shall the sighs of Octavia blow the fire up in
Caesar, and, as I said before, that which is the strength   **130**
of their amity shall prove the immediate author of
their variance. Antony will use his affection where it
is. He married but his occasion here.

Menas: And thus it may be. Come, sir, will you aboard?
I have a health for you.   **135**

Enobarbus: I shall take it, sir. We have used our
throats in Egypt.

Menas: Come, let's away.   ***Exeunt.***

ACT TWO, SCENE SEVEN

[On board Pompey's galley, off Misenum.]

Music plays. Enter two or three Servants with a banquet.

1 Servant: Here they'll be, man. Some o' their plants
are ill-rooted already. The least wind i'th' world will
blow them down.

2 Servant: Lepidus is high-colored.

1 Servant: They have made him drink alms-drink.   **5**

131–32. "author . . . variance": cause of their falling out.

132. "use his affection": satisfy his sexual passion.

133. "but his occasion": only his political opportunity.

135. "health": toast, drink to your health.

136. "take": drink.

136. "used": practiced, trained.

S.D. 1. "*banquet*": dessert with fruit and wine.

1. "Here they'll be": they are coming here (for their after-dinner dessert).

1. "plants": a quibble: (1) soles of feet (*planta*, in Latin), (2) seedlings (a metaphor for the new agreements among the parties).

4. "high-colored": flushed (from drinking).

5. "alms-drink": Although its precise meaning is unclear because the term is used only here, the Second Servant's reply indicates that as the others irritate

2 Servant: As they pinch one another by the
    disposition, he cries out "No more," reconciles them to
    his entreaty and himself to th' drink.

1 Servant: But it raises the greater war between him
    and his discretion.   **10**

2 Servant: Why, this it is to have a name in great
    men's fellowship. I had as lief have a reed that will
    do me no service as a partisan I could not heave.

1 Servant: To be called into a huge sphere, and not to
    be seen to move in't, are the holes where eyes should   **15**
    be, which pitifully disaster the cheeks.

---

one another, Lepidus, seeking to keep peace, urges them to stop their bickering, for which they toast his every effort, forcing him to accept yet another round of drinks pledging friendship.

6. "pinch": harass, irritate, find fault.

6–7. "by the disposition": according to their personal tendencies.

10. "discretion": good sense. While Lepidus, ironically, tries to live up to his name (literally, "pleasantly agreeable"), his attempted peacemaking puts him at war with his common sense.

11–12. "a name . . . fellowship": a title only, without any ability or power (as a triumvir).

12. "had as lief": would just as soon.

13. "partisan": long-handled, double-edged sword.

13. "heave": lift, throw.

15. "are": are like.

16. "disaster": strike with calamity (an astronomical term for an unfavorable aspect or condition of a star or planet).

14–16. "To be called . . . cheeks": to be called to a great position but have no function or authority is like having eye sockets without eyes. The terms "huge sphere," "move," and "disaster" refer to Ptolemaic astronomy, according to which the planets move in concentric spheres around the earth. Lepidus resembles a planet that is not seen to move in its sphere and, by further analogy, can cause only calamity by giving the pitiful appearance of pits instead of eyes. The reduction of the cosmic to the personal seems to reflect the reduction of Rome's political institutions to the persons of its rulers and their purely personal foibles, tastes, traits, interests, and abilities, as we see prominently in this scene.

A sennet sounded. Enter Caesar, Antony, Pompey, Lepidus, Agrippa,
Maecenas, Enobarbus, Menas, with other Captains and a Boy.

Antony: Thus do they, sir: they take the flow o'th' Nile
     By certain scales i'th' Pyramid; they know
     By th'height, the lowness, or the mean if dearth
     Or foison follow. The higher Nilus swells,   **20**
     The more it promises. As it ebbs, the seedsman
     Upon the slime and ooze scatters his grain,
     And shortly comes to harvest.

Lepidus: You've strange serpents there?

Antony: Ay, Lepidus.   **25**

S.D. 17. "*sennet*": notes on a trumpet announcing the ceremonial entrance of some great person(s).

17. "take": measure.

17. "the flow o'th' Nile": the height of the river at its annual flood.

18. "By certain ... Pyramid": "[T]he isle of measure, in which isle (according to the inundation of Nilus) they have a kind of device invented by the ancient Egyptians whereby they most certainly foresee the plenty or scarcity of the year following" (Joannes Leo Africanus, *A Geographical History of Africa*, trans. John Pory [London: Impensis Georg. Bishop, 1600; rpt. Amsterdam: Da Capo Press, 1969], 312).

19. "mean": middle.

20. "foison": plenty.

20–21. "The higher . . . promises": According to Antony, the greater the Nile's flood, the greater its fertility. Antony, however, is mistaken. While the quantity of Egypt's food depends on the quantity of the Nile's floods, the Nile produces dearth when it floods too much as well as too little. Just as a small overflow impedes planting by limiting the ground covered by the mud, a large overflow retards planting by retiring too slowly. "If the water reaches only to the fifteenth cubit of [a specific] pillar," Leo Africanus writes," [Egyptians] hope for a fruitful year following; but if it stays between the twelfth cubit and the fifteenth, then the increase of the year will prove but mean. . . . But if it arises to the eighteenth cubit, there is likely to follow great scarcity in regard to too much moisture; and if the eighteenth cubit be surmounted, all Egypt is in danger to be swallowed by the inundation of Nilus" (Leo Africanus, 312; see also Pliny, 5.58). For Antony, in contrast, more is never too much.

21. "seedsman": farmer sowing seeds.

Lepidus: Your serpent of Egypt is bred now of your
    mud by the operation of your sun; so is your crocodile.

Antony: They are so.

Pompey: Sit, and some wine. A health to Lepidus!

[*They sit and drink.*]

Lepidus: I am not so well as I should be, but I'll ne'er   **30**
    out.

Enobarbus: [*aside*] Not till you have slept. I fear me
    you'll be in till then.

Lepidus: Nay, certainly, I have heard the Ptolemies'
    pyramises are very goodly things. Without contradiction   **35**
    I have heard that.

Menas: [aside to Pompey] Pompey, a word.

Pompey: [*aside to Menas*]   Say in mine ear what is't.

Menas: [*Whispers in his ear*]
    Forsake thy seat, I do beseech thee, captain,
    And hear me speak a word.

Pompey: [*aside to Menas*]
    Forbear me till anon.—This wine for Lepidus!   **40**

---

26. "Your": a colloquially indefinite pronoun, affecting thorough knowledge of the subject. "Though in this instance the *your* may seem literally justified, the repetition of it indicates a colloquial vulgarity which suits the character of Lepidus" (Abbott, §221).

26–27. "Your serpent . . . crocodile": On the belief held by some Egyptians that the inundated Egyptian soil, warmed by the blaze of the sun, generates living animals, including snakes and crocodiles, see Diodorus, 1.7.3–5, 1.10.1–7; Ovid, *Metamorphoses*, 1.416–37; see also 1.3.69–70n.

31. "out": give up, quit.

32. "fear me": fear.

33. "in": in drink, drunk (a play on Lepidus' "out").

34–35. "Ptolemies' pyramises": royal pyramids ("pyramises" is Lepidus' drunken plural).

36. "I have heard that": On Egyptian pyramids as marvels, see Diodorus, 1.63.2–9.

40. "Forbear me till anon": let me alone for a little while.

Lepidus: What manner o' thing is your crocodile?

Antony: It is shaped, sir, like itself, and it is as broad
  as it hath breadth. It is just so high as it is, and
  moves with it own organs. It lives by that which
  nourisheth it, and the elements once out of it, it   **45**
  transmigrates.

Lepidus: What color is it of?

Antony: Of it own color too.

Lepidus: 'Tis a strange serpent.

Antony: 'Tis so, and the tears of it are wet.   **50**

Caesar: Will this description satisfy him?

Antony: With the health that Pompey gives him, else
  he is a very epicure.

---

41. "What manner . . . your crocodile": Its mixture of contrary extremes makes
the crocodile seem especially exotic. No other animal grows so large from so small
an egg. It is the only land animal without a tongue, and the only one that bites
by moving only its upper jaw. Its skin is completely covered with scales, making it
invincible against all blows. Although it devours any other animal that approaches
it, it lets a certain small bird (the plover or trochilus) clean its mouth of leeches. In
some places the Egyptian regard the crocodile as sacred; in others they kill and eat
it (Pliny, 8.89; Diodorus, 1.35.2–6).

44. "it own": its own (archaic form).

45. "elements": the four fundamental natural elements—fire, air, earth, and water—
thought to constitute the material of a living body (see, further, 5.2.288–89n).

45–46. "it transmigrates": According to Herodotus, the Egyptians believe that animals are depositories of the soul and life. When an animal dies, the soul, which
they hold to be immortal, enters the body of another creature just as it is being
born (Herodotus, 2.123).

50. "tears . . . wet": Antony's sly taunt. In a Roman fable handed down from antiquity, crocodiles are said to shed tears ("crocodile tears") in order to lure unsus-
pecting prey, whom they then catch and quickly devour. For Antony's opinion of
Lepidus, see *JC*, 4.1.12–40.

52. "health": toast.

52. "else": otherwise.

53. "a very epicure": a man with unshakable opinions (hence, could drink as much
as Lepidus and still not believe anything he is told). Epicurus reduced his teach-
ing to a series of short summaries which his followers could memorize, so that
they would have them always, no matter what they might hear, and consequently

Pompey: [*aside to Menas*] Go hang, sir, hang! Tell me of that? Away!
  Do as I bid you.—Where's this cup I called for?   **55**

Menas: [*aside to Pompey*] If for the sake of merit thou wilt hear me,
  Rise from thy stool.

Pompey: [*aside to Menas*] I think th'art mad! The matter?

[Rises, and walks aside with Menas.]

Menas: I have ever held my cap off to thy fortunes.

Pompey: Thou hast served me with much faith. What's else to say?—
  Be jolly, lords.

Antony: These quicksands, Lepidus,   **60**
  Keep off them, for you sink.

Menas: Wilt thou be lord of all the world?

Pompey: What sayst thou?

Menas: Wilt thou be lord of the whole world?
  That's twice.

Pompey: How should that be?

Menas: But entertain it,
  And though thou think me poor, I am the man   **65**
  Will give thee all the world.

"never, either in waking or in dream, . . . be disturbed" (Epicurus, *Letter to Herodotus*, 36, 82, 83, *Letter to Pythocles*, 85, 95, *Letter to Menoeceus*, 135).

54. "Go hang": a strong expression of dismissal.

54. "Tell . . . that?": still harping on that.

56. "merit": my past service. Pompey's best naval commanders are freedmen inherited from his father (Appian, 5.79, 96; Velleius Paterculus, 2.73.3).

58. "held my cap off to": showed great respect or deference for (the image reflects the practice of servants removing their caps in the presence of their masters).

60. "quicksands": a warning to Lepidus, who is about to collapse, not to drink again.

64. "But entertain it": only accept my offer.

66. "all the world": Eight of the play's forty-four mentions of the word "world" occur in this scene, including three ending lines for emphasis in the Menas-Pompey exchange. In addition, "all" and "whole" modify "world," once implicitly and thrice explicitly (lines 62, 63, 66, 74). Note also lines 69–70, 73. For the episode, see Plutarch, *Antony*, 32.4–5; Appian, 5.73.

Pompey: Hast thou drunk well?

Menas: No, Pompey, I have kept me from the cup.
    Thou art, if thou dar'st be, the earthly Jove.
    Whate'er the ocean pales or sky inclips
    Is thine, if thou wilt ha't.

Pompey: Show me which way.   **70**

Menas: These three world-sharers, these competitors,
    Are in thy vessel. Let me cut the cable,
    And when we are put off, fall to their throats.
    All there is thine.

Pompey: Ah, this thou shouldst have done
    And not have spoke on't! In me 'tis villainy;   **75**
    In thee't had been good service. Thou must know
    'Tis not my profit that does lead mine honor;
    Mine honor, it. Repent that e'er thy tongue
    Hath so betrayed thine act. Being done unknown,
    I should have found it afterwards well done,   **80**
    But must condemn it now. Desist and drink.

Menas: [*aside*] For this,

---

69. "pales": encompasses, encloses.
69. "inclips": embraces, encircles.
71. "competitors": partners (the triumvirs).
72. "cable": anchor cable.
73. "are put off": have left the shore (a nautical term).
73. "fall to": cut.
74. "All there is": all that the triumvirs possess.
75. "on't": of it.
76. "Thou must know": I would have you know, you must let me tell you.
79. "betrayed": revealed.
79–81. "Being done . . . now": Pompey evidently feels bound by his agreement (2.6.57). Nevertheless, he would have thought well of the deed and had no objections to accepting its benefits if only he did not know of it beforehand. Like his father, Pompey refuses to act to obtain something to which he has no legitimate claim, but would gladly accept it if handed to him (see 2.6.14–23n). Although claiming to champion the republican cause, Pompey would readily become the sole ruler of the world if only given the power.

I'll never follow thy palled fortunes more.
Who seeks and will not take when once 'tis offered
Shall never find it more.

Pompey: This health to Lepidus!   **85**

Antony: Bear him ashore. I'll pledge it for him, Pompey.

Enobarbus: Here's to thee, Menas!

Menas: Enobarbus, welcome.

Pompey: Fill till the cup be hid.

Enobarbus: [*pointing to the Servant carrying Lepidus*] There's a strong
     fellow, Menas.

Menas: Why?   **90**

Enobarbus: 'A bears the third part of the world, man. Seest not?

Menas: The third part, then, is drunk. Would it were all,
     That it might go on wheels!

---

83. "palled": weakened, diminished.

84–85. "Who seeks . . . more": Appian (who refers to him as Menodorus) describes
Menas as "a traitor by nature" (Appian, 5.96; W. B., 349). Yet Pompey seems to take
his loyalty for granted. He seems to fail to consider that Menas' loyalty may depend
not upon his gratitude or good will toward Pompey, as Menas initially suggested
(lines 56–59), but upon Pompey's ability and willingness to satisfy his desire to
command an army and a province. Menas' decision to abandon Pompey is the first
of many desertions in the play.

86. "him": Lepidus.

86. "pledge it for him": respond (to Pompey's toast) by drinking for Lepidus.

91. "'A": he (a colloquialism).

91. "the third . . . world": a scornful allusion to Lepidus as one of the three triumvirs (cp. 1.1.12n).

92–93. "Would it . . . on wheels": would that the whole world were drunk so that
it would spin wildly. One might suppose that if all the triumvirs and Pompey were
drunk, Menas could carry out his plan quite easily. Unwilling to follow Pompey's
fortunes any longer, he might follow his own and do for himself what he would
have done for Pompey. But Menas, who is now drinking (see lines 87ff.), wants
only to enjoy the party. Although disloyal by both nature and circumstances, he
does not have unbounded ambition. He may want to add to what he already has,
but he seems content with lieutenancy. Even though he offers to give the world to
Pompey, he continues to be dependent on a superior. Treachery and dependence
go together with the former slave.

Enobarbus: Drink thou. Increase the reels!

Menas: Come!   **95**

Pompey: This is not yet an Alexandrian feast.

Antony: It ripens towards it. Strike the vessels, ho!
    Here's to Caesar.

Caesar: I could well forbear't
    It's monstrous labor when I wash my brain
    And it grows fouler.   **100**

Antony: Be a child o'th' time.

Caesar: Possess it, I'll make answer.
    But I had rather fast from all, four days,
    Than drink so much in one.

Enobarbus: [*to Antony*]   Ha, my brave emperor,
    Shall we dance now the Egyptian bacchanals
    And celebrate our drink?   **105**

Pompey: Let's ha't, good soldier.

Antony: Come, let's all take hands

---

94. "reels": staggering, revels.

96. "Alexandrian feast": such as you would have in Alexandria. The play's only example of Alexandrian revelry takes place entirely in a Roman context.

97. "Strike the vessels": open more wine casks.

98. "could well forbear't": would gladly abstain (from drinking the toast).

99. "monstrous": unnatural.

99. "wash my brain": drink copiously (a jocular expression for wine drinking).

100. "it grows fouler": Caesar does not express a traditional Roman's contempt for immoderate pleasures, but rather his fear that his body is not up to the effects of heavy drinking. Fear, not pride, prompts his moderation. As Gibbon writes, "[Caesar's] virtues, and even his vices, [are] artificial" (Gibbon, 3, 1:63).

101. "Be a child . . . answer": Both Antony and Caesar voice what could be their mottos. Antony: submit to the pleasures of the moment; Caesar: master the situation.

102. "fast . . . four days": abstain altogether for four days in a row. Contrary to his wish, Caesar accommodates himself to the others here, if only because he thinks he must.

104. "bacchanals": wild dances in honor of Bacchus, the Roman god of wine. Romans link dancing with drinking. "No one dances unless he is drunk (or out of his mind)" (Cicero, *For Murena*, 13).

Till that the conquering wine hath steeped our sense
In soft and delicate Lethe.

Enobarbus: All take hands.
Make battery to our ears with the loud music,
The while I'll place you; then the boy shall sing.   **110**
The holding every man shall beat as loud
As his strong sides can volley.

Music plays. Enobarbus places them hand in hand.

The Song

Boy: Come, thou monarch of the vine,
Plumpy Bacchus, with pink eyne.
In thy fats our cares be drowned.   **115**
With thy grapes our hairs be crowned.

All: Cup us till the world go round!
Cup us till the world go round!

Caesar: What would you more? Pompey, good night. Good brother,

---

107. "Till that": until.

108. "Lethe": forgetfulness, oblivion (see 2.1.26–27n). Traditional Roman wakefulness has given way to the stupor and languor of the East. Egyptian softness, sensuality, and oblivion replace Roman hardness, austerity, and alertness. Rather than conquering one's bodily desires, one surrenders to the conquering wine.

109. "Make battery to": batter, assault.

110. "place": position.

111. "holding": burden, or refrain, of a song (here, the song's repeated last line).

111. "beat": beat out the rhythm of.

112. "volley": discharge (as with the noise of many firearms). Enobarbus' military metaphors (lines 109–12) adulterate the language of war.

114. "pink eyne": half-shut eyes ("pink," from the Dutch *pinken* ["to blink"], "eyne," an archaic form of "eyes").

115. "fats": vats, vessels.

117. "Cup us": fill our cups.

113–18. The celebratory song incongruously resembles a Christian hymn addressed to the Holy Spirit. It begins with an appeal to a deity, proceeds in lines of four stresses, and seeks a divine gift to make men other than themselves. See Richmond Noble, *Shakespeare's Use of Song with the Texts of the Principal Songs* (London: Oxford University Press, 1923), 127–28.

119. "brother": brother-in-law (Antony).

Let me request you off. Our graver business   **120**
Frowns at this levity. Gentle lords, let's part.
You see we have burnt our cheeks. Strong Enobarb
Is weaker than the wine, and mine own tongue
Splits what it speaks. The wild disguise hath almost
Anticked us all. What needs more words? Good night.   **125**
Good Antony, your hand.

Pompey: I'll try you on the shore.

Antony: And shall, sir. Give's your hand.

Pompey: O, Antony, you have my father's house.
But what? We are friends! Come down into the boat.   **130**

Enobarbus: Take heed you fall not.

[*Exeunt all but Enobarbus and Menas.*]

Menas, I'll not on shore.

Menas: No, to my cabin. These drums, these trumpets, flutes!
What!
Let Neptune hear we bid a loud farewell
To these great fellows. Sound and be hanged. Sound out!

---

120. "off": come ashore (with me).

122. "burnt": reddened.

124. "Splits": mispronounces.

124. "wild disguise": (1) wild playacting of the dance itself, (2) the disorderly drunkenness that makes us unlike ourselves.

125. "Anticked": made into antics (hence grotesque fools).

127. "try you": test further (your drinking capacity).

128. "shall": you shall (a drinking contest replaces a military contest, which Pompey was likely to have won).

128. "Give's": give me.

129. "my father's house": see 2.6.26–27n.

130. "what": so what.

130. "boat": the boat that takes them from the galley to the shore.

131. "not": not go.

132–34.: The Folio gives this speech to Enobarbus, which seems a mistake. He cannot have a cabin on Pompey's ship.

132. "These drums . . . flutes": fanfare for departing honored guests.

133. "Neptune": the Roman god of the sea; cp. 2.1.1–2n.

Sound a flourish, with drums.

Enobarbus: Hoo, says 'a! There's my cap! [*Flings his cap in the air.*] **135**
Menas: Hoo! Noble captain, come.   **Exeunt.**

---

136. "come": Although he no doubt had intended to cut his throat along with those of the triumvirs, Menas invites Enobarbus for more drinking in his cabin, and Enobarbus, as always, accepts.

ACT THREE, SCENE ONE

[A plain in Syria.]

Enter Ventidius as it were in triumph, the dead body of Pacorus borne before him, with Silius and Soldiers.

Ventidius: Now, darting Parthia, art thou struck, and now
Pleased Fortune does of Marcus Crassus' death
Make me revenger. Bear the King's son's body

S.D. 1. "*as it were*": A triumph could be formally celebrated only in Rome; see 3.6.1–2n.

S.D. 1. Ventidius' victory over the Parthians is the defeat of the last foreign enemy seriously able to threaten Rome. With the victory, the East is essentially secured, as the West now is, following Pompey's agreement. Rome, however, has always been in danger from itself when it has had no foreign enemies to contend with. "[E]ven now are we in greatest danger, being at this pass that we have left ourselves none to fear" (Plutarch, *How to Profit by One's Enemies*, 3 [88a]; Holland, 1:239). No enemy remains who could force the Romans to unite for the common good. While Ventidius alone in the play fights Rome's enemy instead of fellow Romans, his victory, ironically, ensures that he will be the last to do so. For the present Parthian danger, see 1.2.105–9n.

S.D. 1. Pacorus is the son of the Parthian king, Orodes.

1. "darting Parthia": "Darting" puns on the Parthians' famous weapon and tactic—their arrows and their flight. After shooting their arrows at the enemy, the Parthians flee to avoid close combat, but then turn in their saddles and shoot their arrows behind them as they go (Horace, *Odes*, 2.13.17–18; Virgil, *Georgics*, 3.31).

1. "struck": conquered, punished (with a tactic similar to the Parthians' darting; see Dio, 49.19–20). The Folio reads "stroke," a spelling variant.

2–3. "Marcus Crassus' death . . . revenger": Ventidius' triumph is Rome's long-sought revenge. Crassus (115–53), a member of the first triumvirate with Julius Caesar and Pompey the Great, led an army into Parthia in 53. He was defeated, with 20,000 Romans killed and another 10,000 taken prisoners, and Crassus himself was treacherously killed by King Orodes during a conference. The Parthians then ridiculed a Roman triumph, dressing Roman prisoners as women and "singing . . . songs of mockery and derision of Crassus's womanish cowardice" (Plutarch, *Crassus*, 32.1–2; Tudor, 4:88). After decapitating Crassus, in addition to pouring molten gold into his gaping mouth to mock him for his greed (see 2.5.34–35n), they used his head as a stage prop in a farcical performance of Euripides' *Bacchae*. "This noble exploit," Plutarch says of Ventidius' victory, "as famous as ever any was, was a full revenge to the Romans of the shame and loss they had received before by the death of Marcus Crassus" (Plutarch, *Antony*, 34.2; Spencer, 217–18).

Before our army. Thy Pacorus, Orodes,
Pays this for Marcus Crassus.

Silius: Noble Ventidius,   **5**
Whilst yet with Parthian blood thy sword is warm,
The fugitive Parthians follow. Spur through Media,
Mesopotamia, and the shelters whither
The routed fly. So thy grand captain, Antony,
Shall set thee on triumphant chariots and   **10**
Put garlands on thy head.

Ventidius: O, Silius, Silius,
I have done enough. A lower place, note well,
May make too great an act. For learn this, Silius:
Better to leave undone than by our deed
Acquire too high a fame when him we serve's away.   **15**
Caesar and Antony have ever won

1–5. Ventidius, exulting in his victory, addresses Parthia and Orodes as though they were actually before him. Illustrating spiritedness' tendency to animate the inanimate in order to punish it, he apostrophizes both while also personifying Parthia, so that he can punish them—or imagine he is doing so—to their faces.

7. "The fugitive Parthians follow": pursue the fleeing Parthians.

7. "Spur": ride swiftly (using your spurs).

7. Media, home of the Medes, is located southwest of the Caspian Sea and north of Parthia (modern northwest Iran).

8. Mesopotamia is the land between the Tigris and Euphrates Rivers (modern Iraq), south of Parthia.

7–9. "Spur through . . . fly": Such a pursuit, if successful, would drive the Parthians back, deep within their original territory.

9–11. "So thy grand . . . head": On Roman triumphs, see 1.3.102–3n. During the Republic, only the Senate, not an individual Roman, could grant one (Polybius, 6.15.8).

12. "lower place": subordinate officer.

12–15. Throughout the Republic, fame was the spur to and reward for noble action. To advance, a Roman needed to please Rome, not his superior, with whom he in fact competed and whose position his success threatened (see *Cor.*, 1.1.258–71). Ventidius, however, serves Antony, not Rome. To advance or even to maintain his position, he must please his superior and avoid appearing to rival him. And so it is better to curtail one's own campaign than to win too much fame for oneself.

16. "ever": always.

More in their officer than person. Sossius,
One of my place in Syria, his lieutenant,
For quick accumulation of renown,
Which he achieved by th' minute, lost his favor.   20
Who does i'th' wars more than his captain can
Becomes his captain's captain; and ambition,
The soldier's virtue, rather makes choice of loss
Than gain which darkens him.
I could do more to do Antonius good,   25
But 'twould offend him. And in his offence
Should my performance perish.

Silius: Thou hast, Ventidius, that
Without the which a soldier and his sword
Grants scarce distinction. Thou wilt write to Antony?   30

Ventidius: I'll humbly signify what in his name,
That magical word of war, we have effected;
How, with his banners and his well-paid ranks,
The ne'er-yet-beaten horse of Parthia

---

17. "More . . . than person": more by the deeds of their officers than by their own actions.

18. "place": rank.

18. "his": Antony's.

20. "by th' minute": quickly and continually. C. Sosius (original spelling) captured Jerusalem in 37 and installed Herod as king (Dio, 49.22.3–6).

21. "Who": whoever.

23–24. "rather makes choice . . . him": prefers a military loss to a victory which would diminish his captain's glory. Sosius evidently learned his lesson. In the following year, "Sosius dreaded [Antony's] jealousy and anger, [and] spent the time in devising means, not for achieving some success and incurring his enmity, but for pleasing him without engaging in any activity" (Dio, 49.23.2).

26. "in his offence": as the result of his taking offence.

27. "perish": come to nothing.

28–30. "Thou hast . . . distinction": without discretion a soldier can hardly be distinguished from his sword. Silius answers like a thoroughly post-republican Roman. A soldier's virtue is no longer knowing how to win in battle, but now includes knowing when not to win in order not to lose his captain's favor.

32. "word of war": in whose name they are fighting.

34. "horse": cavalry.

We have jaded out o'th' field.

Silius: Where is he now?   **35**

Ventidius: He purposeth to Athens, whither, with what haste
      The weight we must convey with's will permit,
      We shall appear before him. On there, pass along!   ***Exeunt.***

ACT THREE, SCENE TWO

[Rome. Caesar's house.]

Enter Agrippa at one door, Enobarbus at another.

Agrippa: What, are the brothers parted?

Enobarbus: They have dispatched with Pompey; he is gone.
      The other three are sealing. Octavia weeps
      To part from Rome. Caesar is sad, and Lepidus,
      Since Pompey's feast, as Menas says, is troubled   **5**
      With the green-sickness.

Agrippa: 'Tis a noble Lepidus.

Enobarbus: A very fine one. O, how he loves Caesar!

Agrippa: Nay, but how dearly he adores Mark Antony!

Enobarbus: Caesar? Why, he's the Jupiter of men.

---

35. "jaded out o'th' field": driven out of the field like worn-out nags. Although he is "the only man that ever triumphed [over] the Parthians until this present day" (Plutarch, *Antony*, 34.5; Spencer, 219), Ventidius sacrifices his glory to his discretion.

36. "purposeth": intends to go.

37. "weight": burden (spoils, baggage, equipment).

37. "with's": with us.

38. "On": go on.

1. "are the brothers parted": have the brothers-in-law, Caesar and Antony, departed.

2. "dispatched": finished their business.

3. "sealing": affixing seals to their agreements.

4. "sad": serious.

6. "green-sickness": a mocking description of Lepidus' hangover as the symptom of a kind of anemia thought to affect love-sick young women: the infatuated Lepidus is besotted with Caesar and Antony.

Agrippa: What's Antony? The god of Jupiter.   **10**

Enobarbus: Spake you of Caesar? Hoo! The nonpareil!

Agrippa: O Antony! O thou Arabian bird!

Enobarbus: Would you praise Caesar, say "Caesar." Go no further.

Agrippa: Indeed, he plied them both with excellent praises.

Enobarbus: But he loves Caesar best, yet he loves Antony.   **15**
    Hoo! Hearts, tongues, figures, scribes, bards, poets, cannot
    Think, speak, cast, write, sing, number—hoo!—
    His love to Antony! But as for Caesar,
    Kneel down, kneel down, and wonder!

Agrippa: Both he loves.

Enobarbus: They are his shards and he their beetle.

                            [*Trumpet within.*]
                            So,   **20**

---

11. "nonpareil": peerless, without an equal.

12. "Arabian bird": the mythological Phoenix, of which only one existed at any time, and which regenerated itself out of its own ashes after a life span of 500 years (Pliny, 10.3–5).

13. "Would you": if you wish to.

13. "Would you praise ... further": Enobarbus' joke on Lepidus elevates Caesar's name to the highest possible praise. To have the name "Caesar" is to have an unsurpassable distinction. For Julius Caesar's ambition for his name, see *Julius Caesar*, ed. Blits, xix.

16–17. "Hearts, . . . number": hearts cannot think, tongues cannot speak, figures of speech cannot articulate (or numbers cannot calculate), scribes cannot write, bards cannot sing, poets cannot versify. Enobarbus makes his ridiculously excessive rhetoric even more excessive by his parodic rhetorical figures of repetition, concision, succession, analogy, and denial.

20. "They are . . . beetle": an obscene summary of Lepidus' professed love of Caesar and Antony. According to Plutarch, the Egyptians hold that there are no female beetles, "but all the males do blow or cast their seed into a certain globus or round matter [of dung] in form of balls, which they drive from them and roll to and fro contrariwise, like as the sun, when he moves himself from the West to the East, seems to turn about the Heaven clean contrary" (Plutarch, *Isis and Osiris*, 74 [381a]; Holland, 1071). Lepidus, scurrying back and forth with fulsome praise between Caesar in the West and Antony in the East, resembles a beetle generating by rolling a ball of dung backwards and forwards, just as the sun seems to travel west by day and east by night. Lepidus, a triumvir of the world, resembles nothing so much as a ludicrous, loathsome, low insect attempting to emulate the motions of the sun in the sky (cp. 2.7.14–16n).

This is to horse. Adieu, noble Agrippa.

Agrippa: Good fortune, worthy soldier, and farewell.

Enter Caesar, Antony, Lepidus, and Octavia.

Antony: No further, sir.

Caesar: You take from me a great part of myself.
Use me well in't. Sister, prove such a wife   25
As my thoughts make thee, and as my farthest bond
Shall pass on thy approof. Most noble Antony,
Let not the piece of virtue which is set
Betwixt us, as the cement of our love
To keep it builded, be the ram to batter   30
The fortress of it. For better might we
Have loved without this mean, if on both parts
This be not cherished.

Antony: Make me not offended
In your distrust.

Caesar: I have said.

Antony: You shall not find,
Though you be therein curious, the least cause   35
For what you seem to fear. So the gods keep you,
And make the hearts of Romans serve your ends.
We will here part.

---

21. "This . . . horse": the trumpet signal to mount their horses.

23. "No further, sir": you need not (1) accompany us further, or (2) urge your point further.

25. "Use": treat.

26–27. "As my thoughts . . . approof": as I will pledge my utmost credit on your proving to be (the commercial language of a promissory note). The Folio reads "band," which in Shakespeare's day was synonymous with "bond."

28. "piece": masterpiece, exemplar.

30. "ram": battering ram.

32. "mean": (1) means, (2) intermediary.

28–33. "Let not . . . cherished": On Caesar's pedestrian mode of everyday, informal speech, see Suetonius, *Augustus*, 87.

34. "In": by.

34. "I have said": on the finality of the phrase, see 1.2.59n.

35. "curious": (1) minutely inquisitive, (3) intrusive.

36. "keep": protect, guard.

Caesar: Farewell, my dearest sister, fare thee well.
The elements be kind to thee and make   **40**
Thy spirits all of comfort. Fare thee well.

Octavia: My noble brother!   **[*She weeps.*]**

Antony: The April's in her eyes. It is love's spring,
And these the showers to bring it on. Be cheerful.

Octavia: Sir, look well to my husband's house, and—   **45**

Caesar: What, Octavia?

Octavia: I'll tell you in your ear.

                    [*She whispers to Caesar.*]

Antony: Her tongue will not obey her heart, nor can
Her heart inform her tongue—the swan's-down feather
That stands upon the swell at the full of tide
And neither way inclines.   **50**

Enobarbus: [*aside to Agrippa*] Will Caesar weep?

Agrippa: [*aside to Enobarbus*]   He has a cloud in's face.

Enobarbus: [*aside to Agrippa*]
He were the worse for that were he a horse;
So is he being a man.

---

40. "The elements": (1) the four elements which compose the world (see 2.7.45n),
or (2) the elements of earth (land) and water on which she will travel.

41. "all": completely.

43–44. "April's . . . bring it on": her tears will nourish her young love (an allusion
to the proverbial effect of April showers bringing forth May flowers).

45. "my husband's house": Since she is a recent widow (2.6.112), Octavia may be
referring to Antony's house or to her first husband's.

48. "inform": instruct.

49. "stands": floats.

48–50. "the swan's-down . . . inclines": Her love divided equally between them,
Octavia's heart is balanced between her sorrow at parting from her brother and
her desire to accompany her husband. Like a feather on still water just before
the full tide turns, she is not inclined either way. Antony speaks of the fullness of
Octavia's love for both men ("the swell at full tide"), but, ominously, the tide, now
at its height, will soon begin to decline, and the water will flow in one direction.

51–53. "a cloud . . . man": just as a horse is less valuable for having a dark patch or
spot ("a cloud") on its face, so too is a man (since weeping ["a cloud"] is a sign of

Agrippa: [*aside to Enobarbus*] Why, Enobarbus,
    When Antony found Julius Caesar dead,
    He cried almost to roaring. And he wept   **55**
    When at Philippi he found Brutus slain.

Enobarbus: [*aside to Agrippa*]
    That year indeed he was troubled with a rheum.
    What willingly he did confound he wailed,
    Believe't, till I weep too.

Caesar: No, sweet Octavia,
    You shall hear from me still. The time shall not   **60**
    Outgo my thinking on you.

Antony: Come, sir, come,
    I'll wrestle with you in my strength of love.
    Look, here I have you [*embracing him*], thus I let you go,
    And give you to the gods.

---

unmanliness). A dark patch on a horse's face was thought to indicate a bad temper.

54–56. "When Antony . . . slain": Agrippa fabricates or exaggerates. Antony did not cry when he found either Caesar or Brutus slain (*JC*, 3.1.148ff., 5.5.69–76), though his eyes "[began] to water" when he saw Octavius' servant weep at the sight of Caesar's corpse, and he did feign tears at Caesar's funeral (*JC*, 3.1.283–85, 3.2.116).

57. "rheum": a running of the eyes.

58. "confound": destroy.

55–58. "And he wept . . . wailed": Agrippa and Enobarbus say that Antony wept at Philippi at the destruction he eagerly sought (as Caesar will at the sight of the sword that kills Antony [5.1.24–27]). Such displays of tears, whether simulated or real, enjoy a long ancient tradition, following Alexander's enormous conquests and sudden death at an early age. The tears are meant to acknowledge the mutability of Fortune and the uncertainty of human affairs. "Is there any man living, my friends," Aemilius Paullus asks his men after defeating the Macedonian king Perseus in 168, "who having fortune at will, should therefore boast and glory in the prosperity of his doings, for that he has conquered a country, city or realm; and not rather to fear the inconstancy of Fortune?" (Plutarch, *Aemilius Paulus*, 27.1–2; Tudor, 2:228). However great the present conquest, the conqueror may become the conquered. See 5.1.28–30n.

60. "still": always, continually.

61. "Outgo": outpace.

61. "on": of.

62–64. Throughout the scene, unlike when accepting the marriage proposal, Antony addresses Caesar, as Caesar continues to address him, only with the distant pronoun "you"; cp. 2.2.158n.

Caesar: Adieu, be happy.

Lepidus: Let all the number of the stars give light   **65**
  To thy fair way!

Caesar: Farewell, farewell!   **[*Kisses Octavia.*]**

Antony: Farewell!

                                    Trumpets sound. Exeunt.

ACT THREE, SCENE THREE

[Alexandria. Cleopatra's Palace.]

Enter Cleopatra, Charmian, Iras, and Alexas.

Cleopatra: Where is the fellow?

Alexas: Half afeard to come.

Cleopatra: Go to, go to.

            Enter the Messenger as before.

            Come hither, sir.

Alexas: Good Majesty,
  Herod of Jewry dare not look upon you
  But when you are well pleased.

Cleopatra: That Herod's head

65–66. "Let all . . . fair way": Lepidus' surprisingly lyrical words—his only words in
the scene and his last in the play—ironically echo his first words. There, Antony's
faults resembled the stars (1.4.12–13); here, the stars will guide Octavia's way.
Contrary to what Lepidus evidently intends, Antony's faults will, in fact, determine
her way.

2. "Go to": here, an expression of derisive impatience.

S.D. 2. "*as before*": nervous, as when he brought the news of Antony's marriage.

3. "dare not": would not dare to.

3–4. "Herod of Jewry . . . pleased": even the terrifying Herod the Great, notorious
for cruelty, is intimidated by Cleopatra except when she is pleased with him; see
1.2.29–31n.

  I'll have! But how, when Antony is gone,   **5**
  Through whom I might command it?—Come thou near.

Messenger: Most gracious Majesty!

Cleopatra: Did'st thou behold Octavia?

Messenger: Ay, dread queen.

Cleopatra: Where?

Messenger: Madam, in Rome.
  I looked her in the face and saw her led
  Between her brother and Mark Antony.   **10**

Cleopatra: Is she as tall as me?

Messenger: She is not, madam.

Cleopatra: Didst hear her speak? Is she shrill-tongued or low?

Messenger: Madam, I heard her speak. She is low-voiced.

Cleopatra: That's not so good. He cannot like her long.

Charmian: Like her? O Isis, 'tis impossible!   **15**

Cleopatra: I think so, Charmian: dull of tongue, and dwarfish.
  What majesty is in her gait? Remember,
  If e'er thou look'dst on majesty.

Messenger: She creeps.
  Her motion and her station are as one.
  She shows a body rather than a life,   **20**
  A statue than a breather.

---

5. "But how": but how can I have it.

4–6. "That Herod's head . . . command it": Herod is Cleopatra's bitter rival for control over the kingdom of Judea, which was part of the Ptolemaic Empire a century and a half ago, and Cleopatra wishes to recover. But Egypt depends on Rome—or on one of its leaders—for its power against foreign enemies. Without Antony, Cleopatra is powerless as well as loveless (see, further, 1.5.32n and 2.5.108n). On the hostility between Cleopatra and Herod and Cleopatra's reliance on Antony for needed support, see Josephus, *The Jewish War*, 7.300–303.

14. "not so good": not so good for her.

17. "gait": manner of walking.

19. "station": standing still.

20. "shows": appears to be.

21. "breather": living being.

Cleopatra: Is this certain?

Messenger: Or I have no observance.

Charmian: Three in Egypt
    Cannot make better note.

Cleopatra: He's very knowing.
    I do perceive't. There's nothing in her yet.
    The fellow has good judgment.

Charmian: Excellent.   **25**

Cleopatra: Guess at her years, I prithee.

Messenger: Madam,
    She was a widow—

Cleopatra: Widow? Charmian, hark!

Messenger: And I do think she's thirty.

Cleopatra: Bear'st thou her face in mind? Is't long or round?

Messenger: Round even to faultiness.   **30**

Cleopatra: For the most part, too, they are foolish that are so.
    Her hair what color?

Messenger: Brown, madam, and her forehead
    As low as she would wish it.

Cleopatra: There's gold for thee.
    Thou must not take my former sharpness ill.
    I will employ thee back again. I find thee   **35**
    Most fit for business. Go, make thee ready.

---

22. "observance": powers of observation.

22–23. "Three . . . better note": there are not three people in Egypt who can observe better than he.

24. "in her": to her.

27. "a widow": of Caius Marcellus; see 2.6.112n.

28. "she's thirty": Cleopatra will soon turn thirty-nine. This is the Messenger's only answer which Cleopatra passes over in silence. "Cleopatra . . . neither excelled Octavia in beauty, nor yet in young years" (Plutarch, *Antony*, 57.3; Spencer, 246).

29. "in mind": in memory.

33. "As low . . . wish it": she would not want it any lower.

35. "back": to go back.

Our letters are prepared.   **[Exit Messenger.]**

Charmian: A proper man.

Cleopatra: Indeed he is so. I repent me much
    That so I harried him. Why, methinks, by him,
    This creature's no such thing.

Charmian: Nothing, madam.   **40**

Cleopatra: The man hath seen some majesty, and should know.

Charmian: Hath he seen majesty? Isis else defend,
    And serving you so long!

Cleopatra: I have one thing more to ask him yet, good Charmian,
    But 'tis no matter. Thou shalt bring him to me   **45**
    Where I will write. All may be well enough.

Charmian: I warrant you, madam.   **Exeunt.**

ACT THREE, SCENE FOUR

[Athens. Antony's house.]

Enter Antony and Octavia.

Antony: Nay, nay, Octavia, not only that.
    That were excusable—that and thousands more
    Of semblable import—but he hath waged
    New wars 'gainst Pompey; made his will and read it
    To public ear;   5
    Spoke scantly of me; when perforce he could not

---

37. "proper": fine, admirable.
39. "harried": harassed, mistreated.
39. "by him": from his account.
40. "no such thing": nothing to be concerned about.
42. "else defend": forbid that it be otherwise.
47. "warrant": assure.
3. "semblable": similar.
6. "scantly": slightingly, grudgingly.
6. "perforce": of necessity.

But pay me terms of honor, cold and sickly
He vented them; most narrow measure lent me;
When the best hint was given him, he not took't,
Or did it from his teeth.

Octavia: O, my good lord,   **10**
Believe not all, or if you must believe,
Stomach not all. A more unhappy lady,
If this division chance, ne'er stood between,
Praying for both parts.
The good gods will mock me presently   **15**
When I shall pray "O, bless my lord and husband!"
Undo that prayer by crying out as loud
"O, bless my brother!" Husband win, win brother

---

8. "vented": expressed.

8. "most narrow . . . me": gave me minimal credit.

9. "hint": cue, opportunity (to praise).

10. "from his teeth": through his clenched teeth (not from the heart).

4–10. Caesar agreed at Misena to let Pompey have Sicily and Sardinia in exchange for his clearing the sea of pirates and sending wheat to Rome (2.6.34–39). Now, however, he has waged new wars against Pompey, has made his will, read it in public, presumably promising large bequests to the people (as Antony did to inflame the crowd at Caesar's funeral [*JC*, 3.2.234–42]), and has spoken only grudgingly of Antony when he could not avoid saying something. Antony sees Caesar's actions as his preparation for a final break. Ventidius' victory over the Parthians, which was won in Antony's name, seems to have forced Caesar to act at this time. He needs a victory redounding to his own glory and a way of preventing Antony's triumphant return to Rome. A final victory over Pompey promises both.

12. "Stomach": resent, take offense at.

13. "chance": occur, come about.

14. "Praying . . . parts": In *Coriolanus*, Volumnia describes her misery at being divided between her son and her country. She cannot pray for one, she says, without praying against the other. But forced to choose between them, she chooses her country (*Cor.*, 5.3.104–25). Like Volumnia, Octavia cannot pray without praying against her prayers. But she faces a fundamentally different dilemma. She is torn not between the public and the private, but between two private loves or concerns. Neither here nor anywhere else does Ocatavia mention Rome or speak of her country (or anything like it). Although she is not at all selfish, "my" is by far her most frequent word, eleven of sixteen times referring to either Antony or Caesar.

15. "presently": instantly.

17. "Undo": and then undo.

Prays and destroys the prayer; no midway
'Twixt these extremes at all.

Antony: Gentle Octavia,   **20**
Let your best love draw to that point which seeks
Best to preserve it. If I lose mine honor,
I lose myself; better I were not yours
Than yours so branchless. But, as you requested,
Yourself shall go between's. The meantime, lady,   **25**
I'll raise the preparation of a war
Shall stain your brother. Make your soonest haste,
So your desires are yours.

Octavia: Thanks to my lord.
The Jove of power make me, most weak, most weak,
Your reconciler. Wars 'twixt you twain would be   **30**
As if the world should cleave, and that slain men

18–19. "Husband win . . . prayer": to pray that husband and that brother win is to pray and then to destroy the prayer ("prayer" could mean the person who prays as well as the prayer that is made).

19–20. "no midway . . . at all": In republican Rome, the city tied the citizens together. Rome made them who they were. Romans were citizens first and private individuals second. In praying for any Roman, a Roman was praying for Rome as well. In post-republican Rome, there is nothing higher than private goods. Octavia, not the city, unites the two men, and so she is left with nothing between them except herself and her prayers. In the absence of a public realm, everything goes to the private and consequently to the extreme. The moderating, mediating middle is missing.

21–22. "Let your . . . preserve it": move your greater love to that man ("point") who will best preserve it (the image of the needle of a compass).

22–23. "If I lose . . . myself": Like a traditional Roman, Antony finds his identity in his honor. He cannot be himself unless his retains his honor. Antony thus uses the word "honor" in its characteristically Roman double sense. It is at once his moral worth and his public reputation. Who—or what—he is depends on how others regard him (see, further, 3.11.49n; also 3.11.19–20n).

24. "branchless": lopped, bare.

25. "between's": between us (as mediator).

27. "Shall stain": that will eclipse (Caesar's preparations or his reputation).

28. "So your . . . yours": so that you can achieve what you desire.

30. "'twixt you twain": between you two.

31. "that": as if.

Should solder up the rift.

Antony: When it appears to you where this begins,
Turn your displeasure that way, for our faults
Can never be so equal that your love   **35**
Can equally move with them. Provide your going;
Choose your own company, and command what cost
Your heart has mind to.   *Exeunt.*

ACT THREE, SCENE FIVE

[Athens. Another room in Antony's house.]
Enter Enobarbus and Eros.

Enobarbus: How now, friend Eros?

Eros: There's strange news come, sir.

Enobarbus: What, man?

Eros: Caesar and Lepidus have made wars upon Pompey.

Enobarbus: This is old. What is the success?   **5**

Eros: Caesar, having made use of him in the wars
'gainst Pompey, presently denied him rivality, would
not let him partake in the glory of the action; and,

---

32. "Should": would be needed to.

33. "where this begins": who began this quarrel.

34–36. "our faults . . . with them": the faults of Caesar and Antony cannot be so evenly balanced that her love can remain evenly balanced between them. Antony denies the possibility of Octavia's reconciling her loves. She must choose between her husband and her brother.

36. "Provide your going": make arrangements for your departure.

37 "what": whatever.

S.D. 1. Eros is a former slave of Antony, "whom he loved and trusted much" (Plutarch, *Antony,* 76.4; Spencer, 277).

5. "success": outcome, sequel (not necessarily good).

6. "him": Lepidus.

7. "presently": immediately (as soon as Pompey was defeated).

7. "rivality": equality, partnership.

not resting here, accuses him of letters he had
formerly wrote to Pompey; upon his own appeal, seizes   **10**
him. So the poor third is up, till death enlarge his
confine.

Enobarbus: Then, world, thou hast a pair of chaps, no more,
And throw between them all the food thou hast,
They'll grind the one the other. Where's Antony?   **15**

Eros: He's walking in the garden, thus, and spurns
The rush that lies before him; cries "Fool Lepidus!"
And threats the throat of that his officer
That murdered Pompey.

---

9. "not resting here": not stopping with this.

10. "wrote": written.

10. "upon his own appeal": on the basis only of his own accusation.

11. "up": shut up, imprisoned.

11–12. "enlarge his confine": set him free.

6–12. Having deceived Pompey with the pretense of peace and Lepidus with that of friendship (Tacitus, *Annals*, 1.10.3), Caesar used Lepidus, whose naval forces he needed, to defeat Pompey in Sicily. Then, having used him, he refused to reward him, accusing Lepidus, instead, of secretly dealing with Pompey (cp. 2.4.7–9n), stripped him of his triumviral powers and, after Lepidus begged for his life, banished him forever to an isolated promontory in southwest Italy (Suetonius, *Augustus*, 16). No longer needed, Lepidus was no longer kept. See *JC*, 4.1.19–27, where Antony suggests to Octavius this treatment of Lepidus.

13. "chaps": chops, jaws.

13. "no more": no more than two, no third partner.

14–15. "And throw . . . other": no matter how much empire they have, the two sides will continue to grind against each other and to grind each other down until each has consumed the other.

16. "thus": Eros imitates Antony's angry walk.

16. "spurns": kicks (a strong term).

17. "rush": plant, reed.

18. "threats": threatens.

18. "that his officer": that officer of his.

17–19. Lepidus and Pompey, whatever their weaknesses, helped to provide a balance of power among the Roman rulers. Caesar and Antony could not successfully battle each other if the other had the support of Lepidus or Pompey. The delicate balance kept the peace, though not without sporadic lapses—lapses which were largely kept in check by the fear of a combined opposition. The danger of all-out

Enobarbus: Our great navy's rigged.

Eros: For Italy and Caesar. More, Domitius: **20**
My lord desires you presently. My news
I might have told hereafter.

Enobarbus: 'Twill be naught,
But let it be. Bring me to Antony.

Eros: Come, sir.   **Exeunt.**

ACT THREE, SCENE SIX

[Rome. Caesar's house.]

Enter Agrippa, Maecenas, and Caesar.

Caesar: Contemning Rome, he has done all this and more
In Alexandria. Here's the manner of 't:

---

war was limited by the ever-shifting alliances of the weaker parties. As with first triumvirate of Caesar, Pompey, and Crassus, when the three parties are reduced to two, the two quickly become one (Plutarch, *Caesar*, 29.1, *Pompey*, 53.6). Sextus fled from Sicily after Agrippa defeated him at sea at Naulochus and was forced to surrender to M. Titius, the governor of Syria, who, though previously spared by Sextus, put him to death (Appian, 5.118–22, 133–45).

19–20. "Our great navy's . . . Caesar": The elimination of Pompey and Lepidus removes a final impediment to Caesar's plans against Antony. With war between them now unavoidable, Antony evidently wants to act quickly to gain the initiative and fight Caesar in Italy.

20. "More": I have more to say.

20. "Domitius": Enobarbus' first name.

22. "hereafter": later.

22. "naught": (1) nothing, (2) disastrous. The ambiguous word will prove to mean both. Antony will not proceed to Italy, and his failure will prove disastrous.

1. "Contemning": treating with contempt.

1–2. "Contemning Rome . . . Alexandria": Antony has put off fighting Caesar in Italy and returned to Alexandria, where he has celebrated his victory over the king of Armenia (see lines 36–37). The celebration, which his enemies in Rome have portrayed as a Roman triumph performed in a foreign city, "was too arrogant and insolent a part, and done (as a man would say) in derision and contempt of the Romans" (Plutarch, *Antony*, 54.3; Spencer, 242; see, further, lines 8–19n).

I'th' marketplace, on a tribunal silvered,
Cleopatra and himself in chairs of gold
Were publicly enthroned. At the feet sat 5
Caesarion, whom they call my father's son,
And all the unlawful issue that their lust
Since then hath made between them. Unto her
He gave the stablishment of Egypt, made her
Of lower Syria, Cyprus, Lydia, 10
Absolute queen.

Maecenas: This in the public eye?

Caesar: I'th' common showplace where they exercise.
His sons he there proclaimed the kings of kings.
Great Media, Parthia, and Armenia

---

3. "tribunal silvered": a platform shining with silver (raised high above the huge crowd).

5. "enthroned": seated on thrones (of gold). Affronting the Roman's abhorrence of kings, Antony presented himself publicly as an oriental monarch proclaiming a dynasty.

6. "Caesarion . . . son": Caesar, whose position as a triumvir rests in no small part on Julius Caesar's name and parentage, tries to cast doubt on Caesarion's paternity as Julius Caesar's son. As the Roman people's honoring Sextus Pompey for his father's deeds seems to show, imperial rule tends to be hereditary rule (see 1.2.194–96n). After defeating Antony, Caesar will waste no time to hunt down and kill the thirteen-year-old Caesarion. "Too many Caesars is not good" (Plutarch, *Antony*, 81.2; Spencer, 285).

9. "stablishment": confirmed possession.

10. Lower Syria ("Coele Syria") is bounded by the Euphrates on the east, the Mediterranean on the west, Syria proper on the north, and Judea on the south (roughly the lower half of modern Syria).

10. Cyprus is a large island in the eastern Mediterranean near the coast of Syria. The island passed back and forth between Roman and Ptolomaic rule in the first century. Caesar will annex it after defeating Antony.

10. Lydia is a territory in western Asia Minor (modern Turkey).

12. "I'th' . . . exercise": The gymnasium is Alexandria's "most beautiful building, with porticos more than a stadium [c. 600 ft.] in length" (Strabo, 17.1.10 [795]). It is one of the most splendid and ample buildings in the whole Mediterranean world.

13. "kings of king": a common title for Oriental kings, also a New Testament designation for God; see 4.8.16n.

14. Great Media, Parthia, Armenia are recently conquered lands, surrounding the southern half of the Caspian Sea. Alexander (Alexander Helios) is Antony and Cleopatra's six-year-old son.

He gave to Alexander; to Ptolemy he assigned   **15**
Syria, Cilicia, and Phoenicia. She
In th' habiliments of the goddess Isis
That day appeared, and oft before gave audience,
As 'tis reported, so.

Maecenas: Let Rome be thus informed.   **20**

Agrippa: Who, queasy with his insolence already,
Will their good thoughts call from him.

Caesar: The people knows it and have now received

15–16. Syria is bordered by the Mediterranean and Phoenicia on the west, Cilicia and Cappadocia on the north, Mesopotamia on the east, and Coele Syria on the south. Cilicia is the eastern portion of modern Turkey's southern coast, a center of piracy suppressed by Pompey the Great in 67 and made a Roman province in 63. Phoenicia is a narrow strip of land along the eastern Mediterranean, also conquered by Pompey in 67 and made a province in 63. Ptolemy (Ptolemy Philadelphus) is Antony and Cleopatra's two-year-old son.

17. "habiliments": robes.

16–18. For centuries, Ptolemaic queens have associated or identified themselves with Isis. Cleopatra, however, evidently went further. "[S]he did not only wear at that time, but at all other times else when she came abroad, the apparel of the goddess Isis, and so gave audience unto all her subjects as a new Isis" (Plutarch, *Antony*, 54,6; Spencer, 243). For a description of Isis' robes, with their variegated colors symbolizing her ability to become and receive everything, see Plutarch, *Isis and Osiris*, 77 (382c).

8–19. Instead of presenting his spoils to Capitoline Jupiter, Antony gave them to Cleopatra as she sat on the throne dressed like the Egyptian goddess Isis. He celebrated in Egypt a sacred victory that could be celebrated only in Rome. "This greatly offended the Romans . . . when they saw that for Cleopatra's sake he deprived his country of [its] due honor and glory, only to gratify the Egyptians" (Plutarch, *Antony*, 50.4: Spencer, 238–39). See Dio, 49.40, 50.25.2–4.

21. "queasy": disgusted, nauseated.

22. "Will their . . . him": will withdraw their support for him.

23. "knows": know (old plural form).

23. "The people knows it": "Octavius Caesar reporting all these things unto the Senate, and oftentimes accusing him to the whole people and assembly in Rome, he thereby stirred up all the Romans against him" (Plutarch, *Antony*, 55.1; Spencer, 243). The accusations that Antony denied the Romans the spoils that were properly theirs and submitted himself to a foreign queen presenting herself as a foreign goddess were major parts of Caesar's propaganda war against him; see, further, 3.7.5n.

His accusations.

Agrippa: Who does he accuse?

Caesar: Caesar, and that, having in Sicily   **25**
    Sextus Pompeius spoiled, we had not rated him
    His part o'th' isle. Then does he say he lent me
    Some shipping, unrestored. Lastly, he frets
    That Lepidus of the triumvirate
    Should be deposed and, being, that we detain   **30**
    All his revenue.

Agrippa: Sir, this should be answered.

Caesar: 'Tis done already, and the messenger gone.
    I have told him Lepidus was grown too cruel,
    That he his high authority abused
    And did deserve his change. For what I have conquered, **35**
    I grant him part; but then in his Armenia
    And other of his conquered kingdoms I
    Demand the like.

Maecenas: He'll never yield to that.

Caesar: Nor must not then be yielded to in this.

---

24. "Who": whom.

26. "spoiled": despoiled (seized the land that had been his).

26. "we": the royal "we."

26. "rated him": assigned to him.

28. "shipping, unrestored": ships, which I did not return to him.

29. "of": from.

30. "being": being deposed.

30. "detain": retain.

33–35. "I have told . . . change": "Octavius Caesar answered [Antony] again, that, for Lepidus, he had indeed deposed him, and taken his part of the Empire from him, because he did overcruelly use his authority" (Plutarch, *Antony*, 55.2; Spencer, 243–44). Plutarch does not specify Caesar's allegation.

35. "For": as for.

36–38. "in his Armenia . . . the like": Caesar is demanding lands which include much of those he will soon accuse Antony of having given to foreign kings. His proposed exchange would thus cost Antony the political, military, and financial support of those new allies (see lines 69–77n).

Enter Octavia with her Train.

Octavia: Hail, Caesar, and my lord! Hail, most dear Caesar.   **40**

Caesar: That ever I should call thee castaway!

Octavia: You have not called me so, nor have you cause.

Caesar: Why have you stol'n upon us thus? You come not
    Like Caesar's sister. The wife of Antony
    Should have an army for an usher and   **45**
    The neighs of horse to tell of her approach
    Long ere she did appear. The trees by th' way
    Should have borne men, and expectation fainted,
    Longing for what it had not. Nay, the dust
    Should have ascended to the roof of heaven,   **50**
    Raised by your populous troops. But you are come
    A market-maid to Rome, and have prevented
    The ostentation of our love, which, left unshown,
    Is often left unloved. We should have met you
    By sea and land, supplying every stage   **55**
    With an augmented greeting.

Octavia: Good my lord,
    To come thus was I not constrained, but did it
    On my free will. My lord, Mark Antony,

---

41. "castaway": (1) someone who has been discarded or rejected, (2) a ruined person.

43. "stol'n": come furtively.

44. "Like": in a manner or fashion appropriate to.

46. "horse": horses (plural).

47. "by th' way": along the roadside.

52–53. "prevented The ostentation": forestalled the grand display.

53. "our": Caesar's (the royal "we").

53–54. "love, . . . left unloved": love which is not displayed is (1) not thought to exist, or (2) not returned.

54. "should": would.

55. "stage": stopping place (of the journey).

44–56. Caesar, with uncharacteristic bombast, describes a triumphant general's magnificent return to Rome, whose glory is measured by the numbers and quality of the people turning out to greet him, and by the place where he is met: the greater the distance from Rome, the greater the honor (see, for example, Appian, 5.130).

57. "constrained": forced, compelled.

Hearing that you prepared for war, acquainted
My grieved ear withal, whereon I begged   **60**
His pardon for return.

Caesar: Which soon he granted,
Being an abstract 'tween his lust and him.

Octavia: Do not say so, my lord.

Caesar: I have eyes upon him,
And his affairs come to me on the wind.
Where is he now?

Octavia: My lord, in Athens.

Caesar: No,   **65**
My most wronged sister. Cleopatra hath
Nodded him to her. He hath given his empire
Up to a whore, who now are levying
The kings o'th' earth for war. He hath assembled
Bocchus, the King of Libya, Archelaus   **70**
Of Cappadocia, Philadelphos, King
Of Paphlagonia, the Thracian king, Adallas,
King Manchus of Arabia, King of Pont,
Herod of Jewry, Mithridates, King
Of Comagen, Polemon and Amyntas,   **75**
The Kings of Mede and Lycaonia,
With a more larger list of scepters.

---

60. "withal": with the news.

60. "whereon": and because of this.

61. "pardon for": permission to.

62. "abstract": shortening (of the distance or the time to accommodate his desires). Some editors change the Folio's "abstract" to "obstruct," referring not to Antony's permission, but to Octavia's obstructing his desires.

62. "his lust": the object of his lust, Cleopatra.

63. "eyes": a network of spies.

64. "on the wind": For Caesar's speeding up the delivery of reports from the provinces, see Suetonius, *Augustus*, 49.3.

67. "Nodded him": summoned him with a nod.

68. "who now": and they now.

77. "more larger": larger (a double comparative for added emphasis).

69–77. "He hath . . . scepters": Caesar lists ten kings and kingdoms to whom Antony has given land and power. They stretch from the lands west and east of Egypt

Octavia: Ay me, most wretched,
That have my heart parted betwixt two friends
That does afflict each other!

Caesar: Welcome hither.   **80**
Your letters did withhold our breaking forth
Till we perceived both how you were wrong led
And we in negligent danger. Cheer your heart.
Be you not troubled with the time, which drives
O'er your content these strong necessities,   **85**
But let determined things to destiny
Hold unbewailed their way. Welcome to Rome,

(Libya and Arabia), to the eastern Mediterranean coast (Judea), to Asia Minor (Cappadocia, Paphlagonia, Pont [Pontus], Comagen, and Lycaonia), to the western side of the Bosporus, facing Pontus (Thrace), and to land north of Parthia and south of the Caspian Sea (Media). While accusing Antony of squandering Roman provinces on an Egyptian whore, Caesar ignores that Antony's actions serve Antony's political and military interests. While punishing client kings who had previously sided with the Parthians, the grants replace them with kings who belong to no established dynasty and therefore owe their positions to Antony (Appian, 5.75). They will fight for him at Actium (Plutarch, *Antony*, 61.1–2). Caesar will adopt a similar policy in the East (Dio, 54.9.2–3).

80. "does": do.

78–80. Ay me, . . . each other": Octavia, who still calls Antony her love ("friend"), says nothing about his abandoning her. Her heart is broken not by his betrayal, but by her having to choose between two warring loves. Octavia's lack of recrimination will only add to the people's love and pity for her and their hostility toward Antony. Unintentionally, she will damage Antony by not blaming him. "[T]hinking no hurt, she did Antony great hurt. For her honest love and regard to her husband made every man hate him when they saw he did so unkindly use so noble a lady" (Plutarch, *Antony*, 54.2; Spencer, 241–42).

81. "withhold . . . forth": restrain my beginning military action.

82. "wrong led": misled (by Antony).

83. "in negligent danger": in danger through negligence.

84. "time": state of affairs.

85. "content": happiness.

85. "strong necessities": harsh inevitabilities.

86–87. "let determined . . . way": let predetermined events continue unlamented to their fated conclusion.

83–87. Caesar urges Stoic resignation or patience. Except for (disingenuously) blaming Antony's end on their "[u]nreconciliable" "stars" (5.1.46–47), Caesar

Nothing more dear to me. You are abused
Beyond the mark of thought, and the high gods,
To do you justice, makes his ministers   **90**
Of us and those that love you. Best of comfort,
And ever welcome to us.

Agrippa: Welcome, lady.

Maecenas: Welcome, dear madam.
Each heart in Rome does love and pity you;
Only th'adulterous Antony, most large   **95**
In his abominations, turns you off
And gives his potent regiment to a trull
That noises it against us.

Octavia: Is it so, sir?

Caesar: Most certain. Sister, welcome. Pray you
Be ever known to patience. My dear'st sister!   ***Exeunt.***   **100**

---

nowhere else alludes to necessity or destiny. Elsewhere, when he says that something has been "[d]etermine[d]," he means chosen by him (5.1.59). Here, he tries to present his choosing to go to war as impersonal destiny. It is Fate that has determined the situation, and one should not lament what cannot be avoided; for the Stoic doctrine, see Cicero, *On Fate*; Seneca, *On Providence*, 5.8; see, further, 3.13.83–85n.

88. "abused": mistreated, deceived.

89. "mark": reach, limits.

89–90. "the high gods . . . justice": This is Caesar's sole mention of "justice" (or anything like it). For his only mention of law, which Caesar, using the subjunctive ("as [if] a law"), implicitly identifies with his will, see 3.12.33. For his only other mentions of gods, see line 17, 5.1.27. "[T]he high gods," here, seems to be a collective term, used for emphasis (hence the singular verb "makes").

90. "ministers": agents.

95. "large": unrestrained, prodigal (with implication of licentious).

96. "off": away.

97. "his potent regiment": his powerful rule.

97. "trull": whore.

98. "noises it": cries out, clamors.

100. "Be ever . . . patience": always endure your misfortune with patience.

100. "My dear'st sister": This is the last time Caesar ever mentions Octavia. The nearest he will come will be to refer to Antony as "[his] brother," after learning of his death (5.1.42). Note especially 5.2.357–59.

ACT THREE, SCENE SEVEN

[Antony's camp. Near Actium.]

Enter Cleopatra and Enobarbus.

Cleopatra: I will be even with thee, doubt it not.

Enobarbus: But why, why, why?

Cleopatra: Thou hast forspoke my being in these wars
       And say'st it is not fit.

Enobarbus: Well, is it, is it?

Cleopatra: Is't not denounced against us? Why should not we   5
       Be there in person?

Enobarbus: Well, I could reply:
       If we should serve with horse and mares together,
       The horse were merely lost. The mares would bear
       A soldier and his horse.

Cleopatra: What is't you say?

S.D. 1. Actium is a promontory on the northwest coast of Greece.

1. "even": indeed (used to underscore an answer in the affirmative).

3. "forspoke": spoken against.

5. "denounced against us": Caesar has declared ("denounced") war not against Antony, but only against Cleopatra. He means to emphasize that the war is not a civil war, but a foreign conflict between Rome and Egypt. The war's purported purpose is to prevent Cleopatra from becoming the Egyptian empress of Rome. Moreover, fully expecting him to remain with and fight for her, Caesar seeks to present Antony as a traitor to Rome (Dio, 50.4.3–4, 6.1).

5. "us . . . we": the royal "we."

7. "serve": go to battle.

7. "horse": (male) horses.

8. "were merely lost": would utterly lose their military function.

8–9. "bear . . . his horse": support the mounting stallion and its rider (see 1.5.22n).

9. "What . . . say?": Editors often mark Enobarbus' previous speech as an aside. Cleopatra's question leaves unclear whether she did not hear it or simply pretends not to have. In the sequel, Enobarbus bowdlerizes rather than repeats what he said.

Enobarbus: Your presence needs must puzzle Antony,   10
    Take from his heart, take from his brain, from 's time
    What should not then be spared. He is already
    Traduced for levity, and 'tis said in Rome
    That Photinus an eunuch and your maids
    Manage this war.

Cleopatra: Sink Rome, and their tongues rot   15
    That speak against us! A charge we bear i'th' war,
    And as the president of my kingdom will
    Appear there for a man. Speak not against it.
    I will not stay behind.

---

10. "puzzle": confuse, distract, leave him at a loss what to think or do.

11. "heart": courage.

13. "Traduced": condemned.

14. The name Photinus (or North's "Pothinus") seems an error. The eunuch Photinus was Cleopatra's determined enemy. Regent for her young brother and co-ruler, he turned Ptolemy XIII against her and drove her out of Egypt, bringing on the civil war which Julius Caesar ended. Earlier, after pretending to offer Pompey the Great asylum, Photinus arranged for his murder when he landed in Egypt following his defeat at Pharsalus. Hoping to win his favor, he presented Caesar with Pompey's head when he arrived, but, instead, filled Caesar with grief and disgust. Caesar soon afterwards punished Photinus with death (Plutarch, *Pompey*, 77–80; Appian, 2.84–86, 90).

13–15. "'tis said . . . this war": "Caesar said furthermore that Antonius was not master of himself, but that Cleopatra had brought him beside himself by her charms and amorous poisons, and that they that should make war with them should be Mardian the eunuch, Pothinus, and Iras, a woman of Cleopatra's bedchamber that frizzled her hair and dressed her head, and Charmian, the which were those that ruled all the affairs of Antonius' empire" (Plutarch, *Antony*, 60.1; Spencer, 248–49).

16. "charge": (1) responsibility (as queen), (2) expense.

16. "A charge . . . i'th' war": Cleopatra has furnished 200 ships, 20,000 talents, and provisions to maintain the whole army during the war (Plutarch, *Antony*, 56.1).

17. "president": presiding sovereign.

18. "for a man": as though, in the capacity of, a man. It is striking that Cleopatra, who has mentioned Fulvia more than anyone else has (eight times, to Antony's six), does not cite her as a Roman precedent (see 1.1.21n).

Enter Antony and Canidius.

Enobarbus: Nay, I have done.
Here comes the Emperor.

Antony: Is it not strange, Canidius,   **20**
That from Tarentum and Brundusium
He could so quickly cut the Ionian Sea
And take in Toryne? You have heard on't, sweet?

Cleopatra: Celerity is never more admired
Than by the negligent.

Antony: A good rebuke,   **25**

S.D. 19. P. Canidus is Antony's victorious lieutenant in Armenia and commander of all his land forces at Actium (Plutarch, *Antony*, 34.6, 63.3).

20. "the Emperor": This is the first time a sober Roman calls either Antony or Caesar Emperor (cp. 2.7.103). The title will now become frequent.

21. Tarentum and Brundusium are ports in southern Italy (modern Taranto and Brindisi), located on opposite sides of the heel of the boot of Italy, west of Actium. Both are strategically vital cities throughout antiquity as principal routes to Greece and the East.

22. The Ionian Sea is part of the Mediterranean, lying between Sicily and the boot of Italy on the west and Greece on the east. It is south of, or the southern part of, what is now called the Adriatic Sea. (There is no clear line of demarcation between the two seas.)

23. "take in": take, occupy.

23. Toryne is a small town not far north of Actium, on the western Greek coast. Caesar gains the advantage of time and place. Speed and surprise are the crux of his plan.

23. "on't": about it.

24. "admired": wondered at, envied.

24–25. "Celerity . . . the negligent": Antony's negligence is (at least) twofold. "[A]mong the greatest faults that ever Antonius committed, [his critics] blamed him most for that he delayed to give Caesar battle [during the previous summer]. For he gave Caesar leisure to make his preparations, and also to appease the complaints of the people [angry about his excessive taxation]" (Plutarch, *Antony*, 58.1; Spencer, 246). And, at present, he has allowed Caesar to lead his army down Italy to the southern ports and cross to western Greece. "Now whilst Antonius rode at anchor, lying idly in harbor at the head of Actium, . . . Caesar had quickly passed the sea Ionium and taken a place called Toryne, before Antonius understood that he had taken ship" (Plutarch, *Antony*, 62.3; Spencer, 252).

Which might have well becomed the best of men,
To taunt at slackness. Canidius, we will fight
With him by sea.

Cleopatra: By sea, what else?

Canidius: Why will my lord do so?

Antony: For that he dares us to't.

Enobarbus: So hath my lord dared him to single fight.   **30**

Canidius: Ay, and to wage this battle at Pharsalia,
  Where Caesar fought with Pompey. But these offers,
  Which serve not for his vantage, he shakes off,
  And so should you.

Enobarbus: Your ships are not well manned,

---

26. "becomed": become, been appropriate to.

25–27. "A good rebuke . . . slackness": Antony commends Cleopatra for speaking like a manly man, fit for command.

29. "Why . . . do so": Antony's forces have often fought successfully on land, but never a major battle at sea. And Caesar's navy has recently defeated, and been augmented by, Pompey's formidable fleet (Plutarch, *Antony*, 63.4).

29. "For that": because.

30. "dared him . . . fight": Rome has a long tradition of single combat, stretching back to the days of Rome's third king, Tullus Hostilius (c. 650) (Livy, 1.24–26). "[Romans] have done valiantly and courageously, where without any necessity, they enter voluntarily and fight man-to-man in single combat" (Polybius, 6.54.4; *History of Polybius*, trans. Edward Grimeston [London: Simon Waterson, 1634], 301). Note *Cor.*, 1.1.228–30, 1.8.1–16. However, all of the very few instances of a formal duel deciding the outcome of a battle, let alone of a war, are probably mythical.

31–32. Pharsalia (Pharsalus) is where Julius Caesar defeated Pompey the Great in 48. On Antony's distinguishing himself brilliantly in that battle, see 2.1.36n.

33. "for his vantage": to his advantage.

32–34. "But these offers . . . you": since Caesar acts only for his advantage, you should ignore his challenge (for there is no honor at stake in a challenge coming from someone simply calculating his advantage and trying to trap you into fighting from your weakness). Caesar generally employed a cautious cost-benefit calculation in choosing and conducting wars. "His saying was, That neither battle nor war was once to be undertaken unless there might be evidently seen more hope of gain than fear of damage" (Suetonius, *Augustus*, 25.4; Holland, 1:100).

Your mariners are muleteers, reapers, people   35
Engrossed by swift impress. In Caesar's fleet
Are those that often have 'gainst Pompey fought.
Their ships are yare, yours heavy. No disgrace
Shall fall you for refusing him at sea,
Being prepared for land.

Antony: By sea, by sea.   40

Enobarbus: Most worthy sir, you therein throw away
The absolute soldiership you have by land,
Distract your army, which doth most consist
Of war-marked footmen, leave unexecuted
Your own renowned knowledge, quite forgo   45
The way which promises assurance, and
Give up yourself merely to chance and hazard
From firm security.

Antony: I'll fight at sea.

Cleopatra: I have sixty sails, Caesar none better.

Antony: Our overplus of shipping will we burn,   50

---

35. "muleteers": mule drivers.

35. "reapers": migrant crop gatherers.

36. "Engrossed . . . impress": rounded up and forcibly enlisted without careful selection.

38. "yare": light, swift, and easy to handle.

39. "fall": befall, occur to.

42. "absolute soldiership . . . by land": "having so great skill and experience of battles by land" (Plutarch, *Antony*, 53.4; Spencer, 254).

43. "Distract": divide (therefore confuse and demoralize).

43. "most": mostly.

44. "war-marked footmen": veteran infantry, foot soldiers (not sailors or marines).

44. "unexecuted": unused.

46. "assurance": certainty of success.

47. "merely": utterly, entirely.

49. "I have sixty . . . better": Plutarch suggests that Antony wants the victory won by the fleet so that Cleopatra could have the glory: "[T]hough he was a great deal the stronger by land, yet for Cleopatra's sake he would needs have this battle tried by sea" (Plutarch, *Antony*, 62.1; Spencer, 250–51).

50. "overplus": surplus.

And with the rest full-manned, from th'head of Actium
Beat th'approaching Caesar. But if we fail,
We then can do't at land.

Enter a Messenger.

Thy business?

Messenger: The news is true, my lord; he is descried.
Caesar has taken Toryne.   **55**

Antony: Can he be there in person? 'Tis impossible;
Strange that his power should be. Canidius,
Our nineteen legions thou shalt hold by land,
And our twelve thousand horse. We'll to our ship.
Away, my Thetis!

Enter a Soldier.

How now, worthy soldier?   **60**

Soldier: O noble emperor, do not fight by sea!
Trust not to rotten planks. Do you misdoubt

---

51. "the rest full-manned": Antony has a shortage of sailors, not a surplus of ships. He will burn some of his ships so he can fully man the rest.

51. "head": headland, promontory.

51–53. Antony's strategy is to fight Caesar's approaching ships by staying close to the shore. For this to work, Antony's crews must maintain a tight formation and deny Caesar sea room to use his superior numerical strength and greater agility. His ships must prevent letting the enemy outflank or sail through their formation and engage them on both sides at once (Plutarch, *Antony*, 65.5). Antony, while permitting Caesar to take the offensive and strike first, seems to assume that his land troops will remain loyal even if his ships are defeated.

54. "is descried": has been sighted, observed.

57. "power": armed forces.

58–59. "Our nineteen legions . . . our ship": "Antony had . . . a hundred thousand footmen and twelve thousand horsemen" (Plutarch, *Antony*, 61.1; Spencer, 259). This large army is to remain in battle formation but stay out of action while Antony's comparatively small navy fights.

60. Thetis, the most famous of the Nereides (and mother of Achilles), is a sea nymph or sea goddess, able to take on any shape she pleases, whose beauty is so great that Jupiter himself sought to marry her (Ovid, *Metamorphoses*, 11.221–65; Apollodorus, 1.11, 136). Women dressed as the Nereides served Cleopatra when she captured Antony's heart on the Cydnus (2.2.216–19). Antony's fond moniker for her seems foreboding as well as fitting, however. According to one famous account, Thetis and her lover, Peleus, were finally united only in death (Euripides, *Andromache*, 1255ff.).

62. "misdoubt": mistrust.

This sword and these my wounds? Let th'Egyptians
And the Phoenicians go a-ducking. We
Have used to conquer standing on the earth   **65**
And fighting foot to foot.

Antony: Well, well, away!

Exeunt Antony, Cleopatra and Enobarbus.

Soldier: By Hercules, I think I am i'th' right.

Canidius: Soldier, thou art, but his whole action grows
Not in the power on't. So our leader's led,

62–63.:"Do you misdoubt … wounds": For the Soldier, who is devoted to Antony and has evidently fought for him many times before, the issue is not a matter of tactics, but of trust. The man's wounds are witness to his loyalty and courage. See, further, lines 65–66n.

64. "a-ducking": a contemptuous pun: (1) dive (into the water), (2) cringe or bow (from fear).

63–64. "Let th'Egyptians … a-ducking": The Egyptians and the Phoenicians were both sea-going peoples. From an early time, the Egyptians maintained fleets for commerce and defense in the Mediterranean and the Red Sea, with a canal linking the two (Herodotus, 2.158). In Cleopatra's day, Alexandria was a major shipbuilding and trading center. On the advantages to Alexandria of the sea, see Strabo, 17.1.7. The Phoenicians were an ancient maritime people, famous for shipbuilding, maritime trade and far-reaching naval exploration, including excursions beyond the Pillars of Hercules and perhaps circumnavigating Africa in 610–595 (Herodotus, 4.42). Carthage, which Rome finally defeated and destroyed in 146 (after three wars, including one led by Hannibal), was originally a Phoenician settlement.

65. "Have used": are accustomed.

65–66. "conquer standing … foot": To the Romans, fortune rather than virtue often decides battles at sea. "In contests on land, valor … is able to gain the upper hand when no unusual misfortune interferes. But in naval battles there are many causes of various kinds that, contrary to reason, defeat those whose valor would otherwise certainly have won the day" (Diodorus, 20.51.5). Moreover, acts of virtue are difficult to distinguish at sea. When men go down with their ships, the sea tends to obscure "the distinction between courage and cowardice, wisdom and folly, calculation and chance" (Tacitus, *Annals*, 1.70.3). Consequently, no one can gain glory—or much glory—by dying at sea. Hence, Achilles, Alexander, and Julius Caesar, although fearless on land, all feared dying by drowning (Homer, *Iliad*, 21.273–83; Plutarch, *Alexander*, 60.3; Lucan, 5.665–86). They feared not death, but an obscure death.

68–69. "his whole action … on't": his whole course of action disregards his military strengths.

And we are women's men.

Soldier: You keep by land   **70**
    The legions and the horse whole, do you not?

Canidius: Marcus Octavius, Marcus Justeius,
    Publicola, and Caelius are for sea,
    But we keep whole by land. This speed of Caesar's
    Carries beyond belief.

Soldier: While he was yet in Rome,   **75**
    His power went out in such distractions as
    Beguiled all spies.

Canidius: Who's his lieutenant, hear you?

Soldier: They say one Taurus.

Canidius: Well I know the man.

Enter a Messenger.

Messenger: The Emperor calls Canidius.

69–70. "So our leader's . . . men": Where a traditional Roman is a man's man, Antony has made his men unmanly or womanish. The difficulty, Canidius seems to think, is not simply that Antony is led by a woman's whim, but that her whim favors an unmanly manner of war, as the Soldier just protested. Tactics and character go together. Just as the Roman army has traditionally depended on its leaders for its valor (see, for example, *Cor.*, 4.6.76–80, 91–96, 104–9), Antony unmans the whole from the top.

70–71. "keep . . . whole": keep the entire infantry and the entire cavalry intact and held in reserve.

72–73. Antony has split the fleet's command among four lieutenants (two on the left flank, two in the center), while he takes the right flank. Evidently looking for the important action to occur on the wings, he seeks to increase the fleet's quickness and agility there (Plutarch, *Antony*, 65.1).

75. "Carries": advances, pushes forward (a military metaphor of a projectile's forward motion).

76–77. "His power . . . spies": Caesar's forces, divided into small groups, were able to avoid being seen by Antony's spies. His detachments ("distractions") served as diversions ("distractions"), making his ruse appear as his rapidity.

78. Statilius Taurus, second only to Agrippa as Caesar's commander and administrator, fought against Pompey in Sicily in 36. After driving him to North Africa, he crossed the sea and secured the province of Africa, for which he was awarded a triumph in 34 and the construction in his name of Rome's first amphitheater. At Actium, he is in charge of Caesar's land forces (Plutarch, *Antony*, 65.2).

Canidius: With news the time's in labor, and throws forth   **80**
        Each minute some.   *Exeunt.*

ACT THREE, SCENE EIGHT

[A plain near Actium.]

Enter Caesar [and Taurus] with his army, marching.

Caesar: Taurus!

Taurus: My lord?

Caesar: Strike not by land, keep whole. Provoke not battle
        Till we have done at sea. Do not exceed
        The prescript of this scroll. Our fortune lies   **5**
        Upon this jump.   *Exeunt.*

ACT THREE, SCENE NINE

[Another part of the plain.]

Enter Antony and Enobarbus.

Antony: Set we our squadrons on yond side o'th' hill
        In eye of Caesar's battle, from which place

---

80. "in labor": The Folio reads "with labor."

80–81. "throws forth ... some": gives painful birth to one after another (the metaphor of an animal giving birth to a litter of offspring).

3. "whole": intact.

3–4. "Provoke not ... sea": Antony expects to fight on land if he falters at sea; Caesar, to fight on land after he is done at sea. Where a land battle is Antony's backup plan, it is Caesar's mop-up plan.

4. "exceed": depart from.

5. "prescript of this scroll": written instructions. On Caesar's general reliance on communicating by writing, see Suetonius, *Augustus*, 84.2.

6. "jump": venture, hazard. Caesar evidently believes that Antony's land forces will have no heart to fight after losing at sea, and so the sea battle will decide the final outcome.

1. "squadrons": land forces drawn up in square formations.

2. "In eye": in sight.

2. "battle": battle line of ships in battle array.

We may the number of the ships behold
And so proceed accordingly. **Exeunt.**

ACT THREE, SCENE TEN

[Another part of the plain.]

*Canidius marcheth with his land army one way over the stage, and
Taurus, the lieutenant of Caesar, the other way. After their going in, is
heard the noise of a sea fight.*

Alarum. Enter Enobarbus.

Enobarbus: Naught, naught, all naught! I can behold no longer.
Th'Antoniad, the Egyptian admiral,
With all their sixty, fly and turn the rudder.
To see't mine eyes are blasted.

Enter Scarus.

Scarus: Gods and goddesses,
All the whole synod of them!

3–4. "We may . . . proceed accordingly": While Caesar gives his officer written orders, Antony directs Enobarbus to act according to what he sees of Caesar's forces. Where Caesar's battle plan is fixed, Antony's is flexible. The difference is tactical as well as characteristic. While an offensive force knows what it wants, a defensive force must adjust its actions to its opponent's. Permitting Caesar to take and keep the initiative, Antony must await developments.

S.D. 1. "*going in*": leaving the stage.

S.D. 1. The battle of Actium (Sept. 2, 31), although not a major military engagement, ranks as one of the Western world's most significant sea battles. Notwithstanding the later fighting at Alexandria (4.7.1–12.13), it amounts to Caesar's final victory in his rise to sole power, preparing the way for the institution of the Augustan Principate. It also reestablishes or reaffirms Rome's command over the East. Although largely over before it begins, it marks a turning point for the world.

1. "naught": lost, ruined, reduced to nothing; see 3.5.22n.

1. "behold": watch.

2. "admiral": flagship (called The Antoniad).

3. "their sixty": the sixty Egyptian ships (see 3.7.49; Plutarch, *Antony*, 64.1).

4. "blasted": stricken, blinded (as if by a blast of lightning).

S.D. 4. Some commentators argue that Scarus, who is named only in the speech headings and not in the dialogue, is the same character as the Soldier who urges Antony not to fight at sea (3.7.60–81), who is never named.

5. "synod": assembly.

Enobarbus: What's thy passion?   **5**

Scarus: The greater cantle of the world is lost
 With very ignorance. We have kissed away
 Kingdoms and provinces.

Enobarbus: How appears the fight?

Scarus: On our side, like the tokened pestilence,
 Where death is sure. Yon ribaudred nag of Egypt,   **10**
 Whom leprosy o'ertake, i'th' midst o'th' fight,
 When vantage like a pair of twins appeared
 Both as the same—or, rather, ours the elder—
 The breeze upon her like a cow in June
 Hoists sails and flies.   **15**

Enobarbus: That I beheld.
 Mine eyes did sicken at the sight and could not
 Endure a further view.

Scarus: She once being loofed,
 The noble ruin of her magic, Antony,

---

5. "thy passion": the cause of your distress.

6. "cantle": portion (a segment of a sphere).

7. "With very ignorance": through absolute folly.

7. "kissed away": said goodbye to, lost by kissing (bitter wordplay).

9. "tokened pestilence": the final stage of the plague when fatal spots (called "God's tokens") appear on the skin.

10. "ribaudred nag": This much-disputed phrase seems to mean "ribald-rid nag" (a whore anyone can ride).

11. "leprosy": a loathsome disease affecting the skin (mistakenly thought to be sexually transmitted).

11. "o'ertake": seize.

12–13. "When vantage . . . elder ": when both sides had equal advantage—or, rather, ours had the edge. Scarus' temporal formulation reflects the traditional Roman view that the elder appear as the larger, the greater, the superior (*maiores*) and the younger as the smaller, the less important, the inferior (*minores*). See H. Wagenvoort, *Roman Dynamism* (Oxford: Basil Blackwell, 1947), 121.

14. "breeze": (1) gadfly (an insect which attacks cattle), (2) wind (filling her sails).

18. "loofed": luffed (a nautical term: the head of her ship brought nearer to the wind, so she could sail away).

Claps on his sea-wing and, like a doting mallard,   **20**
Leaving the fight in height, flies after her.
I never saw an action of such shame.
Experience, manhood, honor ne'er before
Did violate so itself.

Enobarbus: Alack, alack.

Enter Canidius.

Canidius: Our fortune on the sea is out of breath   **25**
And sinks most lamentably. Had our general
Been what he knew himself, it had gone well.
O, he has given example for our flight
Most grossly by his own.

Enobarbus: Ay, are you thereabouts?
Why then goodnight indeed.   **30**

Canidius: Toward Peloponnesus are they fled.

Scarus: 'Tis easy to't, and there I will attend
What further comes.

---

20. "Claps . . . sea-wing": sets more sail to increase the speed of his flight.

20. "doting mallard": a lovesick male duck.

21. "in height": at its height, when most intense.

9–21. Scarus' despairing description consists in a series of similes and metaphors, for likenesses lend themselves especially well to hyperbole (see Aristotle, *Rhetoric*, 1413a18–35; Quintilian, 8.6.67–76). He also uses the vivid present tense.

23–24. "Experience, . . . violate so itself": "There Antonius showed plainly that he had not only lost the courage and heart of an Emperor, but also of a valiant man, and that he was not his own man" (Plutarch, *Antony*, 66.4; Spencer, 258).

24. "Alack": expression of grief, condemnation, and alarm.

26–27. "Had our general . . . himself": See 1.1.58–60n and lines 35–37n.

28–29. "O, he has . . . own": Antony's flight will set in motion many desertions to follow. See, further, Introduction, xiv.

29. "thereabouts": near to that (thinking of deserting).

30. "Why then . . . indeed": then our cause is finished.

31. Peloponnesus is the large peninsula of southern mainland Greece, not far south of Actium.

32. "to't": to get there.

32–33. "attend . . . comes": await what happens. Scarus stays loyal and fights again for Antony at Alexandria (see 4.7–8, 10, 12).

Canidius: To Caesar will I render
  My legions and my horse. Six kings already
  Show me the way of yielding.

Enobarbus: I'll yet follow   **35**
  The wounded chance of Antony, though my reason
  Sits in the wind against me.   **[*Exeunt separately.*]**

ACT THREE, SCENE ELEVEN

[Alexandria. Cleopatra's palace.]

Enter Antony with attendants.

Antony: Hark, the land bids me tread no more upon't.
  It is ashamed to bear me. Friends, come hither.
  I am so lated in the world that I
  Have lost my way forever. I have a ship
  Laden with gold. Take that, divide it. Fly,   **5**
  And make your peace with Caesar.

All: Fly? Not we!

---

33. "render": surrender.

34–35. "Six kings . . . yielding": on Romans behaving like foreigners, not like
fellow citizens, see Introduction, xiv.

36. "chance": fortunes.

35–37. "I'll yet . . . against me": Defending his nobility by dividing himself,
Enobarbus identifies himself ("I," "me") with his loyal part, while alienating his
calculating part ("my reason") as though it were external to himself. He protects
his sense of loyalty by presenting his ambivalence as a conflict between himself and
another. What would otherwise shame him is not part of him. Enobarbus' psychic
self-division also manifests spiritedness' tendency to simplify or oversimplify the
moral world by reducing wholes to parts and taking parts for wholes (hence, the
frequency of synecdoche and metonymy in the play). See, further, 1.1.58–60n and
3.11.7n.

1–2. "Hark, the land . . . bear me": the land is now ashamed for me and will not
support me (because I refused to fight on land and ignominiously fled at sea).

3. "lated": belated (the metaphor of a traveler overtaken by the darkness of night).

6. "Fly? Not we": As Antony is generous in defeat and solicitous for their safety, his
men are devoted to him. "They answered him weeping that they would neither
[take the gold] nor yet forsake him" (Plutarch, *Antony*, 67.6; Spencer, 260).

Antony: I have fled myself and have instructed cowards
     To run and show their shoulders. Friends, be gone.
     I have myself resolved upon a course
     Which has no need of you. Be gone.   **10**
     My treasure's in the harbor; take it. O,
     I followed that I blush to look upon.
     My very hairs do mutiny, for the white
     Reprove the brown for rashness, and they them
     For fear and doting. Friends, be gone. You shall   **15**
     Have letters from me to some friends that will
     Sweep your way for you. Pray you look not sad,
     Nor make replies of loathness. Take the hint
     Which my despair proclaims. Let that be left
     Which leaves itself. To the seaside straightway!   **20**

---

7. "I have fled myself": (1) I fled from battle, because (2) I fled from myself. Like Enobarbus, Antony separates himself from himself, but in the contrary fashion. He reverses the loyal and disloyal parties. "I" is the shameful Antony; "myself," the noble Antony. Antony preserves his noble self, by separating it and making it the abandoned, offended party. Where Enobarbus, not yet having acted ignobly, separated the corrupting part by identifying himself with the uncorrupted part, Antony, having acted ignobly, alienates the uncorrupted part by identifying himself with the corrupted part. Both preserve their noble self by separating it, Enobarbus by identifying himself with it, Antony by distinguishing himself from it. Despite his overbearing sense of shame, Antony—if only momentarily—seeks to maintain his nobility; cp. 3.10.35–37.

7. "instructed": taught by example.

8. "shoulders": upper part of their backs (as they fled).

9–10. "a course . . . of you": a hint at suicide.

12. "that": what.

13. "mutiny": rise against each other.

14. "they them": the brown reprove the white.

17. "Sweep your way": clear your path.

18. "loathness": reluctance.

18. "hint": opportunity.

19–20. "Let that . . . leaves itself": Antony replaces the previous personal pronouns "I," "me," "my," "myself" (lines 7–19) with the impersonal pronouns "that" and "itself," pronouns which, moreover, lack an antecedent. Just as he finds his existence in his honor, Antony loses it in his dishonor: "If I lose mine honor, / I lose myself" (3.4.22–23). See, further, line 49n.

20. "straightway": right away.

I will possess you of that ship and treasure.
Leave me, I pray, a little—pray you, now,
Nay, do so; for indeed I have lost command.
Therefore I pray you. I'll see you by and by.

[Exeunt attendants. Antony] sits down.

Enter Cleopatra led by Charmian, [Iras,] and Eros.

Eros: Nay, gentle madam, to him, comfort him.   25

Iras: Do, most dear queen.

Charmian: Do? Why, what else?

Cleopatra: Let me sit down. O Juno!

Antony: No, no, no, no, no!

Eros: See you here, sir?   30

Antony: Oh fie, fie, fie!

Charmian: Madam!

Iras: Madam, O good empress!

Eros: Sir, sir!

Antony: Yes, my lord, yes. He at Philippi kept   35
His sword e'en like a dancer, while I struck

---

21. "possess you": put you in possession of.

22–24. Antony demonstrates as well as states his inability to command. He uses the beseeching "pray" four times in the speech, thrice in the last three lines, the only times he mentions the word (note his similar use of "prithee" [4.14.130]). No longer able to command, he is forced to beg his men to do what he asks.

24. "by and by": before long.

28. Juno is queen of the Roman gods, Jupiter's (Jove's) wife.

35. "Yes, my lord, yes": Though probably addressed to Caesar, Antony's words are not addressed to anyone around him. Utterly hopeless, he neither hears Eros nor notices Cleopatra. This is the only time he addresses anyone as "lord."

35. "He": Caesar.

35–36. "kept . . . like a dancer": kept it in its sheath, never drew it. Plutarch says that Caesar never fought at Philippi: "As for Octavius Caesar himself, he was not in his camp, because he was sick" (Plutarch, *Brutus*, 41.1; Spencer, 156). Shakespeare shows Caesar before and after the battle, but not during it (*JC*, 5.1.62–65, 5.5.53).

The lean and wrinkled Cassius, and 'twas I
That the mad Brutus ended. He alone
Dealt on lieutenantry, and no practice had
In the brave squares of war, yet now—no matter.　　**40**

Cleopatra: Ah, stand by.

Eros: The Queen, my lord, the Queen.

Iras: Go to him, madam; speak to him.
　　He's unqualitied with very shame.

Cleopatra: Well, then, sustain me. O!　　　　　　**45**

Eros: Most noble sir, arise. The Queen approaches.
　　Her head's declined, and death will seize her but
　　Your comfort makes the rescue.

No one in *Antony and Cleopatra* mentions Caesar's courage except to deny it (lines 38–40, 4.7.2, 4.15.15).

37. "The lean . . . Cassius": see 2.6.15n and *JC* 1.2.193.

38. "The mad Brutus": "mad," because he sacrificed his friend to his country and his country to his Stoic ideals.

36–38. "I struck . . . Brutus ended": Buried in anguished thoughts, Antony can do nothing but think of his glorious past, but not without grossly exaggerating or distorting it. He did not strike Cassius at Philippi, and he ended Brutus only in the sense that Brutus killed himself after losing to him (*JC*, 5.3.36–46, 5.5.45–52; also *A&C*, 3.2.55–56; Plutarch, *Antony*, 22.3–4, *Brutus*, 43.5–6, 52).

38. "He": Caesar.

38. "alone": was the only one who.

39. "Dealt on lieutenantry": fought through his lieutenants rather than by his own presence and actions. Antony overlooks his own practice of fighting and winning through his subordinates (2.3.31, 39–41; 3.1.16–17; 4.6.1).

40. "brave squares": splendid squadrons; see 3.9.1n.

41. "stand by": stand near me (Cleopatra evidently fears that she is about to faint; see line 45).

44. "unqualitied with very shame": stripped by absolute shame of the qualities that make him who or what he is, deprived of his nature or character. "Very," placed before a noun, implies the fullest sense of the term.

45. "sustain": help, support.

47. "but": unless.

48. "comfort": comforting her.

Antony: I have offended reputation,
  A most unnoble swerving.

Eros: Sir, the Queen.   **50**

Antony: O, whither hast them led me, Egypt? See
  How I convey my shame out of thine eyes,
  By looking back what I have left behind
  'Stroyed in dishonor.

Cleopatra: O, my lord, my lord,
  Forgive my fearful sails! I little thought   **55**
  You would have followed.

Antony: Egypt, thou knew'st too well
  My heart was to thy rudder tied by th' strings,

---

49. "reputation": honor. Whereas we moderns tend to distinguish between moral worth and public reputation, Antony, speaking in Rome's long-standing manner, closely identifies virtue and reputation. Life in republican Rome was public in every respect. Because they held that the only thing in life worth seeking is what is worthy of public praise and renown, the Romans believed that a person's actions should be governed by the estimation of others. The good citizen was the citizen thought to be good (see Cicero, *Brutus*, 281, *Stoic Paradoxes*, 12–13). Paradoxically, Antony sounds very much like a traditional Roman when he is "unqualitied with very shame." Shame at what he has become makes him sound like what he is not (see, further, 1.2.115–17n).

50. "swerving": deviation, departure, transgression.

52. "convey": withdraw, remove.

52. "out of": away from.

53. "back": back at.

54. "'Stroyed": destroyed.

51–54. "See . . . in dishonor": Antony claims that his looking back on the ruins of his past prevents Cleopatra from seeing the shame in his face. Where pride seeks public display, shame seeks privacy or concealment. Heightened by the sense of an onlooker's gaze, shame dwells largely in the face (see 1.1.30–33n). Thus, when ashamed we tend to cover or avert our face, for the face is a synecdoche for the self. We try literally to save face (see, for example, Livy, 9.6.8). Yet, by turning his face away from Cleopatra so she cannot directly see his shame, Antony only stresses what his effort aims to avoid. Hence, his self-contradictory imperative: "See / How I convey my shame out of thine eyes." Antony directs Cleopatra to see what he putatively prevents her from seeing and how he prevents her.

And thou shouldst tow me after. O'er my spirit
Thy full supremacy thou knew'st, and that
Thy beck might from the bidding of the gods   **60**
Command me.

Cleopatra: O, my pardon!

Antony: Now I must
To the young man send humble treaties, dodge
And palter in the shifts of lowness, who
With half the bulk o'th' world played as I pleased,
Making and marring fortunes. You did know   **65**
How much you were my conqueror, and that
My sword, made weak by my affection, would
Obey it on all cause.

Cleopatra: Pardon, pardon!

Antony: Fall not a tear, I say; one of them rates
All that is won and lost. Give me a kiss.   **[They kiss.]**   **70**

---

58. "shouldst": would certainly.

57–58. "My heart . . . me after": Antony mixes heartstrings and a ship's towline.
Both pull another irresistibly in its own direction. Note the parallel uses of "rudder," literally for "[t]h' Antoniad," figuratively for Antony (3.10.2–3; line 57).

60. "beck": a silent nod or gesture.

60. "bidding": spoken orders.

58–61. "O'er my spirit . . . me": Love, by its nature, commands. Cleopatra knew
that, owing to the power of Antony's love for her, a mere silent gesture from her
would have prevailed over the spoken orders of the gods.

62. "the young man": In *Julius Caesar* Antony disparaged Octavius for his young
age (*JC*, 4.1.18). This is the first of several times in *A&C* when he does so. But, in
contrast to Antony's air of superiority in *Julius Caesar*, here Octavius' young age
only adds to the humiliation of Antony's defeat, as Cleopatra foreshadowed when
she taunted him by belittling Caesar as "scarce-bearded" (1.1.22).

62. "treaties": entreaties to negotiate peace.

62–63. "dodge And palter": haggle and equivocate.

63. "the shifts of lowness": the expedients of those who are poor or weak.

67. "My sword": my heroic sword (a metonymy for valor and masculinity).

67. "affection": passion.

68. "on all cause": no matter the cause at stake.

69. "Fall": let fall.

69. "rates": is worth.

Even this repays me.
We sent our schoolmaster. Is a come back?
Love, I am full of lead. Some wine
Within there, and our viands! Fortune knows
We scorn her most when most she offers blows.   75

[*Exeunt.*]

ACT THREE, SCENE TWELVE

[Near Alexandria. Caesar's camp.]

Enter Caesar, Agrippa, [Thidias], and Dolabella, with others.

Caesar: Let him appear that's come from Antony.
Know you him?

Dolabella: Caesar, 'tis his schoolmaster;
An argument that he is plucked, when hither
He sends so poor a pinion of his wing,
Which had superfluous kings for messengers   5
Not many moons gone by.

---

71. "Even this repays me": this single kiss alone is enough to repay me.

72. "our schoolmaster": see 3.12.2–6n.

72. "a": he.

73. "lead": the heaviness of sorrow.

74. "viands": food.

74–75. "Fortune knows . . . offers blows": the greater the misfortune, the greater the scorn for Fortune. Antony blames Fortune for his debacle.

3. "An argument": sign, evidence.

3. "plucked": stripped of his feathers.

4. "pinion": feather (a term of falconry for feathers).

5. "which": who.

2–6. Antony and Cleopatra were forced to send as their messenger to Caesar the teacher of their children "because they had no other men of estimation about them, for that some were fled, and those that remained, they did not greatly trust them" (Plutarch, *Antony*, 72.1; Spencer, 268).

Enter Ambassador from Antony.

Caesar: Approach, and speak.

Ambassador: Such as I am, I come from Antony.
   I was of late as petty to his ends
   As is the morn-dew on the myrtle leaf
   To his grand sea.

Caesar: Be't so. Declare thine office.   **10**

Ambassador: Lord of his fortunes he salutes thee, and
   Requires to live in Egypt, which not granted,
   He lessens his requests, and to thee sues
   To let him breathe between the heavens and earth,
   A private man in Athens. This for him.   **15**
   Next, Cleopatra does confess thy greatness,
   Submits her to thy might, and of thee craves
   The circle of the Ptolemies for her heirs,
   Now hazarded to thy grace.

Caesar: For Antony,
   I have no ears to his request. The Queen   **20**

---

8. "as petty to his ends": as insignificant to his purposes.

10. "To his grand sea": compared to the grand sea from which the dewdrop origi-
nated. No doubt overwhelmed by his extraordinary circumstances, the Ambassador
speaks with an incongruous mixture of showy language and self-disparagement.

10. "Declare thine office": state the business for which you have come.

11. "Lord": as lord.

12. "Requires": requests.

12. "which not granted": and if that is not granted.

13. "lessens": The Folio reads "lessons," which some editors retain and gloss as
"disciplines," as might fit a schoolmaster.

13. "sues": petitions.

14. "breathe": live.

17. "her": herself.

18. "circle of the Ptolemies": crown of Egypt.

19. "hazarded to thy grace": at the disposal of your favor ("hazarded" is a gambling
term, meaning "staked and lost" [Schmidt, s.v. "hazard," vb.]).

19. "For": as for.

Of audience nor desire shall fail, so she
From Egypt drive her all-disgraced friend,
Or take his life there. This if she perform,
She shall not sue unheard. So to them both.

Ambassador: Fortune pursue thee!

Caesar: Bring him through the bands.   **25**

[*Exit Ambassador.*]

[*to Thidias*] To try thy eloquence now 'tis time. Dispatch.
From Antony win Cleopatra. Promise,
And in our name, what she requires; add more,
From thine invention, offers. Women are not
In their best fortunes strong, but want will perjure   **30**

20–21. "The Queen . . . fail": the Queen shall lack neither a hearing nor the fulfill-
ment of her wishes.

21. "so": provided that.

22. "friend": lover.

19–24.: Political prudence as well as personal hatred speaks against both Antony's
and Cleopatra's requests. Caesar cannot grant either of Antony's requests without
endangering his settlement of the East and his position as sole ruler of the world.
Even as a private man in Athens, Antony would pose a serious potential threat.
Cleopatra's request is similarly problematic. In addition to Caesarion's representing a powerful challenge to Caesar's claim to be Julius Caesar's legitimate heir, a
Ptolemic dynasty in Egypt would conflict with Caesar's rule of the East and hence
of the world. Moreover, Caesar seeks to acquire the enormous Egyptian royal
treasury. Cleopatra's fruitless request is the last time the name of the Ptolemies is
mentioned.

25. "Bring him . . . bands": Escort him through the troops.

26. Thidias (Thyreus) is one of Caesar's freedmen (Dio, 51.8.6).

26. "try": test.

26. "Therewithal [Caesar] sent Thyreus one of his [freed]men unto her, a very wise
and discreet man, who, bringing letters of credit from a young Lord unto a noble
Lady, and that besides greatly liked her beauty, might easily by his eloquence have
persuaded her" (Plutarch, *Antony*, 73.1; Spencer, 269).

28. "in our name": on my authority.

28. "what she requires": whatever she requests.

29. "invention": devising, improvising.

30. "In their best fortunes": in their most fortunate circumstances.

The ne'er-touched vestal. Try thy cunning, Thidias.
Make thine own edict for thy pains, which we
Will answer as a law.

Thidias: Caesar, I go.

Caesar: Observe how Antony becomes his flaw,
And what thou think'st his very action speaks   **35**
In every power that moves.

Thidias: Caesar, I shall.   **Exeunt.**

ACT THREE, SCENE THIRTEEN

[Alexandria. Cleopatra's palace.]

Enter Cleopatra, Enobarbus, Charmian, and Iras.

Cleopatra: What shall we do, Enobarbus?

Enobarbus: Think, and die.

30–31. "want will perjure . . . vestal": need will make a vestal virgin break her vows. Vestal virgins were six priestesses who tended the sacred fire of Vesta, the goddess of the domestic hearth. A vestal was bound to maintain the strictest sexual purity during the minimum of thirty years of service and would be buried alive for violating her vow of chastity (Ovid, *Fasti*, 6.456–60).

31. "cunning" skill, cleverness.

32–33. "Make thine own . . . law": decree your own reward for your (successful) efforts, which I will pay it as if were a law. On Caesar's mention of law, see 3.6.89–90n.

34. "becomes his flaw": bears himself in, adapts himself to, his disaster (a "flaw" is a sudden blast of wind).

35. "speaks": indicates.

36. "In every . . . moves": in every motion he makes. Caesar knows that Antony is characteristically at his best in great adversity (see 1.4.56–72). He might yet rally his spirit.

1. "shall": The word denotes not mere futurity, but inevitable futurity. It implies "must" (Abbott, §315).

1. "we": I (the royal "we").

1. "Think, and die": brood on what has happened and die of despair (cp. 4.6.35–37).

Cleopatra: Is Antony or we in fault for this?

Enobarbus: Antony only, that would make his will
    Lord of his reason. What though you fled
    From that great face of war, whose several ranges   5
    Frighted each other? Why should he follow?
    The itch of his affection should not then
    Have nicked his captainship, at such a point,
    When half to half the world opposed, he being
    The mered question. 'Twas a shame no less   10
    Than was his loss, to course your flying flags
    And leave his navy gazing.

Cleopatra: Prithee, peace.

Enter the Ambassador with Antony.

Antony: Is that his answer?

Ambassador: Ay, my lord.

Antony: The Queen shall then have courtesy, so she   **15**
    Will yield us up?

---

2. "in fault": at fault.

3. "will": desire, esp. sexual desire.

5. "ranges": battle lines of opposing ships.

7. "affection": sexual passion.

8. "nicked": cut short, snipped off (hence emasculated).

8. "captainship": generalship.

8. "point": crisis.

10. "mered question": sole or entire ground of dispute. Enobarbus vindicates his original judgment that women are not fit to fight and men will be distracted by their presence, and he tacitly dismisses the fact that the war was declared against Cleopatra and not against Antony (3.7.6–12, 16–18).

11. "course": chase, pursue.

12. "gazing": looking on intently with astonishment: "Many plainly saw Antonius fly, and yet could hardly believe it, that he . . . would so have forsaken them, and have fled so cowardly" (Plutarch, *Antony*, 68.2; Spencer, 261). So, too, the enemy: "For the enemies themselves wondered much to see them sail in that sort, with full sail towards Peloponnesus" (Plutarch, *Antony*, 66.4; Spencer, 258).

12. "peace": silence.

15. "courtesy": kindness, generosity.

15. "so": so long as.

16. "us": the royal "we."

Ambassador: He says so.

Antony: Let her know't.
To the boy Caesar send this grizzled head,
And he will fill thy wishes to the brim
With principalities.

Cleopatra: That head, my lord?

Antony: To him again. Tell him he wears the rose   **20**
Of youth upon him, from which the world should note
Something particular. His coin, ships, legions
May be a coward's, whose ministers would prevail
Under the service of a child as soon
As i'th' command of Caesar. I dare him therefore   **25**
To lay his gay caparisons apart
And answer me declined, sword against sword,
Ourselves alone. I'll write it. Follow me.

                 [*Exeunt Antony and the Ambassador.*]

Enobarbus: [*aside*] Yes, like enough, high-battled Caesar will
Unstate his happiness and be staged to th' show   **30**
Against a sworder! I see men's judgments are

---

17. "grizzled": somewhat gray.

20. "To": go to.

20–22. "Tell him . . . particular": Antony now uses Caesar's youth as a reason for the world to expect some distinctive achievement from him. As a man in the bloom of youth, Caesar should show his nobility by some brave action, as young Roman men traditionally have (see 4.4.26–27; and see, further, Polybius, 6.53.9–54.5).

23. "ministers": agents, subordinates.

24. "Under": in.

26. "gay caparisons": splendid trappings, defensive armor (of a horse).

27. "answer": meet to fight.

27. "declined": fallen, diminished, perhaps also aged (modifies "me").

20–28. This is Antony's second challenge to Caesar to fight a duel of valor for rule of the world; the first was before the battle; see 3.7.30 and n.

29. "like": likely.

29. "high-battled": supported by great armies.

30–31. "Unstate his happiness . . . sworder": cast aside the advantages of his good fortune and be exhibited upon a public stage as though fighting a gladiator.

A parcel of their fortunes, and things outward
Do draw the inward quality after them
To suffer all alike. That he should dream,
Knowing all measures, the full Caesar will   **35**
Answer his emptiness! Caesar, thou hast subdued
His judgment too.

                    Enter a Servant.

Servant: A messenger from Caesar.

Cleopatra: What, no more ceremony? See, my women,
Against the blown rose may they stop their nose   **40**
That kneeled unto the buds. Admit him, sir. [***Exit Servant.***]

Enobarbus: [*aside*] Mine honesty and I begin to square.
The loyalty well held to fools does make

---

32. "parcel of": of a piece with.

32–33. "things outward . . . after them": external circumstances shape one's inner
being. Enobarbus implicitly answers Antony's claim to be able to scorn the worst
misfortunes (3.11.74–75).

34. "To suffer all alike": so that all (both one's circumstances and one's inner being)
suffer to the same degree.

35. "Knowing all measures": "thoroughly acquainted with the diverse changes and
fortunes of battles" (Plutarch, *Antony*, 68.2; Spencer, 261–62).

35. "full": abounding in power, at full measure.

36. "Answer his emptiness": agree to fight someone as weak as he. Caesar would
have nothing to gain. If he won, he would keep what he already has. If he lost, he
would lose what he has.

39. "ceremony": locution of honor, expressing deference or respect (cp., for example, 1.5.9, 41; 2.5.98, 106; 3.3.2, 7, 8; 3.11.26, 33).

40. "blown": no longer in bloom, now decaying.

40. "stop": hold.

42. "honesty": sense of honor.

42. "square": quarrel. Enobarbus again divides and simplifies himself, but trans-
poses the former terms. Where he previously identified himself with his loyalty
and distinguished himself from his calculation (3.10.35–37), he now identifies
himself ("I") with the corrupted party, while alienating "[his] honesty." Closer
now to acting dishonorably, he, like Antony (3.11.7), separates his honesty from his
corrupted self in order to preserve it.

Our faith mere folly. Yet he that can endure
To follow with allegiance a fall'n lord 45
Does conquer him that did his master conquer,
And earns a place i'th' story.

Enter Thidias.

Cleopatra: Caesar's will?

Thidias: Hear it apart.

Cleopatra: None but friends. Say boldly. 50

Thidias: So haply are they friends to Antony.

Enobarbus: He needs as many, sir, as Caesar has,
  Or needs not us. If Caesar please, our master
  Will leap to be his friend. For us, you know
  Whose he is we are, and that is Caesar's.

Thidias: So. 55
  Thus then, thou most renowned: Caesar entreats

---

44. "faith": faithfulness.

44. "mere": pure, undiluted.

46. "master": Before Actium, the word "master" appeared only once, referring to Pompey's control of the sea (2.2.172–73). Now, in the aftermath of Actium, the word appears nineteen times, always as a title or term of address, all but twice designating someone with absolute command of, or authority over, another person or other people. For the two exceptions, see 4.3.24, 27.

44–47. "Yet he . . . i'th' story": nevertheless, loyalty to a fallen lord may bring renown. In Rome's earlier day, when disloyalty was considered unpardonable, loyalty was taken for granted and would not have won fame. But men, no longer fighting for their country, are now largely free to switch their loyalties according to their own interests. And so willingly to endure his master's defeat can earn a man honorable renown, precisely because it demonstrates the strength to disregard ordinary self-interest.

49. "apart": in private.

50. "None but friends": only friends are here.

51. "haply": perhaps.

53. "Or": or else.

54. "For": as for.

55. "Whose . . . we are": we are friends of Antony's friends.

56. "entreats": entreats you.

> Not to consider in what case thou stand'st
> Further than he is Caesar.

Cleopatra: Go on; right royal.

Thidias: He knows that you embrace not Antony
> As you did love, but as you feared him.

Cleopatra: Oh!   **60**

Thidias: The scars upon your honor therefore he
> Does pity as constrained blemishes,
> Not as deserved.

Cleopatra: He is a god and knows
> What is most right. Mine honor was not yielded,
> But conquered merely.   **65**

Enobarbus: [*aside*] To be sure of that, I will ask Antony.
> Sir, sir, thou art so leaky
> That we must leave thee to thy sinking, for
> Thy dearest quit thee.   ***Exit Enobarbus.***

---

57. "in what . . . stand'st": your present situation.

56–58. "Caesar entreats . . . he is Caesar": Combining generous language and an empty promise, Thidias leaves unclear whether Cleopatra should take for granted Caesar's generosity or his power over her. Caesar is, literally and figuratively, the beginning and the end of the promise.

58. "right royal": Caesar speaks like a true king.

62. "constrained": forced.

61–63. "The scars . . . as deserved": In the eyes of a Roman, a woman's honor consists in sexual respectability, for which intention does not count (see, for example, Cicero, *On the Ends of Good and Evil*, 2.73; Valerius Maximus, 6.1.1–3). However, since fear constrains or compels, and people are responsible only for what they could have done otherwise, Cleopatra's fear of Antony frees her from deserved dishonor.

64. "right": true.

65. "merely": only. Cleopatra's tone and tenor are uncertain. She may be playing false to Antony or playacting to Thidias. Always on stage but never transparent, Cleopatra, the only title character in a Shakespeare tragedy without a soliloquy, typically remains hidden even when in full public view. Like Isis, she is always veiled or enshrouded (Apuleius, *Metamorphoses*, 11.5; see, further, 3.6.16–18n).

67. "Sir, sir": Antony.

67–69. "so leaky . . . quit thee": an allusion to rats deserting a sinking ship.

Thidias: Shall I say to Caesar
What you require of him? For he partly begs   70
To be desired to give. It much would please him
That of his fortunes you should make a staff
To lean upon. But it would warm his spirits
To hear from me you had left Antony
And put yourself under his shroud,   75
The universal landlord.

Cleopatra: What's your name?

Thidias: My name is Thidias.

Cleopatra: Most kind messenger,
Say to great Caesar this in deputation:
I kiss his conqu'ring hand. Tell him I am prompt
To lay my crown at's feet, and there to kneel.   80
Till from his all-obeying breath I hear
The doom of Egypt.

Thidias: 'Tis your noblest course.
Wisdom and fortune combating together,
If that the former dare but what it can,

---

70. "require": request.

70. "partly": in some measure (as much as suits his dignity).

70–71. "partly begs ... to give": To be asked to give shows superiority and strength, while to ask another acknowledges inferiority and need. "[To tell] men that value themselves upon their titles, or positions, and have the world at will, . . . *that ever they stood in need of, or were beholden to any man*, is to strike them to the very heart" (Cicero, *On Duties*, 2.69; *Tully's Offices*, trans. Sr. Roger L'Estrange, 5th edn. [London: Tonson, Knaplock and Hindmarsh, 1699], 116 [translator's italics]). See, further, 2.2.31–33n.

75. "shroud": protection.

76. "universal landlord": "Landlord" is a commercial rather than a political designation. Universal conquest has turned politics into commerce. Everything now is private, and everyone is, in effect, Caesar's tenant. Rome's sovereignty has become the property of a single proprietor (see 1.1.12n).

78. "in deputation": as my deputy.

80. "at's": at his.

81. "all-obeying": obeyed by all.

82. "doom of Egypt": judgment (not condemnation) on me, the Queen of Egypt.

84. "If that": if.

No chance may shake it. Give me grace to lay   **85**
My duty on your hand.

Cleopatra: [*Offers him her hand.*] Your Caesar's father oft,
When he hath mused of taking kingdoms in,
Bestowed his lips on that unworthy place
As it rained kisses.

Enter Antony and Enobarbus.

Antony: Favors? By Jove that thunders!   **90**
What art thou, fellow?

Thidias: One that but performs
The bidding of the fullest man and worthiest
To have command obeyed.

Enobarbus: [*aside*]   You will be whipped.

Antony: [*Calls for servants.*] Approach there!—Ah, you kite!—Now,
gods and devils,
Authority melts from me. Of late when I cried "Ho!"   **95**

83–85. "Wisdom and fortune . . . shake it": Thidias, affecting Stoic wisdom, twists
the central Stoic tenet. Stoicism places happiness in virtue and virtue in what a
man himself can control. Although no one can control the vicissitudes of fortune,
a man can control his disposition toward their effects. So long as nothing external
breaks into his will or affects his judgment, no misfortune can touch his soul or
disturb his happiness. Wisdom renders him immune to the blows of fortune (see,
for example, Cicero, *Tusculan Disputations*, 5.42–43). Thidias speaks of "wisdom,"
but he means pragmatic calculation. So long as one runs no risks beyond what one
knows one is able to accomplish, no misfortune can shake one's security. The constancy of Stoic virtue becomes the expediency of utilitarian acquiescence. Mastery
of fortune becomes submission to Caesar.

86. "duty": homage (a respectful kiss).

87. "Your Caesar's father": Julius Caesar.

88. "mused of": pondered.

88. "taking kingdoms in": conquering kingdoms.

90. "As": as if.

91. "What": who.

91. "fellow": a worthless person (a term of contempt).

92. "fullest": best and most fortunate.

94. "kite": a rapacious bird of prey (Pliny, 10.28), by implication, a whore.

Like boys unto a muss kings would start forth
And cry "Your will?"

Enter Servant[s].

Have you no ears? I am
Antony yet. Take hence this jack and whip him.

Enobarbus: [*aside*] 'Tis better playing with a lion's whelp
Than with an old one dying.

Antony: Moon and stars!   **100**
Whip him! Were't twenty of the greatest tributaries
That do acknowledge Caesar, should I find them
So saucy with the hand of she here—what's her name
Since she was Cleopatra? Whip him, fellows,
Till like a boy you see him cringe his face   **105**
And whine aloud for mercy. Take him hence.

Thidias: Mark Antony—

Antony: Tug him away! Being whipped,
Bring him again. The jack of Caesar's shall
Bear us an errand to him.   ***Exeunt [Servants] with Thidias.***
You were half blasted ere I knew you. Ha!   **110**
I my pillow left unpressed in Rome,
Forborne the getting of a lawful race,

---

96. "muss": a game in which boys scramble for small objects thrown down.

98. "jack": menial, underling.

99. "lion's whelp": young lion.

101. "tributaries": dependent kings (who pay tribute).

103. "saucy": presumptuous (a strong word).

103. "she here": a nameless woman.

103–4. "what's her name . . . Cleopatra": Antony insists that he retains his identity despite his betrayal of his men (lines 97–98), but says that Cleopatra has lost hers because of her (suspected) betrayal of him.

105. "like a boy": Antony intends to unman Thidias (for unmanning him).

105. "cringe": twist (from pain).

110. "blasted": withered, blighted.

110. "ere": before.

112. "Forborne . . . lawful race": gave up having legitimate children.

And by a gem of women, to be abused
By one that looks on feeders?

Cleopatra: Good my lord—

Antony: You have been a boggler ever.   **115**
    But when we in our viciousness grow hard—
    O, misery on't!—the wise gods seel our eyes,
    In our own filth drop our clear judgments, make us
    Adore our errors, laugh at's while we strut
    To our confusion.

Cleopatra: O, is't come to this?   **120**

Antony: I found you as a morsel cold upon
    Dead Caesar's trencher; nay, you were a fragment
    Of Gnaeus Pompey's, besides what hotter hours,
    Unregistered in vulgar fame, you have
    Luxuriously picked out. For I am sure,   **125**
    Though you can guess what temperance should be,
    You know not what it is.

---

113. "abused": deceived.

114. "looks on feeders": looks favorably on (1) servants (those who serve food to the great), (2) parasites (those who eat at the table of the great); here, the two senses are hard to distinguish (see Schmidt, s.v. "feeder").

115. "boggler": one who is shifty, equivocates, plays fast and loose.

116. "grow hard": become hardened.

117. "seel": sew shut, hoodwink (a term in falconry for hawks being trained).

119. "at's": at us.

120. "confusion": destruction. Antony seems to be alluding to the practices of Ate, the Homeric goddess of moral blindness and ruin (Homer, *Iliad*, 19.91–94). For Antony's only previous moralizing, see 1.2.115–17.

121. "morsel": Antony echoes Cleopatra's own ribald description of herself as well as Pompey's and Enobarbus' crude allusions to her (1.5.32; 2.6.64–65, 128).

122. "trencher": plate or platter.

121–22. "morsel . . . a fragment": leftovers from her previous lovers' dishes.

123. "Gnaeus Pompey's": the son of Pompey the Great (see 1.5.32n).

124. "vulgar fame": common gossip.

125. "Luxuriously picked out": chosen for your lascivious pleasures.

126. "Though": even if.

125–27. "For I am sure . . . it is": Anger is always self-righteous. In his futile fury, Antony sanctimoniously accuses Cleopatra, whose immoderation he has always

Cleopatra: Wherefore is this?

Antony: To let a fellow that will take rewards
   And say "God quit you!" be familiar with
   My playfellow, your hand, this kingly seal   **130**
   And plighter of high hearts! O, that I were
   Upon the hill of Basan, to outroar
   The horned herd! For I have savage cause,
   And to proclaim it civilly were like
   A haltered neck which does the hangman thank   **135**
   For being yare about him.

Enter a Servant with Thidias.

                    Is he whipped?

Servant: Soundly, my lord.

Antony: Cried he? And begged 'a pardon?

Servant: He did ask favor.

Antony: [*to Thidias*] If that thy father live, let him repent
   Thou wast not made his daughter; and be thou sorry   **140**
   To follow Caesar in his triumph, since

relished, of being ignorant of the moderation that he himself has never shown or sought.

129. "God quit you": a beggar's phrase of thanks for a tip or alms (to "quit" is to reward, requite).

130–31. "your hand ... plighter": that which ratifies and pledges (see 2.2.157n).

131. "high": noble.

131–33. "O, that I ... horned herd." Antony, who considers himself to have been cuckolded by Thidias' kiss, compares himself to the roaring beasts on the biblical hill of Basan (Psalm 22:12–13) and imagines himself the champion of the horned herd. On cuckolds as horned, see 1.2.4–5n.

133. "savage cause": cause enough to become savage.

134. "civilly": in a civil manner.

135. "haltered neck": neck of a man about to be hanged.

136. "yare": quick and nimble.

137. "'a": he (or perhaps the indefinite article).

138. "favor": for kindness.

139. "If that": if.

139. "repent": regret.

139–40. "repent ... daughter": because you have been reduced to a girl (see line 105n).

141. "in his triumph": in his triumphal procession through Rome.

Thou hast been whipped for following him. Henceforth
The white hand of a lady fever thee;
Shake thou to look on't. Get thee back to Caesar.
Tell him thy entertainment. Look thou say   **145**
He makes me angry with him; for he seems
Proud and disdainful, harping on what I am,
Not what he knew I was. He makes me angry,
And at this time most easy 'tis to do't,
When my good stars that were my former guides   **150**
Have empty left their orbs and shot their fires
Into th'abysm of hell. If he mislike
My speech and what is done, tell him he has
Hipparchus, my enfranched bondman, whom

---

142. "for following him": Thidias is punished for Caesar's victory as well as for kissing Cleopatra's hand. Both have emasculated Antony.

143–44. "The white hand . . . on't": may the sight of a woman's hand make you shiver (with fright) as if you had a fever.

145. "entertainment": reception.

145. "Look thou say": look to it that you say.

146–49. "He makes . . . to do't": In Plutarch, Antony sends Thidias back to Caesar with the complaint that "[Thidias] showed himself proud and disdainful toward him, and now specially when he was easy to be angered, by reason of his present misery" (Plutarch, *Antony*, 73.2; Spencer, 271). In Shakespeare, Antony makes the complaint about Caesar. He punishes the emissary for the emperor's affront. Just as subordinates win battles for generals, they also are punished for them. The intended harm is the insult to the emperor, not the stripes inflicted on his underling.

150. "stars": planets, sun, and moon.

150. "my former guides": gave me good fortune.

151. "orbs": the spheres in which the heavenly bodies orbit the earth (in Ptolemaic astronomy); see 2.7.14–16n.

150–52. "When . . . hell": Antony makes the first of many allusions throughout the rest of the play to the biblical apocalypse: "And the fifth Angel blew the trumpet, and I saw a star fall from heaven unto the earth, and to him was given the key of the bottomless pit. And he opened the bottomless pit [*abussos*]" (Rev. 9:1–2; also 6:13).

152. "mislike": dislike.

154. "enfranched bondman": enfranchised bondsman; freed slave who is now a citizen. On Roman commanders granting Roman citizenship along with freedom to slaves, see 4.14.80–81n.

He may at pleasure whip, or hang, or torture,   **155**
As he shall like to quit me. Urge it thou.
Hence with thy stripes! Be gone!

Exit Thidias [with Servant.]

Cleopatra: Have you done yet?

Antony: Alack, our terrene moon is now eclipsed,
And it portends alone the fall of Antony.

Cleopatra: I must stay his time.   **160**

Antony: To flatter Caesar, would you mingle eyes
With one that ties his points?

Cleopatra: Not know me yet?

Antony: Cold-hearted toward me?

Cleopatra: Ah, dear, if I be so,
From my cold heart let heaven engender hail
And poison it in the source, and the first stone   **165**

---

156. "quit": requite, repay.

154–56. "Hipparchus . . . quit me": Plutarch says that Hipparchus was a favorite of Antony, who became the first of his freedmen to defect to Caesar (Plutarch, *Antony*, 67.7). Shakespeare, however, says nothing about his defecting. Shakespeare's silence, which makes Antony betray an innocent man, serves to point up how savage Antony's anger can be (see *JC*, 3.2.254–75). In contrast to his magnanimity elsewhere, Antony's treatments of Thidias and Hipparchus are his most tyrannical acts.

158. "our terrene . . . eclipsed": Cleopatra, as the earthly incarnation of the moon goddess Isis, is now darkened. On Isis as the moon or moon goddess, see Plutarch, *Isis and Osiris*, 49 (372d).

159. "it": the eclipse of the terrene moon.

159. "alone": above all.

158–59. "our terrene . . . Antony": On eclipses of the moon as precursors of the fall of rulers, in particular, and of calamities, in general, see, for example, Cicero, *On Divination*, 1.18; Tacitus, *Annals*, 1.28.1–2; Plutarch, *Aemilius Paulus*, 17.3–4.

160. "stay his time": wait until his fury passes.

161–62. "mingle eyes With": make eyes at.

162. "ties his points": a servant who fastens his clothes (an anachronism).

163–64. "if I . . . let heaven": Cleopatra intends her speech as a heroic oath to underscore her willing loss if she is cold-hearted toward Antony. For a similar use of the optative imperative as expressing the strongest denial, see 1.1.34–35.

Drop in my neck; as it determines, so
Dissolve my life! The next Caesarion smite,
Till by degrees the memory of my womb,
Together with my brave Egyptians all,
By the discandying of this pelleted storm   **170**
Lie graveless till the flies and gnats of Nile
Have buried them for prey!

Antony: I am satisfied.
Caesar sets down in Alexandria, where
I will oppose his fate. Our force by land
Hath nobly held; our severed navy too   **175**
Have knit again, and fleet, threatening most sea-like.
Where hast thou been, my heart? Dost thou hear, lady?
If from the field I shall return once more

---

166. "determines": melts, comes to an end.

167. "The next Caesarion smite": may the next poisoned hailstone kill my eldest son, Caesarion.

168. "memory of my womb": all my children.

169. "brave": splendid.

170. "discandying": melting.

170. "pelleted storm": hailstorm.

171–72. "till the flies . . . for prey": until they have found graves in the stomachs of the flies and gnats of the Nile who have eaten them.

164–72. Cleopatra's imagery draws on that of the apocalypse: "And there fell a great hail, like talents out of heaven upon the men, and men blasphemed God, because of the plague of the hail: for the plague thereof was exceeding great" (Rev. 16:21). See also Exodus, 8:24, 9:23–25.

173. "sets down in": encamps before, lays siege to.

174. "oppose his fate": resist his destiny (to reign supreme). Antony speaks not of defeating Caesar but of opposing his fate. He leaves unclear whether he expects to win or to die nobly resisting him.

175. "held": remained united. "Antonius thought that his army by land, which he left at Actium, was yet whole" (Plutarch, *Antony*, 69.3; Spencer, 263).

176. "fleet": are afloat.

176. "threatening most sea-like": threatening like the sea itself. Antony is silent about his officers and foreign allies (cp. 3.10.33–35).

177. "my heart": my courage, or my spirit (probably not Cleopatra).

178. "field": battlefield.

To kiss these lips, I will appear in blood.
I and my sword will earn our chronicle.　　　　**180**
There's hope in't yet.

Cleopatra: That's my brave lord!

Antony: I will be treble-sinewed, hearted, breathed,
And fight maliciously; for when mine hours
Were nice and lucky, men did ransom lives　　　**185**
Of me for jests. But now I'll set my teeth
And send to darkness all that stop me. Come,
Let's have one other gaudy night. Call to me
All my sad captains. Fill our bowls once more.
Let's mock the midnight bell.

Cleopatra:　　　　　　　　　It is my birthday.　　**190**
I had thought t'have held it poor. But since my lord
Is Antony again, I will be Cleopatra.

Antony: We will yet do well.

Cleoptra: [*to Charmian and Iras*] Call all his noble captains to my lord.

Antony: Do so; we'll speak to them, and tonight I'll force　**195**
The wine peep through their scars. Come on, my queen,
There's sap in't yet. The next time I do fight

179–80. "I will appear . . . our chronicle": Antony again speaks like a traditional Roman. Blood is a sign of bravery, a sword is a metonymy for prowess, a place in history ("our chronicle") is the reward for victory (cp. *Cor.*, 2.2.105–8). Antony says nothing about Cleopatra fighting along with him.

183. "treble-sinewed . . . breathed": thrice myself in strength, courage, and endurance.

184. "maliciously": fiercely.

185. "nice and lucky": soft (perhaps wanton) and happy.

186. "Of me for": from me in exchange for.

186. "jests": trifles.

188. "gaudy night": night of showy, luxurious revelry.

189. "sad": serious, sober.

190. "mock": defy, pay no heed to.

191. "held it poor": done little to celebrate it.

196. "peep": to appear.

197. "sap": life.

I'll make Death love me, for I will contend
Even with his pestilent scythe.

Exeunt [all but Enobarbus].

Enobarbus: Now he'll outstare the lightning. To be furious   **200**
Is to be frighted out of fear, and in that mood
The dove will peck the estridge; and I see still
A diminution in our captain's brain
Restores his heart. When valor preys on reason,
It eats the sword it fights with. I will seek   **205**
Some way to leave him.   *Exit.*

198–99. "contend . . . pestilent scythe": compete in killing people even with Death
in times of plague.

200. "outstare": stare down.

200. "furious": frenzied, raging.

202. "estridge": ostrich (some editors suggest goshawk).

202. "still": always.

203–4. "A diminution . . . his heart": Antony's diminished judgment revives his
courage.

204–5. "When valor . . . fights with": Valor is not valor unless governed by reason.
By consuming reason, it consumes itself. To be valor, it must be emboldened by
more than anger or pain (see Aristotle, *Nicomachean Ethics*, 1116b23–17a1).

ACT FOUR, SCENE ONE

[Before Alexandria. Caesar's camp.]

Enter Caesar, Agrippa, and Maecenas, with his army,
Caesar reading a letter.

Caesar: He calls me "boy," and chides as he had power
To beat me out of Egypt. My messenger
He hath whipped with rods, dares me to personal combat,
Caesar to Antony. Let the old ruffian know
I have many other ways to die; meantime   5
Laugh at his challenge.

Maecenas: Caesar must think,
When one so great begins to rage, he's hunted
Even to falling. Give him no breath, but now
Make boot of his distraction. Never anger   10
Made good guard for itself.

Caesar: Let our best heads

---

1. "as": as if.

4. "to": against.

4. "ruffian": a swaggering violent pimp, thug, or bully characterized by extravagant concern for his personal appearance.

5. "I have ... to die": Not an admission that Antony would kill him if they fought, but a contemptuous dismissal of Antony's desperate challenge. In Plutarch, Caesar answers that Antony has many other ways of dying. North's translation renders the passage ambiguous: "Caesar answered him that he had many other ways to die than so" (Plutarch, *Antony*, 75.1; Spencer, 273).

6. "Laugh": tell him that I laugh.

7. "Caesar": Maecenas' deference is new. This is the first time he has used the title Caesar. On Caesar's newfound emphasis on formal forms of address following the end of the civil wars, see Suetonius, *Augustus*, 25.1; cp., *Caesar*, 67.2.

8. "rage": rave furiously.

9. "falling": the position of a hunted animal unable to flee farther.

9. "breath": time to recover (catch his breath).

10. "Make boot": take advantage.

10. "distraction": disturbed state of mind.

10. "Never": never did.

11. "best heads": chief commanders.

Know that tomorrow the last of many battles
We mean to fight. Within our files there are,
Of those that served Mark Antony but late,
Enough to fetch him in. See it done,   **15**
And feast the army; we have store to do't,
And they have earned the waste. Poor Antony!   *Exeunt.*

ACT FOUR, SCENE TWO

[Alexandria. Cleopatra's palace.]

Enter Antony, Cleopatra, Enobarbus, Charmian, Iras, with others.

Antony: He will not fight with me, Domitius?

Enobarbus: No.

Antony: Why should he not?

Enobarbus: He thinks, being twenty times of better fortune,
He is twenty men to one.

---

13. "files": ranks.

14. "but late": lately.

15. "fetch him in": defeat and capture him.

15. "See it done": Caesar seems to be thinking beyond the upcoming battle. Because generals have needed to win the support of their troops by satisfying their demands (Sallust, *Catiline Conspiracy*, 11–12), the soldiers' discipline has greatly declined during Rome's civil wars. With the end of the wars now in sight, Caesar needs to establish discipline and loyalty among his troops (Suetonius, *Augustus*, 17.3, 24–25.1; Dio, 49.13.1–14.5). Needing a policy that produces both fear and love of him, he will punish Antony's deserters and spare or reward those who have been loyal to him. His punishment will serve to elicit both the loyalists' fear and love. For those spared will love him for fear that he could do to them what he has done to those he punished. On well-managed fear, see Machiavelli, *Discourses on Livy*, 3.21, *Prince*, 17, 19.

16. "store": adequate supplies.

17. "the waste": expense, extravagance. Like Antony, Caesar will reward his army with a feast. But where Antony spoke of enjoying a grand festive night, Caesar assesses the expense. He calculates, where Antony squanders.

1. "fight": in single combat.

1. "Domitius": Enobarbus' personal name.

Antony: Tomorrow, soldier,
  By sea and land I'll fight. Or I will live   **5**
  Or bathe my dying honor in the blood
  Shall make it live again. Woo't thou fight well?

Enobarbus: I'll strike and cry "Take all."

Antony: Well said! Come on!
  Call forth my household servants.   **[*Exit Alexas.*]**
                        Let's tonight
  Be bounteous at our meal.

         Enter three or four Servitors.

                     Give me thy hand;   **10**
  Thou hast been rightly honest. So hast thou,
  Thou, and thou, and thou. You have served me well,
  And kings have been your fellows.

Cleopatra: [*aside to Enobarbus*]   What means this?

Enobarbus: [*aside to Cleopatra*]
  'Tis one of those odd tricks which sorrow shoots
  Out of the mind.

Antony: And thou art honest too.   **15**
  I wish I could be made so many men,

---

5. "Or": either.

7. "Shall": which shall.

5–7. "Or I will . . . live again": either I will live or I will make my honor live again
by dying valiantly.

7. "woo't": will you (colloquial form of "wilt," literally "wilt thou").

8. "Take all": the cry of a gambler staking everything on a final throw of the dice.

S.D. 10. "*Servitors*": male personal attendants.

11. "honest": true, honorable.

13. "fellows": equals. Just as his handshake is a gesture of the attendants' equality
with him, Antony's reminder that kings have done him a similar service implies
their equality with kings. The age of a universal emperor is an age of universal
equality. All men, regardless of rank or position, are the emperor's servants. All are
similar and equal.

14–15. "odd tricks . . . the mind": carried away by sorrow, the mind blurts out
whimsically foolish words without thought or consideration. Sorrow, no less than
love or anger, can disorder the mind.

16. "made so many men": divided into as many men as you are.

And all of you clapped up together in
An Antony, that I might do you service
So good as you have done.

All the Servants: The gods forbid!

Antony: Well, my good fellows, wait on me tonight.   **20**
Scant not my cups, and make as much of me
As when mine empire was your fellow too
And suffered my command.

Cleopatra: [aside to Enobarbus]   What does he mean?

Enobarbus: [aside to Cleopatra]
To make his followers weep.

Antony: Tend me tonight;
May be it is the period of your duty.   **25**
Haply you shall not see me more, or if,
A mangled shadow. Perchance tomorrow
You'll serve another master. I look on you
As one that takes his leave. Mine honest friends,
I turn you not away, but, like a master   **30**
Married to your good service, stay till death.
Tend me tonight two hours—I ask no more—
And the gods yield you for't!

---

17. "clapped up": combined.

19. "as": as that.

20. "my good fellows": Antony calls the men "servants" only before they enter (line 9). Once present, they become "[his] good fellows," "[his] honest friends," "[his] hearty friends," and "[his] hearts" (lines 20, 29, 38, 41).

22. "fellow": fellow servant.

23. "suffered": submitted to.

24. "To make his followers weep": as if Antony had intended the effect (ironical).

25. "May be": it may be that.

25. "period": end.

26. "Haply": perhaps.

26. "if": if you do.

27. "mangled shadow": dismembered ghost.

31. "Married": bound (till death).

33. "yield": repay, reward.

Enobarbus: What mean you, sir,
To give them this discomfort? Look, they weep,
And I, an ass, am onion-eyed. For shame,   **35**
Transform us not to women.

Antony: Ho, ho, ho!
Now the witch take me if I meant it thus!
Grace grow where those drops fall! My hearty friends,
You take me in too dolorous a sense,
For I spake to you for your comfort, did desire you   **40**
To burn this night with torches. Know, my hearts,
I hope well of tomorrow, and will lead you
Where rather I'll expect victorious life
Than death and honor. Let's to supper, come,
And drown consideration.   ***Exeunt.***   **45**

---

34. "discomfort": distress.

34. "they weep": Besides loving him for his generosity, Antony's most loyal followers love him for his passions and his open display of his passions: "[B]eing given to
love, that made him the more desired, and by that means he brought many to love
him" (Plutarch, *Antony*, 4.3; Spencer, 178). His open display at once impressed and
flattered them. See, further, 1.2.183n.

35. "onion-eyed": tearful.

36. "Ho, ho, ho": a call to stop.

37. "the witch take me": may I be bewitched.

38. "Grace": (1) herb of grace (an old name for the herb rue), (2) virtue and goodness.

38. "hearty": (1) noble, (2) kind-hearted, (3) affectionate.

40. "for your comfort": to encourage you.

41. "burn . . . with torches": revel through the night.

45. "drown consideration": drown brooding thoughts (with wine).

10–45. Antony will die tomorrow. His last supper echoes Jesus'. Like Jesus, Antony
thrice asks his followers to tend him during what he expects to be his final hours
(lines 20, 24, 32; cp. Matt. 26:40–45). He thanks them for their loyalty (lines 11–12,
15), though he will be betrayed by Enobarbus, whose closeness he emphasizes by
addressing him by his personal name, "Domitius" (line 1), as he does only here
(cp. Matt. 26:14–16, 20–25, 45–47). He hopes to find a better life in death (lines
6–7; cp. Matt. 10:39). He offers his followers communion with one another and
with him (lines 16–19; cp. Matt. 26:26–29). Inadvertently evoking tears when he
means to give comfort, he tries to transform his followers' suffering or despair into
hope, speaking specifically of Grace (line 38; cp. 2 Cor. 1:3). He addresses those
who serve him as his friends, not his servants (cp. John 15:15). And suggesting that
they are the equals of kings, he points to the universal equality of everyone, kings

ACT FOUR, SCENE THREE

[Alexandria. Before Cleopatra's palace.]

Enter a company of Soldiers.

1 Soldier: Brother, good night. Tomorrow is the day.

2 Soldier: It will determine one way. Fare you well.
     Heard you of nothing strange about the streets?

1 Soldier: Nothing. What news?

2 Soldier: Belike 'tis but a rumor. Good night to you.   **5**

1 Soldier: Well sir, good night.

[*Enter two more Soldiers.*]

2 Soldier: Soldiers, have careful watch.

3 Soldier: And you. Good night, good night.

They place themselves in every corner of the stage.

2 Soldier: Here we; and if tomorrow
     Our navy thrive, I have an absolute hope   **10**
     Our landmen will stand up.

---

and servants alike, in the eyes of God (line 13; cp. Matt.19:30). In addition, no one understands what is happening (lines 13, 23, 33; cp. John 6:60). Enobarbus, who will in fact repent and die not unlike Judas (4.6.21–40; cp. Matt. 27:3–10), admonishes him not to turn his followers into women (lines 35–36). Although Enobarbus is referring only to Antony's having made the men cry, Shakespeare seems to be pointing to the advent of the new religion, with its emphasis on humility, abjectness, and submission.

S.D. 1. "*a company of Soldiers*": Where the previous scene points to the beginning of Christianity, the present scene, with a changing of the guard, marks the end of classical paganism. It is not strange that Shakespeare presents the emergence of Christianity as preceding the end of paganism. The old and the new religions overlap. The human conditions leading to the disappearance of the pagan world continue beyond the beginning of the new religion to which they give rise. This is the only scene in the play without any major or even named characters.

2. "determine one way": decide the outcome one way or the other.

5. "Belike": very likely.

7. "careful": attentive.

9. "Here we": here we are (on station for our watch).

1 Soldier: 'Tis a brave army, and full of purpose.

    Music of the hautboys is under the stage.

2 Soldier: Peace! What noise?

1 Soldier: List, list!

2 Soldier: Hark!   **15**

1 Soldier: Music i'th' air.

3 Soldier: Under the earth.

4 Soldier: It signs well, does it not?

3 Soldier: No.

1 Soldier: Peace, I say. What should this mean?   **20**

2 Soldier: 'Tis the god Hercules, whom Antony loved,
    Now leaves him.

1 Soldier: Walk. Let's see if other watchmen
    Do hear what we do.

2 Soldier: How now, masters?   *Speak together.*

All: How now? How now? Do you hear this?   **25**

1 Soldier: Ay. Is't not strange?

---

12. "brave": splendid, gallant.

12. "purpose": determination, resolution.

S.D. 12. "*hautboys*": a wooden double-reed wind instrument of high pitch (an early oboe).

14. "List": listen.

18. "signs": bodes.

21–22. The pagan demi-god and hero, Hercules, whose "feats . . . exceedingly surpass[ed] all other that ever were comprised by man's memory" (Diodorus, 4.8.1; trans. John Skelton [c. 1489], *The Bibliotheca Historica of Diodorus Siculus* [London: Early English Text Society, 1956], 360), and whom Antony loved and claimed as his ancestor (see 1.3.85n), forsakes the last hero—and Rome itself. Romans and other ancients commonly believed that a defeated city is abandoned by its gods (see, for example, Virgil, *Aeneid*, 2.351–52; Horace, *Odes*, 2.1.25–28). In Plutarch, the music, which is accompanied by a troop of shouting and singing revelers, is associated with Bacchus (Plutarch, *Antony*, 75.4). Shakespeare, omitting all but the mysterious music, substitutes the god embodying manly strength.

24. "masters": fellows (a polite term of address).

S.D. 24. "*Speak together*": all speaking at the same time.

3 Soldier: Do you hear, masters? Do you hear?

1 Soldier: Follow the noise so far as we have quarter.
   Let's see how it will give off.

All: Content. 'Tis strange.   **Exeunt.**

ACT FOUR, SCENE FOUR

[Alexandria. Cleopatra's Palace.]

Enter Antony and Cleopatra, with Charmian, and others.

Antony: Eros! Mine armor, Eros!

Cleopatra: Sleep a little.

Antony: No, my chuck. Eros! Come, mine armor, Eros!

Enter Eros [with armor].

   Come, good fellow, put thine iron on.
   If fortune be not ours today, it is
   Because we brave her. Come.

Cleopatra: Nay, I'll help too.   5
   What's this for?

Antony: Ah, let be, let be! Thou art
   The armorer of my heart. False, false. This, this!

---

28. "we have quarter": our watch extends.

29. "give off": cease.

29. "Content": agreed.

1. "Eros": The felicitously named Eros is Antony's armorer. Except only for Caesar's name (which he mentions twenty-nine times), Antony mentions Eros' name more often (twenty-six times) than any other noun, proper or common. By contrast, he mentions Cleopatra's name seven times. "Armor," which he mentions (lines 1, 2, 7) is also a pun on "amor."

2. "chuck": an intimate term of endearment.

3. "thine iron": the armor you are holding.

5. "brave": defy.

7. "heart": spirit, courage (rather than of his body).

7. "False, false. This, this": Antony corrects a mistake Cleopatra has made in arming him and shows her which is the right piece.

Cleopatra: Sooth, la, I'll help. Thus it must be.

Antony:　　　　　　　　　　　　　Well, well,
We shall thrive now. Seest thou, my good fellow?
Go, put on thy defenses.

Eros:　　　　　　　　Briefly, sir.　　　　　　　**10**

Cleopatra: Is not this buckled well?

Antony:　　　　　　　　　Rarely, rarely.
He that unbuckles this, till we do please
To daff't for our repose, shall hear a storm.
Thou fumblest, Eros, and my queen's a squire
More tight at this than thou. Dispatch. O love,　　**15**
That thou couldst see my wars today, and knew'st
The royal occupation, thou shouldst see
A workman in't.

Enter an armed Soldier.

　　　　　　　Good morrow to thee! Welcome!
Thou look'st like him that knows a warlike charge.
To business that we love we rise betime　　　　**20**
And go to't with delight.

---

8. "Sooth, la": truly, indeed ("la" adds emphasis).

5–8. The Folio combines these lines and assigns them all to Cleopatra. The eighteenth-century editor Sir Thomas Hanmer disentangled them and moved the name "Antony" from the end of line 5 and made it a speech heading for line 6.

10. "defenses": armor.

10. "Briefly": in a moment.

11. "rarely": splendidly.

13. "daff't": doff it, take it off.

14. "squire": a knight's attendant and armor bearer (an anachronism).

15. "tight": skilled.

15. "Dispatch": be quick.

16. "That": if only.

16. "knew'st": understood, could judge (cp. 3.7.1–19).

17. "royal occupation": warfare, the work of kings.

18. "workman": master craftsman.

19. "charge": duty, responsibility (not onset, attack).

20. "betime": betimes, early.

Soldier: A thousand, sir,
Early though't be, have on their riveted trim
And at the port expect you.   ***Shout. Trumpets flourish.***
Enter Captains and Soldiers.

Captain: The morn is fair. Good morrow, general!

All the soldiers: Good morrow, general!

Antony: 'Tis well blown, lads!   **25**
This morning, like the spirit of a youth
That means to be of note, begins betimes.
[*to Cleopatra*] So, so. Come, give me that. This way. Well said.
Fare thee well, dame. Whate'er becomes of me,
This is a soldier's kiss. [*Kisses her.*] Rebukable   **30**
And worthy shameful check it were to stand
On more mechanic compliment. I'll leave thee
Now like a man of steel.—You that will fight,
Follow me close. I'll bring you to't. Adieu.
          Exeunt [all but Cleopatra and Charmian].

Charmian: Please you retire to your chamber?

Cleopatra: Lead me.   **35**
He goes forth gallantly. That he and Caesar might

---

22. "riveted trim": armor.

23. "port": gate.

24. The Folio gives this line to Alexas, but Alexas has already deserted Antony (see 4.6.12–15 and n).

24. "morrow": morning.

25. "'Tis well blown": the morning begins (blossoms) well.

26–27. "the spirit . . . begins betimes": (just as we rise early ["betime"] to do what we love,) a youth seeking renown begins early ("betimes") to become famous. Earliness indicates eagerness (see *Cor.*, 1.3.1–25; 2.2.85–99; see, further, Cicero, *On Duties*, 2.45; Polybius, 6.54).

28. "Well said": well done.

30–32. "Rebukable . . . mechanic compliment": to make much of a prolonged leave-taking, such as common people might think necessary, would deserve rebuke and shameful reproof.

35. "retire": withdraw.

36. "That": if only.

Determine this great war in single fight,
Then Antony—but now—. Well, on.   ***Exeunt.***

ACT FOUR, SCENE FIVE

[Alexandria. Antony's camp.]

Trumpets sound. Enter Antony and Eros, [and a Soldier meeting them].

Soldier: The gods make this a happy day to Antony.

Antony: Would thou and those thy scars had once prevailed
          To make me fight at land.

Soldier: Had'st thou done so,
          The kings that have revolted and the soldier
          That has this morning left thee would have still   **5**
          Followed thy heels.

Antony: Who's gone this morning?

Soldier: Who?
          One ever near thee. Call for Enobarbus,
          He shall not hear thee, or from Caesar's camp
          Say "I am none of thine."

Antony: What sayest thou?

Soldier: Sir,
          He is with Caesar.

Eros: Sir, his chests and treasure   **10**
          He has not with him.

Antony: Is he gone?

Soldier: Most certain.

S.D. 1. This is the soldier who had urged Antony to fight on land at Actium
(3.7.60–66).

1. "happy day to": fortunate day for.

2. "Would": I wish.

2. "once": previously.

4. "revolted": deserted (see 3.10.34–35).

Antony: Go, Eros, send his treasure after. Do it.
    Detain no jot, I charge thee. Write to him—
    I will subscribe—gentle adieus and greetings.
    Say that I wish he never find more cause   **15**
    To change a master. O, my fortunes have
    Corrupted honest men. Dispatch.—Enobarbus!   *Exuent.*

ACT FOUR, SCENE SIX

[Alexandria. Caesar's camp.]

Flourish. Enter Agrippa, Caesar, with Enobarbus and Dolabella.

Caesar: Go forth, Agrippa, and begin the fight.
    Our will is Antony be took alive;

---

13. "Detain no jot": withhold not the smallest amount.

14. "subscribe": sign (the letter).

12–16. Commentators almost always see Antony's action as exhibiting his characteristic magnanimity. But Antony's letter charges Enobarbus with having deserted for Caesar's money and implies that he was so cowardly that he fled too quickly to take his treasure with him. As Enobarbus soon confirms (4.6.21–40), Antony's gesture is a scathing insult and searing punishment. For honor-loving Romans in general, giving is often a form of taking (see 2.2.31–33n).

17. "honest": honorable.

16–17. "O, my fortunes . . . men": Antony speaks as though his loss of the battle rather than the reason for the loss, has corrupted honest men (cp. 3.13.200–206).

2. "took": taken.

2. "Antony be took alive": Earlier, Caesar wanted Antony killed (3.12.23; 3.13.17–19). Now, he wants him captured, presumably so he can parade him through Rome in his triumph. Caesar would thus treat Antony as a non-Roman. No Roman has ever been led captive through Rome in triumph (Valerius Maximus, 2.8.7). Julius Caesar celebrated a triumph in Rome for his defeat of Cato the Younger and other republicans in Africa, but he disguised it as a victory over King Juba of Numidia (Plutarch, *Caesar*, 55.2). Soon afterwards, he celebrated a triumph for his victory over Pompey's sons in Spain, but, although he did not masquerade it as a foreign victory, he still did not parade Romans through Rome (*JC*, 1.1.31–52). Nevertheless, the Romans were outraged: "[T]he triumph he made into Rome . . . did as much offend the Romans, and more, than anything that ever he had done before, because he had not overcome captains that were strangers, nor barbarous kings, but had destroyed the sons of the noblest man in Rome" (Plutarch, *Caesar*, 56.4;

Make it so known.

Agrippa: Caesar, I shall.   **[Exit.]**

Caesar: The time of universal peace is near.   5
Prove this a prosp'rous day, the three-nooked world
Shall bear the olive freely.

Enter a Messenger.

Messenger: Antony
Is come into the field.

Caesar: Go charge Agrippa

Spencer, 76). Despite the lack of precedent, Brutus and Cassius feared that, if they lost at Philippi, Octavius and Antony would lead them "in triumph / Through the streets of Rome" (*JC*, 5.1.108–9). Their own suicides, however, averted that disgrace, if Octavius and Antony had in fact intended it. As Rome becomes universal, the distinction between Roman and non-Roman disappears. While foreigners may now be treated as Romans, Romans may be treated as foreigners. Universal empire obliterates the most basic political distinction.

4. "I shall": stronger than "I will"; see 1.2.204n.

5. "The time of universal peace is near": Jesus, the Prince of Peace (Isaiah, 9.6), will be born during Caesar's rule and the Pax Romana.

6. "Prove this": if this proves, turns out to be.

6. "the three-nooked world": the three nooks, or corners, of the world (Europe, Asia, and Africa).

7. "the olive": the olive branch, a Roman symbol of peace (see Virgil, *Georgics*, 2.420–25).

5–7. Caesar's victory will mean the end of centuries of Rome's continual foreign wars, culminating in its conquest of the world. "All the countries of the world have been reduced under obedience to the Romans" (Polybius, 3.1.4; Grimeston, 102). Dominating the world from Europe, to North Africa, to Asia, Rome will now have no rival power to seriously threaten it. "The temple of Janus Quirinus, which from the foundation of the City before his days had . . . twice been shut, [Caesar] in a far shorter space of time (having peace both by sea and land) shut a third time" (Suetonius, *Augustus*, 22.1; Holland, 1:97). The peace, moreover, will be internal as well. For the last century, Rome's foreign wars, contributing enormously to its generals' wealth and power, have produced domestic conflicts resulting in betrayals, proscriptions, assassinations, and civil wars among rival leaders. Romans have killed one another in the capital in Rome and on battlefields abroad. Leaving Caesar with no domestic rival, the defeat of Antony will put an end to Rome's bloody turmoil.

Plant those that have revolted in the van
That Antony may seem to spend his fury   **10**
Upon himself.

Exeunt [all but Enobarbus].

Enobarbus: Alexas did revolt and went to Jewry on
Affairs of Antony, there did dissuade
Great Herod to incline himself to Caesar
And leave his master Antony. For this pains,   **15**
Caesar hath hanged him. Canidius and the rest
That fell away have entertainment but
No honorable trust. I have done ill,
Of which I do accuse myself so sorely
That I will joy no more.   **20**

8–9. "charge Agrippa Plant": command Agrippa to place.

9. "van": frontline, vanguard.

10. "That": so that.

10–11. "That Antony . . . himself": Caesar repeats his order to use Antony's deserters against Antony (see 4.1.13–15). But, this time, evidently prompted by cruel spite, he wants to make it seem to Antony that his futile fight against Caesar is nothing but his furious fight against himself—his own self-punishment. Throughout the play, Caesar's strength lies in waiting for the right moment to act and taking advantage of other people's weaknesses and mistakes. In his vengeful punishment of Antony, we see that this may be more than simply a cunning tactic.

12. "Jewry": Judea.

13. "dissuade": persuade.

12–15. Antony had sent Alexas to Herod to keep him from changing sides. But Alexas, instead, persuaded Herod to abandon Antony and ally with Caesar, clearing the way for Caesar to enter Egypt from Syria (Plutarch, *Antony*, 72.2–3, 74.1; Josephus, 1.394).

15. "this": these.

15–16. To thank Herod for his support, Caesar confirmed his kingship and bestowed additional honors on him. Yet, despite Herod's plea to spare Alexas, Caesar ordered him hanged (Josephus, 1.391–95). Caesar's implacable hostility likely stems from Alexas' role in luring Antony back to Cleopatra from Octavia (Plutarch, *Antony*, 72.2).

17–18. "have entertainment . . . trust": have employment in Caesar's service, but given no positions of trust.

18. "ill": evil, wrong.

Enter a Soldier of Caesar's.

Soldier: Enobarbus, Antony
    Hath after thee sent all thy treasure, with
    His bounty overplus. The messenger
    Came on my guard, and at thy tent is now
    Unloading of his mules.

Enobarbus: I give it you.   **25**

Soldier: Mock not, Enobarbus.
    I tell you true. Best you safed the bringer
    Out of the host. I must attend mine office
    Or would have done't myself. Your emperor
    Continues still a Jove.   *Exit.*   **30**

Enobarbus: I am alone the villain of the earth,
    And feel I am so most. O Antony,
    Thou mine of bounty, how wouldst thou have paid
    My better service, when my turpitude
    Thou dost so crown with gold! This blows my heart.   **35**
    If swift thought break it not, a swifter mean

---

23. "His bounty overplus": his (generous) gift in addition.

24. "on my guard": while I was on guard.

27. "safed": gave safe passage to.

28. "Out of the host": so he can pass through the army's lines.

28. "office": duty.

30. "a Jove": godlike in his generosity. "[Perseus], . . . the son of Jove, . . . was conceived / By Danae [through] a golden shower" (Ovid, *Metamorphoses*, 4.610–11; Golding, 4.750–51).

31. "alone": beyond all others (Abbott, §18).

32. "feel . . . most": feel most that I am so.

34. "turpitude": extreme baseness, depravity.

31–35. Enobarbus' praise of Antony and contempt for himself are reciprocally related. The more self-contempt, the higher the praise. Enobarbus fails to recognize Antony's gesture as a deliberate affront because he fully accepts its ignominious verdict (see 4.5.12–16n).

35. "blows": swells (to the bursting point).

36. "thought": shameful sorrow.

36. "mean": means.

Shall outstrike thought, but thought will do't, I feel.
I fight against thee? No. I will go seek
Some ditch wherein to die; the foul'st best fits
My latter part of life.   *Exit.*   **40**

ACT FOUR, SCENE SEVEN

[The battlefield between the camps.]

Alarum, Drums and Trumpets. Enter Agrippa,
[and other of Caesar's soldiers].

Agrippa: Retire! We have engaged ourselves too far.
Caesar himself has work, and our oppression
Exceeds what we expected.   *Exeunt.*

Alarums. Enter Antony, and Scarus wounded.

Scarus: O, my brave emperor, this is fought indeed!
Had we done so at first, we had droven them home   **5**
With clouts about their heads.

Antony: Thou bleed'st apace.

Scarus: I had a wound here that was like a T,
But now 'tis made an H.   *[Sound retreat] far off.*

Antony: They do retire.

---

37. "outstrike": strike sooner and stronger (presumably, he means suicide).

39–40. "the foul'st . . . of life": only a foul death fits my foul final acts.

1. "engaged": entangled.

2. "work": trouble, hard work to do.

2. "oppression": the force that opposes us.

5. "done so at first": had we originally fought on land.

5. "droven": driven (old form of past participle).

6. "clouts": (1) heavy blows, (2) bandages.

7–8. "like a T, . . . an H": Scarus, whose own name is a pertinent pun, puns on the pronunciation of H ("ache") and plays on the shapes of the letters T and H: with an additional stroke (wound) at the bottom, H is a T on its side. Scarus' jest unwittingly anticipates the emergence of Christianity, where earthly ("terrene" [3.13.158]) rewards and punishments are superseded by those of Heaven and Hell.

Scarus: We'll beat 'em into bench-holes. I have yet
Room for six scotches more. **10**

Enter Eros.

Eros: They are beaten, sir, and our advantage serves
For a fair victory.

Scarus: Let us score their backs
And snatch 'em up as we take hares, behind.
'Tis sport to maul a runner.

Antony: I will reward thee
Once for thy sprightly comfort and tenfold **15**
For thy good valor. Come thee on.

Scarus: I'll halt after. **Exeunt.**

ACT FOUR, SCENE EIGHT

[Alexandria.]

Enter Antony again in a march; Scarus, with others.

Antony: We have beat him to his camp. Run one before
And let the Queen know of our gests. **[Exit a soldier.]**

---

9. "bench-holes": the holes of privies (desperate places to hide).

10. "scotches": gashes.

11–12. "our advantage ... fair victory": what we have already gained is favorable to our winning a full victory.

12. "score": slash.

13. "behind": from behind.

14. "runner": one who runs away (coward).

15. "sprightly comfort": spirited encouragement.

17. "halt": limp.

1. "beat": beaten.

1. "Antonius made a sally upon [Caesar], and fought very valiantly, so that he drave Caesar's horsemen back, fighting with his men even into their camp" (Plutarch, *Antony*, 74.3; Spencer, 272).

2. "gests": notable deeds, exploits (esp. as narrated or recorded in history). Antony's surprising military success is the first he wins for himself in the play. But eager to

Tomorrow
Before the sun shall see's, we'll spill the blood
That has today escaped. I thank you all,
For doughty-handed are you, and have fought   5
Not as you served the cause, but as't had been
Each man's like mine. You have shown all Hectors.
Enter the city. Clip your wives, your friends.
Tell them your feats, whilst they with joyful tears
Wash the congealment from your wounds and kiss   10
The honored gashes whole.

Enter Cleopatra.

[*to Scarus*] Give me thy hand.
To this this great fairy I'll commend thy acts,
Make her thanks bless thee. [*to Cleopatra*] O, thou day o'th'
world,
Chain mine armed neck. Leap thou, attire and all,
Through proof of harness to my heart, and there   15
Ride on the pants triumphing!   [*They embrace.*]

---

tell Cleopatra, rather than follow up the rout, as he seemed ready to do (cp. 4.7.16),
he will wait until tomorrow. His delay will turn his success into his utter defeat.
The Folio, here, reads "guests."

3. "see's": see us.

5. "doughty-handed": brave, bold fighters.

6–7. "Not as you served . . . mine": not as if you merely served the cause, but as if
the cause had been each man's own, as it is mine.

7. "shown": shown yourselves to be.

7. Hector was a prince of Troy and its greatest warrior in the Trojan War. The
comparison, however, is ominous. Hector was killed by Achilles, marking a turning point in the defense of Troy (Homer, *Iliad*, 22.98 ff.).

8. "Clip": embrace.

11. "whole": made healthy again (by kissing them). A man's bloody wounds are
direct evidence of his valor.

12. "fairy": enchantress (wielding magic powers).

13. "day": light.

14. "Chain": embrace.

15. "proof of harness": armor proved impenetrable.

16. "pants": quick breaths.

16. "triumphing": as if riding on a triumphal chariot.

Cleopatra: Lord of lords!
    O infinite virtue, com'st thou smiling from
    The world's great snare uncaught?

Antony: Mine nightingale,
    We have beat them to their beds. What, girl! Though gray
    Do something mingle with our younger brown,
        yet have we   **20**
    A brain that nourishes our nerves and can
    Get goal for goal of youth. Behold this man.
    Commend unto his lips thy favoring hand.
                    [*She offers Scarus her hand.*]
    Kiss it, my warrior. He hath fought today
    As if a god in hate of mankind had   **25**
    Destroyed in such a shape.

Cleopatra: I'll give thee, friend,
    An armor all of gold. It was a king's.

———————————

16. "Lord of lords": a New Testament designation for God delivering the Last Judgment (Rev. 17:14, 19:16; also 1 Tim. 6:15).

17. "virtue": valor, manliness.

17–18. "com'st . . . uncaught": Although praising Antony's immeasurable virtue, Cleopatra describes his escape rather than his victory. Having expected defeat (see 4.4.38), she counts the avoidance of an ignoble defeat as a triumph. This is only the second time Cleopatra praises Antony to his face (for the first, see 3.13.182).

18. "nightingale": "[H]er voice and words were marvelous pleasant; for her tongue was an instrument of music" (Plutarch, *Antony*, 27.3; Spencer, 203).

19. "beat . . . their beds": To be beaten to one's bed is not just to be defeated, but to be beaten out of one's standing in the world. It is to be unmanned (see *JC*, 4.3.265n).

20. "something": somewhat.

20. "we": I.

21. "nerves": sinews.

22. "Get . . . of youth": match youth in any contest (a sports metaphor); cp. 3.11.13–15.

23. "Commend": entrust, commit.

24. "Kiss it, my warrior": cp. 3.10.7–8. Scarus says not so much as a word throughout the scene.

26. "in": by using.

27. "all of gold": made entirely of gold.

Antony: He has deserved it, were it carbuncled
Like holy Phoebus' car. Give me thy hand.
Through Alexandria make a jolly march.   **30**
Bear our hacked targets like the men that owe them.
Had our great palace the capacity
To camp this host, we all would sup together
And drink carouses to the next day's fate,
Which promises royal peril. Trumpeters,   **35**
With brazen din blast you the city's ear.
Make mingle with our rattling taborins,
That heaven and earth may strike their sounds together,
Applauding our approach.   *[Trumpets sound.] Exeunt.*

ACT FOUR, SCENE NINE

[Caesar's camp.]

Enter a Sentry and his company. Enobarbus follows.

Sentry: If we be not relieved within this hour,
We must return to th' court of guard. The night

---

28. "carbuncled": covered with fire-red jewels. "Among . . . red gems, carbuncles
. . . have their name [for] . . . their likeness unto fire" (Pliny, 37.92; Holland, 616).

29. "holy Phoebus' car": chariot of Phoebus Apollo, the Roman sun god (see
Ovid, *Metamorphoses*, 2.106–10).

30. "jolly": celebratory.

31. "targets": shields.

31. "owe": own.

31. "like . . . owe them": (1) in the spirited fashion appropriate to the men who
own them, (2) as hacked as the men who own them. The men's hacked shields, like
their wounds, reflect their courage.

33. "camp this host": accommodate this army.

34. "carouses": toasts (which drain the cup).

35. "royal peril": (in addition to hunting and, today, horse racing), warfare is the
sport of kings; see 4.4.17n.

36. "brazen": (1) brass, (2) bold.

37. "taborins": small drums.

38. "That heaven . . . sounds together": so that their mingled sounds may echo back
and forth from earth to heaven.

2 "court of guard": guard house (where the guards muster).

Is shiny, and they say we shall embattle
By th' second hour i'th' morn.

1 Watch: This last day was a shrewd one to's.   **5**

Enobarbus: O, bear me witness, night—

2 Watch: What man is this?

1 Watch: Stand close, and list him.   **[*They stand aside.*]**

Enobarbus: Be witness to me, O thou blessed moon,
When men revolted shall upon record   **10**
Bear hateful memory, poor Enobarbus did
Before thy face repent.

Sentry: Enobarbus?

2 Watch: Peace! Hark further.

Enobarbus: O sovereign mistress of true melancholy,   **15**
The poisonous damp of night disponge upon me,
That life, a very rebel to my will,
May hang no longer on me. Throw my heart
Against the flint and hardness of my fault,

---

3. "shiny": bright (lit by a full moon).

3. "embattle": draw up in battle array.

1–4.: Antony spoke of fighting before sunrise (4.8.3). However, Caesar's sentry expects his forces to take up their positions earlier. Caesar, whose forces had a terrible day in the battle, evidently wants to gain the initiative by marshaling his forces early.

5. "shrewd": difficult, dangerous (with a sense of cursed).

5. "to's": for us.

8. "Stand close": remain concealed.

8. "list": listen to.

10. "revolted": who have broken their allegiance.

10. "upon record": in the historical record (cp. 3.13.47).

15. "O sovereign . . . true melancholy": addressed to the moon. On the moon's causing melancholy, see Burton, 1.2.1.4.

16. "poisonous . . . of night": On the moon—particularly a full moon—dropping dew which suffuses and dissolves flesh, see, for example, Plutarch, *Table-Talk*, 3.10 (658A–59E), *On the Face of the Moon*, 25 (940A); Macrobius, *Saturnalia*, 7.16.31–32.

16. "disponge": discharge, squeeze out (as from a wet sponge).

17. "That": so that.

Which, being dried with grief, will break to powder   **20**
And finish all foul thoughts. O Antony,
Nobler than my revolt is infamous,
Forgive me in thine own particular,
But let the world rank me in register
A master-leaver and a fugitive.   **25**
O Antony! O Antony!   [*He sinks down.*]

1 Watch: Let's speak to him.

Sentry: Let's hear him, for the things he speaks may
concern Caesar.

2 Watch: Let's do so. But he sleeps.   **30**

Sentry: Swoons rather, for so bad a prayer as his was
never yet for sleep.

1 Watch: Go we to him.

2 Watch: Awake, sir, awake! Speak to us.

1 Watch: Hear you, sir?   **35**

Sentry: The hand of death hath raught him.   ***Drums far off.***
          Hark! The drums

---

20. "Which": refers to "my heart."

16–20. "damp . . .with grief ": Enobarbus' wishes of dampness and of dryness do
not collide, as some editors say. They are sequential. The dew produced by the
moon may cause extreme melancholy, and melancholy, which is itself cold and dry,
dries and hardens the heart (Burton, 1.1.2.2).

23. "in thine own particular": Antony, you alone should forgive me.

24. "in register": in the history of men's deeds.

25. "master-leaver": (1) one who abandons his master, (2) the greatest of such
deserters.

25. "fugitive": one who has fled.

9–26.: Like Enobarbus, Cleopatra (twice) speaks of dying foully in a ditch. Both
times, however, although explicitly graveless and consumed by insects, she imagines herself dying in Egypt (3.13.171–72, 5.2.56–59). Neither Enobarbus nor
any other Roman in the play thinks of Rome when he thinks of death. Just
as Enobarbus addresses the "blessed moon" rather than a Roman god, the place
where he dies could be anywhere in the world (cp., for example, *Cor.*, 5.3.172–73).
Universalism has made him, like many other Romans, rootless.

32. "for": just before, preparation for.

36. "raught": reached, siezed.

Demurely wake the sleepers. Let us bear him
To th' court of guard; he is of note. Our hour
Is fully out.

2 Watch: Come on then. He may recover yet. **Exeunt [with body].** 40

ACT FOUR, SCENE TEN

[The battlefield.]

Enter Antony and Scarus, with their army.

Antony: Their preparation is today by sea;
  We please them not by land.

Scarus: For both, my lord.

Antony: I would they'd fight i'th' fire or i'th' air;
  We'd fight there too. But this it is: our foot
  Upon the hills adjoining to the city   5
  Shall stay with us—order for sea is given;
  They have put forth the haven—
  Where their appointment we may best discover
  And look on their endeavor.   **Exeunt.**

---

37. "Demurely": in a subdued or solemn manner.

38. "of note": a person of importance.

38–39. "Our hour . . . out": our time of duty is fully complete.

3–4. "I would . . . there too": Antony wishes to fight in all four elements of nature which compose the world—earth (land), water (sea), air, and fire. His wish, replacing prudent military strategy with cosmic swagger, not only disregards his advantage on land but would again concede the initiative to Caesar.

4. "foot": ground forces.

6. "is": has been.

7. "They": Caesar's ships.

7. "Put forth the haven": set out from the harbor.

8. "appointment": (1) direction, purpose, (2) array of ships.

4–9. Antony's plan is to let the naval forces fight first and, seeing how the sea battle proceeds, keep his infantry where he can use them as circumstances develop. This is the plan that failed at Actium (cp. 3.9.1–4).

ACT FOUR, SCENE ELEVEN

[The battlefield.]

Enter Caesar and his army.

Caesar: But being charged, we will be still by land,
   Which, as I take't, we shall, for his best force
   Is forth to man his galleys. To the vales,
   And hold our best advantage.   ***Exeunt.***

ACT FOUR, SCENE TWELVE

[The battlefield.]

Enter Antony and Scarus.

Antony: Yet they are not joined. Where yond pine does stand,
   I shall discover all. I'll bring thee word
   Straight how 'tis like to go.   ***Exit.***

Alarum afar off, as at a sea fight.

Scarus: Swallows have built
   In Cleopatra's sails their nests. The augurs

---

1. "But being charged": unless we are attacked.

1. "still": quiet.

2. "shall": shall be quiet (remain in a defensive posture).

2. "force": power, strength.

3. "forth": ordered, committed.

2–3. "best force . . . galleys": Antony is using his land troops as sailors, as he had at Actium (cp. 3.7.61–66). Ironically, he is again fighting the sea battle as though it were the land battle that it should have been.

3. "vales": low grounds.

4. "hold . . . advantage": take and maintain our most advantageous positions.

1. "joined": in battle.

3. "Straight": straightaway, immediately.

3. "like": likely.

4. "sails": ships.

3–4. "Swallows . . . nests": an ominous sign, suggesting death, particularly portentous for Isis (see Plutarch, *Isis and Osiris*, 16 [357c]).

Say they know not, they cannot tell, look grimly   5
And dare not speak their knowledge. Antony
Is valiant and dejected, and by starts
His fretted fortunes give him hope and fear
Of what he has and has not.

                    Enter Antony.

Antony: All is lost!
This foul Egyptian hath betrayed me.   10
My fleet hath yielded to the foe, and yonder
They cast their caps up and carouse together
Like friends long lost. Triple-turned whore! 'Tis thou
Hast sold me to this novice, and my heart
Makes only wars on thee. Bid them all fly!   15
For when I am revenged upon my charm,
I have done all. Bid them all fly! Be gone!   [*Exit Scarus.*]
O sun, thy uprise shall I see no more.
Fortune and Antony part here; even here

---

5. "grimly": grim.

4–6. A reflection of the orientalizing of Roman divination, no Roman interprets
the sign favorably, and everyone seems to see it as telling their fate rather than as
testing their decision (see S.D. 2.3.10n).

7. "starts": intermittent bursts.

8. "fretted": (1) various, (2) vexed, (3) worn away.

11–13. As at Actium, Antony loses before the battle even begins. "[Antony stood]
upon the hills adjoining unto the city . . . to behold his galleys which departed
from the haven, and rowed against the galleys of his enemies, and so stood still,
looking what exploit his soldiers in them would do. But when by force of rowing
they were come near unto them, they first saluted Caesar's men, and then Caesar's men re-saluted them also, and of two armies made but one, and then did all
together row toward the city" (Plutarch, *Antony*, 76.1; Spencer, 275–76).

13. "Triple-turned whore": from Gnaeus Pompey to Julius Caesar, from Julius
Caesar to Antony, and now from Antony to Octavius Caesar.

14. "sold": betrayed.

14. "this novice": see 3.11.62n.

15. "only wars on": wars only on.

16. "revenged": avenged.

16. "charm": enchantress, witch.

Do we shake hands. All come to this? The hearts   **20**
That spanieled me at heels, to whom I gave
Their wishes, do discandy, melt their sweets
On blossoming Caesar, and this pine is barked
That overtopped them all. Betrayed I am.
O, this false soul of Egypt! This grave charm,   **25**
Whose eye becked forth my wars and called them home,
Whose bosom was my crownet, my chief end,
Like a right gypsy hath at fast and loose
Beguiled me to the very heart of loss.
What Eros, Eros!

                    Enter Cleopatra.

          Ah, thou spell! Avaunt!   **30**

Cleopatra: Why is my lord enraged against his love?

Antony: Vanish, or I shall give thee thy deserving
          And blemish Caesar's triumph. Let him take thee

19–20. "Fortune . . . shake hands": Fortune and Antony, once enemies (3.11.74–75; 4.4.4–5), now part with mutual respect.

21. "spanieled me at heels": fawned at my heels like spaniels.

22. "discandy": dissolve.

22–23. "melt . . . blossoming Caesar": pour their sweet flattery on Caesar now that his fortune is in bloom.

23. "this pine": Antony himself.

23. "barked": stripped bare (and so destroyed).

25. "grave charm": deadly witch.

26. "becked": beckoned (see 3.11.60–61).

27. "Whose bosom . . . chief end": whose love was the crown and chief end of all my efforts and achievements ("*Finis coronat opus*" ["The end crowns the work"], attributed to Ovid).

28. "right gypsy": true gypsy (see 1.1.10n).

28. "fast and loose": a cheating game, of which Egyptians ("gypsies") were thought to be adept, in which a belt or handkerchief was tied apparently fast in a hard knot but really so that it could be loosened easily (see Reginald Scot, *Discoverie of Witchcraft*, XIII.29 [London, 1584]).

29. "loss": ruin, destruction.

30. "Avaunt": begone (an exclamation of abhorrence, uttered to drive one away).

32–33. "give thee . . . Caesar's triumph": Cleopatra's death would deprive Caesar's triumph of its chief trophy; see 5.1.65–66n.

And hoist thee up to the shouting plebeians!
Follow his chariot, like the greatest spot   **35**
Of all thy sex; most monster-like be shown
For poor'st diminutives, for dolts, and let
Patient Octavia plow thy visage up
With her prepared nails!   [*Exit Cleopatra.*]
               'Tis well thou'art gone,
If it be well to live. But better 'twere   **40**
Thou fell'st into my fury, for one death
Might have prevented many. Eros, ho!
The shirt of Nessus is upon me. Teach me,
Alcides, thou mine ancestor, thy rage.
Let me lodge Lichas on the horns o'th' moon,   **45**
And with those hands that grasped the heaviest club

35–36. "spot Of": blemish on.

37. "poor'st diminutives": most insignificant commoners.

37. "dolts": stupidest commoners.

38. "visage": face.

39. "prepared": sharpened.

31–39. This brief exchange, just nine lines, is the only time Antony and Cleopatra are alone, together, on the stage.

41. "Thou fell'st into": you were killed by.

39–42. "'Tis well . . . prevented many": if life is good, it is good that you have escaped my fury, but it would have been better if I had killed you, for your death might have saved many others from death. This is the only time Antony attempts a formal syllogistic argument. He states a conditional major premise ("If . . . "), a minor premise ("for . . . "), and an affirmative conclusion by way of contraries ("But better . . . "). Antony, a man with an enormous appetite for life, may be not so much threatening Cleopatra as trying to persuade himself to kill himself.

43. "The shirt of Nessus": Hercules fatally shot the centaur Nessus with a poisoned arrow for attempting to rape Hercules' wife, Deianira. Dying, Nessus, seeking revenge, gave Deianira a shirt soaked in his poisoned blood, telling her it was a love charm that would bind Hercules to her forever. Deianira, jealous of a rival, gave the shirt to Lichas to give to Hercules. But when Hercules put it on, he went mad from the burning pain. In his rage, he threw the innocent Lichas into the sea and threatened to kill Deianira for conspiring against him (Ovid, *Metamorphoses*, 9.98–272).

44. "Alcides": Herculus.

44. "thou mine ancestor": see 1.3.85n.

46. "heaviest club": Hercules' favorite weapon (see, for example, Apollodorus, 2.71, 75, 79, 108).

Subdue my worthiest self. The witch shall die.
To the young Roman boy she hath sold me, and I fall
Under this plot. She dies for't. Eros, ho!   *Exit.*

ACT FOUR, SCENE THIRTEEN

[Alexandria. Cleopatra's palace.]

Enter Cleopatra, Charmian, Iras, and Mardian.

Cleopatra: Help me, my women! O, he's more mad
Than Telamon for his shield; the boar of Thessaly
Was never so embossed.

Charmian: To th' monument!
There lock yourself and send him word you are dead.

---

47. "worthiest": noblest.

47. "Subdue my worthiest self": kill myself (like Hercules, too noble to allow himself to be subdued by another). For suicide as noble self-conquest, see 4.14.62–63, 4.15.15–16n, 4.15.59–60n; *JC*, 5.5.55–58.

47. "witch": Cleopatra.

2. "Telamon for his shield": Telamon (Ajax) went mad and killed himself when Achilles' arms were awarded to Odysseus rather than to him, as the bravest of the Greeks at Troy (Homer, *Odyssey*, 11.543ff.).

3. "embossed": frenzied and foaming at the mouth (from exhaustion in running; a hunting term).

2–3. "the boar ... embossed": The ferocious boar of Thessaly, whose eyes glowed with blood and fire, was sent by a vengeful Diana (Artemis), showing that wrath can move even the gods, to ravage the fields of Calydon when its king, Oeneus, neglected to sacrifice to her (Ovid, *Metamorphoses*, 8.267–525); see, further, 2.5.77n.

3. "th' monument": a tomb which Cleopatra has built for herself. "Cleopatra had long before made many sumptuous tombs and monuments, as well for excellency of workmanship as for height and greatness of building, joining hard to the temple of Isis" (Plutarch, *Antony*, 74.1; Spencer, 272).

4. "There lock ... are dead": Unlike in Plutarch (*Antony*, 76.2), Charmian thinks of the plan which sets in motion the events that will lead directly to Antony's death. Much earlier, Cleopatra rejected her advice to give Antony his way in everything (1.3.7–13). Now, she follows it. Her discarding her characteristic contrariness will prove fatal.

The soul and body rive not more in parting   **5**
Than greatness going off.

Cleopatra: To th' monument!
Mardian, go tell him I have slain myself.
Say that the last I spoke was "Antony,"
And word it, prithee, piteously. Hence, Mardian,
And bring me how he takes my death. To th' monument!   **10**
                                                    Exeunt.

ACT FOUR, SCENE FOURTEEN

[Cleopatra's palace. Another room.]

Enter Antony and Eros.

Antony: Eros, thou yet behold'st me?

Eros: Ay, noble lord.

Antony: Sometime we see a cloud that's dragonish,
A vapor sometime like a bear or lion,
A towered citadel, a pendent rock,
A forked mountain, or blue promontory   **5**
With trees upon't that nod unto the world

---

5. "rive": tear apart, split.

6. "going off": suddenly departing. Great men can endure the thought of losing their lives more easily than their greatness (cp. 3.13.99–100).

9. "piteously": such as to arouse pity (to quell his anger).

10. "bring me . . . my death": Cleopatra had suggested that a lover can never know this (1.3.65–66). Now she feigns suicide not only to answer Antony's doubts about her love, but her own doubts about his love. The news is meant both as a testimony of her love and as a test of his. However great their love may be, to the end, neither is ever certain of the other's love.

1. "thou yet behold'st me": can you still see me. Antony imagines that, betrayed by Cleopatra, he has no form or substance, that he is as shapeless on the outside as on the inside.

2. "dragonish": shaped like a dragon.

3. "vapor": mist.

4. "pendent": overhanging, protruding.

And mock our eyes with air. Thou hast seen these signs.
They are black vesper's pageants.

Eros: Ay, my lord.

Antony: That which is now a horse, even with a thought
The rack dislimns and makes it indistinct   **10**
As water is in water.

Eros: It does, my lord.

Antony: My good knave Eros, now thy captain is
Even such a body. Here I am Antony,
Yet cannot hold this visible shape, my knave.
I made these wars for Egypt, and the Queen,   **15**
Whose heart I thought I had, for she had mine—
Which whilst it was mine had annexed unto't
A million more, now lost—she, Eros, has
Packed cards with Caesar and false-played my glory
Unto an enemy's triumph.   **20**
Nay, weep not, gentle Eros. There is left us
Ourselves to end ourselves.

                        Enter Mardian.

                        O, thy vile lady!
She has robbed me of my sword.

---

7. "mock": delude, deceive.

7. "signs": images.

8. "black vesper's pageants": illusory spectacles of sunset heralding the darkness of night.

9. "even with a thought": as quick as a thought.

10. "The rack dislimns": the floating cloud effaces (its image; a "rack" is a mass of clouds moving quickly; to "dislimn" is, literally, to "unpaint" or "unportray").

12. "knave": boy, servant (used here fondly).

13. "Here": here and now, at this moment.

15. "Egypt": Cleopatra.

17. "annexed": added, joined.

18. "A million more": a million more hearts (of my followers).

19. "Packed cards": stacked the deck, made a cheating arrangement (to favor Caesar and herself).

19–20. "false-played . . . triumph": falsely played away my glory until my enemy had won it all. The card-playing term "triumph," of which "trump" is a corruption, means a winning card.

23. "robbed . . . my sword": (1) forced me to surrender, (2) emasculated me.

Mardian: No, Antony,
  My mistress loved thee and her fortunes mingled
  With thine entirely.

Antony: Hence, saucy eunuch! Peace!   **25**
  She hath betrayed me and shall die the death.

Mardian: Death of one person can be paid but once,
  And that she has discharged. What thou wouldst do
  Is done unto thy hand. The last she spake
  Was "Antony, most noble Antony."   **30**
  Then in the midst a tearing groan did break
  The name of Antony; it was divided
  Between her heart and lips. She rendered life
  Thy name so buried in her.

Antony: Dead, then?

Mardian: Dead.

Antony: Unarm, Eros. The long day's task is done,   **35**
  And we must sleep. [*to Mardian*] That thou depart'st hence safe
  Does pay thy labor richly. Go.   **Exit Mardian.**
  Off! Pluck off!   **[*Eros unarms Antony.*]**

---

25. "saucy": insolent.

26. "die the death": solemn legal language for the imposition of capital punishment.

27–28. "Death . . . discharged": Mardian, punning on death/debt, shifts to the language of repayment.

28–29. "What thou . . . hand": what you would do has already been done for you. The eunuch thinks that Antony can get full revenge without himself acting.

29. "spake": spoke.

30. "most noble Antony": Cleopatra has never used the word "noble" in speaking to or about Antony; see 4.15.61n.

31. "tearing": harrowing.

33. "rendered": surrendered.

34. "so": thus.

31–34. "Then . . . in her": in a dying groan, Cleopatra cut the name Antony in two, half-pronounced by her lips and half-retained by her heart. She surrendered her life but buried his name in herself.

35. "Unarm": unarm me.

37. "thy labor": as messenger. Such a message might deserve death.

The sevenfold shield of Ajax cannot keep
The battery from my heart. O, cleave, my sides!   **40**
Heart, once be stronger than thy continent;
Crack thy frail case. Apace, Eros, apace!
No more a soldier. Bruised pieces, go.
You have been nobly borne. From me awhile.   *Exit Eros.*
I will o'ertake thee, Cleopatra, and   **45**
Weep for my pardon. So it must be, for now
All length is torture. Since the torch is out,
Lie down and stray no farther. Now all labor
Mars what it does; yea, very force entangles
Itself with strength. Seal, then, and all is done.   **50**
Eros!—I come, my queen.—Eros!—Stay for me.

---

39. "The sevenfold shield of Ajax": Ajax's huge shield was made of brass, backed by six layers of oxhide (Homer, *Iliad*, 7.219–20; Ovid, *Metamorphoses*, 13.1–2).

39–40. "The sevenfold . . . heart": no protection can keep the grievous news from battering my heart. A "battery" is a military bombardment or other succession of heavy blows.

40. "cleave": split apart.

41. "once": for once.

41. "continent": container.

42. "Apace": quickly.

43. "No": I am no.

43. "Bruised pieces": dented armor.

45. "Cleopatra": Antony had not mentioned her name (in his more than 250 lines) since he denied that it was still her name (3.13.104).

46. "Weep . . . pardon": After Actium, Cleopatra wept for his pardon (3.11.68–71). Now, having doubted her love, Antony concludes, as Cleopatra wished, that her (supposed) death was an act of love for him.

47. "All length": all prolongation (of life).

47. "torch": the life of Cleopatra (for Antony, she is the light of the world).

48. "stray": wander, roam.

48–50. "Now . . . strength": all efforts now are futile; indeed, all strong efforts would only impede themselves by their strength (the image of a strong animal entangling itself in a net by its efforts to escape).

50. "Seal": Affixing a seal is the final act in completing an official document. By killing himself, Antony seals his life and Cleopatra's pardon. "Seal" also alludes to the Day of Judgment: "I heard a voice from Heaven saying unto me, 'Seal up those things which the seven thunders have spoken'" (Rev. 10:4; also 5:1).

Where souls do couch on flowers, we'll hand in hand,
And with our sprightly port make the ghosts gaze.
Dido and her Aeneas shall want troops,
And all the haunt be ours. Come, Eros, Eros!   **55**

Enter Eros.

Eros: What would my lord?

Antony: Since Cleopatra died
I have lived in such dishonor that the gods
Detest my baseness. I, that with my sword
Quartered the world and o'er green Neptune's back
With ships made cities, condemn myself to lack   **60**
The courage of a woman; less noble mind
Than she which, by her death, our Caesar tells
"I am conqueror of myself." Thou art sworn, Eros,

---

52. "couch": recline (in the Elysian fields, the abode of the blessed, where the noble are rewarded with an immortality of bliss (Homer, *Odyssey*, 4.563–69; Virgil, *Aeneid*, 6.637–67).

52. "we'll": we will go.

53. "sprightly port": lively (also ghostly) bearing.

54. "want troops": lack admirers.

55. "haunt": (1) a place much frequented, (2) a play on "ghosts" (line 53).

55. "all . . . ours": we shall be the only pair of lovers that all the ghosts throng to behold (cp. 1.1.37–41n).

54–55. Antony reverses the unhappy story of Dido and Aeneas in Hades. Dido's ghost refuses not only to answer but even to look at Aeneas when he greets her there. As she wept for him (and killed herself) when he abandoned her in Carthage to sail for Italy and found Rome, he weeps for her as she leaves him behind in Hades (Virgil, *Aeneid*, 6.450ff.).

57. "in such dishonor": for my cowardice in having outlived her.

59. "Quartered": divided and conquered.

59. "green Neptune's back": the sea (Neptune is the Roman god of the sea).

60. "With ships made cities": assembled fleets so with ships so large they appeared to be cities (see Florus, *Epitome of Roman History*, 2.21.5).

60. "to lack": for lacking.

61. "less noble mind": for having a less noble mind.

62. "which": who.

58–63. "I, that . . . of myself'": "I am sorry that, having been so great a Captain and Emperor, I am indeed condemned to be judged of less courage and noble mind than a woman" (Plutarch, *Antony*, 76.3; Spencer, 277).

That when the exigent should come, which now
Is come indeed, when I should see behind me   65
Th' inevitable prosecution of
Disgrace and horror, that on my command
Thou then wouldst kill me. Do't. The time is come.
Thou strik'st not me; 'tis Caesar thou defeat'st.
Put color in thy cheek.

Eros: The gods withhold me!   70
Shall I do that which all the Parthian darts,
Though enemy, lost aim and could not?

Antony: Eros,
Wouldst thou be windowed in great Rome and see
Thy master thus with pleached arms, bending down
His corrigible neck, his face subdued   75
To penetrative shame, whilst the wheeled seat
Of fortunate Caesar, drawn before him, branded
His baseness that ensued?

---

64. "exigent": exigency, compelling need.

66. "inevitable prosecution": inescapable pursuit.

69. "'tis Caesar thou defeat'st": you thwart Caesar's plan to parade me in his triumph.

70. "Put color . . . cheek": pluck up courage.

70. "withhold": forbid, prevent.

72. "enemy": hostile (an adjective).

71–72. "Parthian darts . . . could not": Eros' protest is Shakespeare's only explicit indication that Antony himself fought against the Parthians. Unlike Ventidius' campaign, for which Antony won credit (3.1.9–27), Antony's ended in disaster (Plutarch, *Antony*, 37–52). Eros, Antony's most loyal officer, may collapse the distinction between who won the victory and who won credit for the victory. In his eyes, Ventidius' victory may truly have been Antony's, his master. On Parthian darts, see 3.1.1n.

73. "windowed": placed in a window.

74–75. "pleached arms . . . corrigible neck": folded arms and bowed neck (the posture of a submissive captive).

76. "penetrative": deep, penetrating.

76. "wheeled seat": chariot.

77–78. "branded . . . that ensued": made conspicuous the baseness of him who followed his chariot. The vanquished, in fact, preceded the victor in a Roman triumph (see Plutarch, *Aemilius Paulus*, 33.3–34.2).

72–78. While shame seeks concealment (see 3.11.51–54n), Caesar would shame Antony publicly before all of Rome. Antony's shame would be literally

Eros: I would not see't.

Antony: Come, then! For with a wound I must be cured.
Draw that thy honest sword, which thou hast worn   **80**
Most useful for thy country.

Eros: O, sir, pardon me!

Antony: When I did make thee free, swor'st thou not then
To do this when I bade thee? Do it at once,
Or thy precedent services are all
But accidents unpurposed. Draw, and come!   **85**

Eros: Turn from me then that noble countenance
Wherein the worship of the whole world lies.

Antony: [*Turns from him.*] Lo thee!

"penetrative." Because it would be seen by everyone, it would penetrate to the core of his soul. Nothing could disgrace him more. Just as celebrating a Roman triumph is a Roman's greatest glory, being led prisoner in a Roman triumph would be the greatest shame. On Romans suffering this indignity, see, further, 4.6.2n.

79. "with a wound . . . cured": To kill oneself by one's sword is a suicide appropriate to a Roman soldier (Martial, *Epigrams*, 1.78.7). And such a dignified death will heal Antony. It will not only forestall his shame, but display his noble courage.

80. "that . . . sword": that honorable sword of yours.

81. "useful": usefully, beneficially.

80–81. "thou . . . thy country": This is the first time anyone has mentioned the word "country." Since the wars of Marius and Sulla (early first century), Roman commanders have granted Roman citizenship along with freedom to slaves they have conscripted into their private armies (see 3.13.154n; also, for example, Suetonius, *Caesar*, 24.2). Eros, a freedman with a Greek name, has consequently come to think not so much of Rome as of Antony's domain as his country.

81. "pardon me": release me (from my sworn oath).

84. "precedent": previous.

85. "accidents unpurposed": unintended actions (none would show his loyalty to Antony).

86–87. "that noble . . . lies": that noble face in which is to be found all that the world reveres. For the Romans, the face is more than a facade, more than the front of the head. "The face is the image of the soul" (Cicero, *Orator*, 18.60). Mirroring the heart of the man himself, the face (*facies*) is not something a man is born with, but something the man himself makes (*facture*; Gellius, 13.30.2). It is at once the surface and the depth manifested by the surface.

88. "Lo thee": look, see (an interjection used to direct attention to something about to be said or done).

Eros: My sword is drawn.

Antony: Then let it do at once
   The thing why thou hast drawn it.

Eros: My dear master,   **90**
   My captain, and my emperor, let me say,
   Before I strike this bloody stroke, farewell.

Antony: 'Tis said, man, and farewell.

Eros: Farewell, great chief. Shall I strike now?

Antony: Now, Eros.

Eros: Why, there, then!   ***Kills himself.***
                    Thus I do escape the sorrow   **95**
   Of Antony's death.

Antony: Thrice nobler than myself,
   Thou teachest me, O valiant Eros, what
   I should and thou couldst not. My queen and Eros
   Have by their brave instruction got upon me
   A nobleness in record. But I will be   **100**
   A bridegroom in my death and run into't
   As to a lover's bed. Come then, and, Eros,

---

90. "why": for which.

98. "I should . . . couldst not": I should do and you could not do (kill me).

99. "brave instruction": brave deed, courageous example. Where Greeks learn
by noble precepts, Romans learn by noble examples (Quintilian, 12.2.30): "[B]y
example of himself . . . others he shall bind" (Ovid, *Metamorphoses*, 15.832; Golding,
15.938). See 3.11.7–8, 4.14.103–4, and 5.1.76–77n.

99–100. "got . . . in record": gained an advantage over me in winning a noble place
in history.

102. "As": as if.

100–102. "But I . . . lover's bed": Antony will lovingly pursue death, for dying is a
necessary condition to be with his love. In this speech as well as in the exchange that
follows (lines 105–11), the speakers repeatedly allude to the new heaven of Christianity: "Let us be glad and rejoice, and give glory to him; for the marriage of the Lamb
is come, and his wife hath made herself ready" (Rev. 19:7). "And I, John, saw the holy
city, new Jerusalem, . . . prepared as a bride trimmed for her husband" (Rev. 21:2). For
Jesus as the bridegroom who will marry the church, see, further, Matt. 9:15, 2 Cor.
11:2, John 3:29, Ephesians 5:25–32, Rev. 21:9, 17. On the new heaven, see 1.1.17n.

102. "Come": "And the Spirit and the bride say, 'Come.' And let him that heareth
say, "Come': and let him that is thirsty come" (Rev. 22:17).

Thy master dies thy scholar. To do thus

[*Falls on his sword.*]

I learned of thee. How, not dead? Not dead?
The guard, ho! O, dispatch me!

Enter a [company of the] Guard [, one of them Dercetus].

1 Guard: What's the noise?   **105**

Antony: I have done my work ill, friends. O, make an end
Of what I have begun!

2 Guard: The star is fall'n.

1 Guard: And time is at his period.

All: Alas, and woe!

Antony: Let him that loves me strike me dead.

1 Guard: Not I!

2 Guard: Nor I!   **110**

3 Guard: Nor anyone!   *Exeunt [all the guards but Dercetus].*

Dercetus: Thy death and fortunes bid thy followers fly.

---

103. "scholar": student, pupil. Antony, in what he supposes are his dying words, intends a paradoxical inversion as a tribute: the high and the low—lord and teacher, slave and student—trade places.

104. "of": from.

105. "What's the noise": "And I heard like a voice of great multitude, and as the voice of many waters, and as the voice of strong thunderings" (Rev. 19.6).

107. "The star is fall'n": "And the stars of heaven fell unto the earth"; "[A]nd there fell a great star from heaven"; "And the fifth Angel blew the trumpet, and I saw a star fall from heaven unto the earth" (Rev. 6:13, 8:10, 9:1).

108. "And time ... period": time is at its end. "And [he] swore ... that time should be no more" (Rev. 10:6).

108. "Alas, and woe": "Woe, woe, woe to the inhabitants of the earth" (Rev. 8:13).

109. "Let him ... me dead": "[I]n those days shall men seek death, and shall not find it, and shall desire to die, and death shall flee from them" (Rev. 9:6).

112. "Thy death ... fly": Dercetus, who (twice) addresses Antony by the informal pronoun "thy," seems to be one of his many subordinates whom he allowed to be informal with him (see 1.2.183n) and one of the many who are eager to win Caesar's favor. Nothing is known of him other than Plutarch's brief account of this episode (Plutarch, *Antony*, 78.1).

This sword but shown to Caesar with this tidings
Shall enter me with him.   [*Takes up Antony's sword.*]
                         Enter Diomedes.

Diomedes: Where's Antony?   **115**

Dercetus: There, Diomed, there.

Diomede: Lives he? Wilt thou not answer, man?

                    [*Exit Dercetus with Antony's sword.*]

Antony: Art thou there, Diomed? Draw thy sword, and give me
     Sufficing strokes for death.

Diomedes: Most absolute lord,
     My mistress Cleopatra sent me to thee.   **120**

Antony: When did she send thee?

Diomedes: Now, my lord.

Antony: Where is she?

Diomedes: Locked in her monument. She had a prophesying fear
     Of what hath come to pass. For when she saw—
     Which never shall be found—you did suspect
     She had disposed with Caesar, and that your rage   **125**
     Would not be purged, she sent you word she was dead;
     But fearing since how it might work, hath sent
     Me to proclaim the truth, and I am come,
     I dread, too late.

---

113. "this": these.

114. "Shall enter . . . him": win his favor, admit me to his service. Dercetus not only betrays and plunders Antony, but symbolically emasculates him. For the importance of the sword to Antony, see 1.3.83; 3.11.67; 3.13.27, 180; 4.14.23, 58–59; also 1.3.101, 2.5.23.

121. "Now": just now.

124. "found": found true of her.

125. "disposed": come to terms.

125–26. "your rage . . . be purged": your insane fury would not be removed (an image of the process of medical phlebotomy; see 1.3.54–55n).

127. "how . . . work": what effect it might have.

128. "truth": a word we have not heard from Cleopatra's own mouth and one she will use only to deceive Caesar (5.2.143). For her single use of "true," see 1.3.28.

Antony: Too late, good Diomed. Call my guard, I prithee. **130**

Diomedes: What ho! The Emperor's guard! The guard, what ho!
Come, your lord calls!

Enter four or five of the Guard of Antony.

Antony: Bear me, good friends, where Cleopatra bides.
'Tis the last service that I shall command you.

1 Guard: Woe, woe are we, sir, you may not live to wear **135**
All your true followers out.

All: Most heavy day!

Antony: Nay, good my fellows, do not please sharp fate
To grace it with your sorrows. Bid that welcome
Which comes to punish us, and we punish it,
Seeming to bear it lightly. Take me up. **140**
I have led you oft; carry me now, good friends,
And have my thanks for all.

Exeunt, bearing Antony [and Eros].

ACT FOUR, SCENE FIFTEEN

[Alexandria. A monument.]

Enter Cleopatra and her maids aloft, with Charmian and Iras.

Cleopatra: O Charmian, I will never go from hence.

---

133. "bides": waits, is to be found.

135–36. "live to wear . . . out": outlive all of your faithful followers (a statement of remorse).

136. "heavy": sorrowful.

138. "To grace it": by honoring or satisfying it (infinitive used as a gerund [Abbott, §356]).

137–38. "do not please . . . sorrows": to deny sorrow is to defy fate.

138–40. "Bid . . . bear it lightly": by welcoming it, we can do to fate ("punish it") what fate has come to us to do ("punish us"). We can rise above our suffering by accepting it. Unable to overcome Fortune by noble action, Antony is reduced to speaking like a Stoic (cp. 3.11.74–75). For the Stoic attitude, see, for example, Seneca, *On the Happy Life*, 4.2.

S.D. 1. "*aloft*": on the upper stage (representing the monument).

Charmian: Be comforted, dear madam.

Cleopatra: No, I will not.
All strange and terrible events are welcome,
But comforts we despise. Our size of sorrow,
Proportioned to our cause, must be as great   5
As that which makes it.

Enter Diomedes [below].

How now? Is he dead?

Diomedes: His death's upon him, but not dead.
Look out o'th' other side your monument.
His guard have brought him thither.

Enter Antony [below, borne by] the Guard.

Cleopatra: O sun,   10
Burn the great sphere thou mov'st in! Darkling stand
The varying shore o'th' world! O Antony, Antony,
Antony! Help, Charmian! Help, Iras, help!
Help, friends below! Let's draw him hither.

Antony: Peace!
Not Caesar's valor hath o'erthrown Antony,   15

4–5. "we . . . our": the royal "we."

3–6. "All strange . . . makes it": In contrast to Antony, Cleopatra denies that death can be defeated by accepting it. Greatness is revealed not by Stoic indifference to death, but by the heroic greatness of one's sorrow. While small things like comforts are to be despised, grief must be as great as its cause—in this instance, the loss of Antony.

10–11. "O sun . . . mov'st in": According to Ptolemaic astronomy, the sun, like the planets, is set in a hollow sphere which revolves around the earth; see 2.7.14–16n.

11. "Darkling stand": in darkness remain.

12. "varying . . . world": the alternation of night and day. If the sun were to burn its sphere, it would wander aimlessly, leaving the world in darkness, without the diurnal alternation of night and day. Cleopatra echoes Revelation's description of the Apocalypse: "And the fourth Angel blew the trumpet, and the third part of the sun was smitten, and the third part of the moon, and the third part of the stars, so that the third part of them was darkened: and the day was smitten, that the third part of it could not shine, and likewise the night" (Rev. 8:12; also 6:12).

But Antony's hath triumphed on itself.

Cleopatra: So it should be that none but Antony
   Should conquer Antony, but woe 'tis so.

Antony: I am dying, Egypt, dying. Only
   I here importune death awhile until   **20**
   Of many thousand kisses the poor last
   I lay upon thy lips.

Cleopatra: I dare not, dear,
   Dear my lord, pardon, I dare not,
   Lest I be taken. Not th'imperious show
   Of the full-fortuned Caesar ever shall   **25**
   Be brooched with me; if knife, drugs, serpents have
   Edge, sting, or operation, I am safe.
   Your wife Octavia, with her modest eyes
   And still conclusion, shall acquire no honor
   Demuring upon me. But come, come, Antony.—   **30**
   Help me, my women! We must draw thee up.
   Assist, good friends!   *[They begin lifting.]*

15–16. "Not Caesar's . . . on itself": Antony's death is not Caesar's triumph, but
his own. Showing that he values honor more than life and has the valor to face
death fearlessly, it is an honorable Roman death; see lines 59–60n. Antony echoes
Ovid's Ajax:" [N]one may Ajax overcome save Ajax" (Ovid, *Metamorphoses*, 13.390;
Golding, 13.472).

17–18. "So it should . . . 'tis so": Cleopatra seconds (and qualifies) Antony's thought
with an elaborate use of rhetorical figures of repetition: *chiasmus, conduplicatio, antis-*
tasis, epanalepsis, ploce, antithesis, and rhyme (see Cicero, *Orator*, 135). She also brings
out more clearly that Antony is the conquered as well as the conqueror.

20. "importune death": beg death to delay.

22. "dare not": dare not come down to you.

24. "th'imperious show": the imperial triumphal procession.

26. "brooched": adorned (as with a broach).

28–29. "modest eyes . . . conclusion": chaste eyes and silent judgment. Antony
warned of Octavia's cutting nails, but Cleopatra fears more her silent judgment—
her loss of face more than the mutilation of her face (see, further, 5.2.53–54).

30. "Demuring": looking with an air of modesty. Cleopatra considers Octavia as
self-righteous and moralistic.

31. "draw thee up": This and her next several lines, all bleakly ironic, bitterly and
piteously echo Cleopatra's much earlier happy pursuits; cp. 2.5.13, 18.

Antony: O, quick, or I am gone!

Cleopatra: Here's sport indeed. How heavy weighs my lord!
     Our strength is all gone into heaviness;
     That makes the weight. Had I great Juno's power,   **35**
     The strong-winged Mercury should fetch thee up
     And set thee by Jove's side. Yet come a little.
     Wishers were ever fools. O, come, come, come!

          They heave Antony aloft to Cleopatra.

     And welcome, welcome! Die when thou hast lived;
     Quicken with kissing. Had my lips that power,   **40**
     Thus would I wear them out.   *[She kisses him.]*

All the Guard: A heavy sight!

Antony: I am dying, Egypt, dying.
     Give me some wine, and let me speak a little.

Cleopatra: No, let me speak, and let me rail so high   **45**

---

33. "sport": entertainment; cp. 1.1.48.

34. "heaviness": (1) weight, (2) sorrow; cp. 1.5.22.

35. Juno is queen of the gods; see 3.11.28n.

36. Mercury is the winged messenger of the gods.

35–37. "Had I . . . Jove's side": Cleopatra alludes to Hercules' apotheosis. "When [Hercules' divine part] is rid from earthly dross, then I will lift it higher, / And take it into heaven" (Ovid, *Metamorphoses*, 9.268–70; Golding, 9.305–6; quoting Jove). Hercules was the son of Jove (Jupiter) and the mortal Alcmene. Juno, Jove's wife, was Hercules' bitter enemy out of jealous anger at his mother and ordered him to perform his famous labors. In order to escape his unbearable pain after his wife, Deianira, accidently poisoned him (see 4.12.43n), Hercules chose to be placed on a pyre. The flames consumed his mortal half, but his divine half ascended to heaven, where he was reconciled to Juno (Ovid, *Metamorphoses*, 9.98–272).

38. "Wishers . . . fools": referring to her impossible wish to have Juno's power.

39. "when": after.

40. "Quicken": revive, return to life.

42. "heavy": sorrowful.

45. "high": loudly, strongly, violently.

That the false huswife Fortune break her wheel,
Provoked by my offense—

Antony: One word, sweet queen:
Of Caesar seek your honor with your safety. Oh!

Cleopatra: They do not go together.

Antony: Gentle, hear me.
None about Caesar trust but Proculeius.   **50**

Cleopatra: My resolution and my hands I'll trust,
None about Caesar.

Antony: The miserable change now at my end
Lament nor sorrow at, but please your thoughts
In feeding them with those my former fortunes   **55**
Wherein I lived the greatest prince o'th' world,
The noblest, and do now not basely die,
Not cowardly put off my helmet to

---

46. "huswife": (1) housewife, (2) hussy (an opprobrious epithet implying faithlessness).

46. "Fortune": the goddess Fortune (who shows her power by showing her inconstancy). For Fortune as a faithless woman, see Machiavelli, *Prince*, 25.

46. "break": may break.

46. "her wheel": (1) the spinning wheel used by a housewife, (2) the wheel on which people's fortunes rise and fall.

45–47. "let me . . . my offense": Cleopatra's offensive language must be strong enough to enrage Fortune, who (unable to punish Cleopatra more than she already has, but looking for an object to punish) would turn her anger against her own wheel. That Cleopatra speaks in the optative imperative ("[L]et me rail so high / That . . . ") stresses her futility.

48. "Of": from.

48. "your": Antony shifts to the formal pronoun (while thinking chiefly of protecting her life and is silent about her being paraded in Rome).

49. "They": her honor and her safety.

49. "Gentle": noble one.

50. "Proculeius": Antony will prove to be mistaken. The disingenuous Proculeius will trap Cleopatra for Caesar (5.1.61–68, 5.2.9–69). On Proculeius, see 5.1.60n.

52. "None": but no one.

54. "Lament": neither lament.

58. "put off my helmet": take off my helmet (a Roman sign of surrender, like our raising a white flag).

My countryman—a Roman by a Roman
Valiantly vanquished. Now my spirit is going;   **60**
I can no more.

Cleopatra: Noblest of men, woo't die?
Hast thou no care of me? Shall I abide
In this dull world, which in thy absence is
No better than a sty? O see, my women,
The crown o'th' earth doth melt. My lord!   **65**

[*Antony dies.*]

O, withered is the garland of the war;
The soldier's pole is fall'n; young boys and girls

59–60. "a Roman . . . Valiantly vanquished": Having vanquished himself, he demonstrates Roman virtue, both as vanquished, by bravely enduring his bloody death, and as victor, by proudly inflicting it. This is the only time Antony uses the word "Roman" as distinguishing a noble action.

61. "no more": Having lived a life of extravagant excess, Antony dies with not only the word "more," but the phrase "no more," on his lips. His endless appetite for more comes to an end only when he is no more. Antony's final words, speaking against themselves, at once epitomize and contradict his life.

61. "Noblest of men": This is the first time Cleopatra calls Antony "noble." Just as she calls him "[m]y Antony" only in his absence (1.5.6, 40), she calls him noble only when he lies on the verge of death.

61. "woo't": wilt thou (see 4.2.7n).

64. "sty": pigsty.

61–64. a series of rhetorical questions (expressing indignation); see 1.3.21n.

66. "garland of war": the wreath used to crown the victor in a war. Various garlands, crowns, and wreaths made of gold and leaves are "the most glorious reward that can be bestowed on military virtue" (Pliny, 16.7).

67. "soldier's pole": the soldier's standard. The standard (or ensign) is at once a long shaft, usually suspending a banner, with an eagle at the top and a spike at the bottom so it can be set firmly in the ground, and the man who holds it and leads a company in battle. The standard was originally devised by Romulus and is emblazoned with an eagle of silver or gold (Plutarch, *Romulus*, 8.6). From the start, it has been sacrosanct and revered (Dio, 40.18). Wars and battles have been fought to recoup captured standards. Antony began his campaign against the Parthians in 36 by demanding the return of the standards that Crassus had lost seventeen years earlier (Plutarch, *Antony*, 37.2), and Octavius Caesar will finally gain their return in 20 (Suetonius, *Augustus*, 21.3).

Are level now with men. The odds is gone,
And there is nothing left remarkable
Beneath the visiting moon.   **[*She faints.*]**

Charmian: O, quietness, lady!   **70**

Iras: She's dead, too, our sovereign.

Charmian: Lady!

Iras: Madam!

Charmian: O madam, madam, madam!

Iras: Royal Egypt! Empress!   **[*Cleopatra stirs.*]**   **75**

Charmian: Peace, peace, Iras.

Cleopatra: No more but e'en a woman, and commanded
     By such poor passion as the maid that milks
     And does the meanest chares. It were for me
     To throw my scepter at the injurious gods,   **80**
     To tell them that this world did equal theirs
     Till they had stolen our jewel. All's but naught.
     Patience is sottish, and impatience does

---

68. "level": equal.

68. "odds": difference (between high and low, great and ordinary).

69. "remarkable": wonderful, extraordinary (a stronger word than in current usage).

70. "visiting": returning in regular phases.

70. "quietness": perhaps (1) urging her to be calm, or (2) seeing her beginning to faint.

77. "No more . . . woman": no longer an empress but just a woman (a reply to Iras at line 75).

77–78. "commanded . . . passion": overcome by such grief.

79. "chares": petty domestic tasks, chores.

79. "were": would be fitting.

80. "injurious": unjustly hostile, willfully harmful.

81–82. "this world . . . our jewel": Antony made the human world rival that of the gods, but the gods punished him jealously for the rivalry (for such divine jealousy, see, for example, Herodotus, 1.34; 3.40; Livy, 5.21.15; Plutarch, *Camillus*, 5.5–7; also 5.2.284–86).

82. "All's but naught": all is worthless, there is no longer any glory in the world (see Augustine, 5.14).

83. "sottish": foolish, stupid.

Become a dog that's mad. Then is it sin
To rush into the secret house of death   **85**
Ere death dare come to us? How do you, women?
What, what, good cheer! Why, how now, Charmian?
My noble girls! Ah, women, women! Look,
Our lamp is spent; it's out. Good sirs, take heart.
We'll bury him; and then, what's brave, what's noble,   **90**
Let's do't after the high Roman fashion
And make death proud to take us. Come, away.
This case of that huge spirit now is cold.
Ah women, women! Come, we have no friend
But resolution and the briefest end.   **95**

Exeunt, bearing off Antony's body.

83–84. "does Become": suits, is characteristic of.

84–86. "Then is it . . . come to us": In a moment, Cleopatra will speak of committing suicide in "the high Roman fashion" (line 91). Here, she poses the question of suicide in a Christian way. While asking whether suicide is a "sin"—the only mention of "sin" in the play—she is silent about honor or shame. On the "sin" of suicide, see Augustine, 1.17, 20, 27.

89. "Our lamp . . . it's out": "And the foolish said to the wife, 'Give us of your oil, for our lamps are out'" (Matt. 25:8).

89. "sirs": sometimes used in addressing women, though here Cleopatra wants the women to act like Roman men.

90. "brave": courageous, splendid.

91. "high Roman fashion": as a noble act in the face of humiliating defeat.

93. "case": body (container).

95. "briefest": swiftest.

ACT FIVE, SCENE ONE

[Alexandria. Caesar's camp.]

Enter Caesar Agrippa, Dolabella, Maecenas, [Gallus, Proculeius, and others], his council of war.

Caesar: Go to him, Dolabella, bid him yield.
Being so frustrate, tell him, he mocks
The pauses that he makes.

Dolabella: Caesar, I shall.   [*Exit.*]

Enter Dercetus with the sword of Antony.

Caesar: Wherefore is that? And what art thou that dar'st
Appear thus to us?

Dercetus: I am called Dercetus.   5
Mark Antony I served, who best was worthy
Best to be served. Whilst he stood up and spoke,
He was my master, and I wore my life
To spend upon his haters. If thou please
To take me to thee, as I was to him   10
I'll be to Caesar; if thou pleasest not,
I yield thee up my life.

---

2. "frustrate": frustrated, baffled.

2–3. "mocks . . . he makes": hesitating to surrender makes him look ridiculous.

3. "I shall": see 1.2.204n.

4. "Wherefore is that": why are you displaying that sword.

4. "what": who.

5. "thus": unannounced, without an escort, and with a bloody, uncovered sword in hand.

5. "us": the royal "we."

4–5. "Wherefore . . . Appear thus to us": "The death of Caesar was ever before his eyes" (Gibbon, 1:63); see, for example, Suetonius, *Augustus*, 35.1–2.

8. "wore": employed (the image suggests that his devoted service can be changed like a suit of clothes).

9. "spend": expend.

9–12. "If thou please . . . my life": Although just rebuffed by Caesar's use of the royal pronoun "us," Dercetus addresses him four times in as many lines with the familiar pronoun "thou"; see, further, 4.14.112n.

Caesar: What is't thou say'st?

Dercetus: I say, O Caesar, Antony is dead.

Caesar: The breaking of so great a thing should make
    A greater crack. The round world   15
    Should have shook lions into civil streets
    And citizens to their dens. The death of Antony
    Is not a single doom; in the name lay
    A moiety of the world.

Dercetus: He is dead, Caesar,
    Not by a public minister of justice,   20
    Nor by a hired knife, but that self hand
    Which writ his honor in the acts it did
    Hath, with the courage which the heart did lend it,
    Splitted the heart. This is his sword.
    I robbed his wound of it. Behold it stained   25
    With his most noble blood.

Caesar: Look you, sad friends,
    The gods rebuke me, but it is tidings
    To wash the eyes of kings.

Agrippa: And strange it is
    That nature must compel us to lament

---

14. "breaking": (1) destruction, (2) disclosure, report.

15. "crack": (1) thunderous sound (as in "crack of doom"; cp. line 18), (2) deep break.

16. "civil": city (also civilized).

16–17. "lions . . . to their dens": see Jeremiah 4:7.

18. "not a single doom": not one person's death (but the crack of doom, the Last Judgment).

19. "moiety": half.

21. "hired knife": hired assassin.

21. "self": same.

26. "Look you, sad friends": The Folio places a comma only at the end of the line. Some editors insert one after "you," as here, others after "sad." Editors often end the line with a question mark.

27. "The": may the.

27. "but it is": if it is not.

Our most persisted deeds.

Maecenas: His taints and honors 30
Waged equal with him.

Agrippa: A rarer spirit never
Did steer humanity, but you gods will give us
Some faults to make us men. Caesar is touched.

Maecenas: When such a spacious mirror's set before him,
He needs must see himself.

Caesar: O Antony, 35
I have followed thee to this, but we do launch
Diseases in our bodies. I must perforce
Have shown to thee such a declining day
Or look on thine. We could not stall together

---

30. "Our most persisted deeds": outcomes we have worked most persistently to achieve.

28–30. In accordance with post-Alexandrian sensibility, the victor weeps over the vanquished for fear that he, too, will one day meet a similar end. Such tears are meant to show the victor's regard for the power of Fortune in human affairs (see 3.2.55–58n). But where in Plutarch Caesar retires into his tent and weeps privately for Antony (Plutarch, *Antony*, 78.2), in Shakespeare he openly displays his tears to the men around him. He seems intent to exhibit his decorous restraint at the moment of the greatest triumph. Rather than exult in his pleasure, he publicly mourns.

31. "Waged equal with": were equally matched in.

32. "steer humanity": guide any person.

32–33. "you gods . . . make us men": you gods insist on giving us faults to keep us human (cp. 4.15.81–82n).

34. "spacious": large, ample.

36. "followed . . . this": pursued you to this end.

36. "launch": lance, cut out (a surgical term).

37. "perforce": necessarily.

38. "shown": exhibited (in my own downfall).

38. "declining": sinking, failing.

39. "look": looked.

39. "stall": dwell.

In the whole world. But yet let me lament   40
With tears as sovereign as the blood of hearts
That thou my brother, my competitor
In top of all design, my mate in empire,
Friend and companion in the front of war,
The arm of mine own body, and the heart   45
Where mine his thoughts did kindle, that our stars
Unreconciliable should divide
Our equalness to this. Hear me, good friends—

Enter an Egyptian.

But I will tell you at some meeter season.

37–40. "I must . . . whole world": one imperial rival must have killed the other or would have been killed by him. Republican Rome had frequent turnover in office. As consuls were elected for just one year, honor did not rest long with any man. "Rome" always had "room enough" for "more than . . . one man" (*JC*, 1.2.151–56). But with the end of the Republic, the battle is for sole rule of Rome, and the winner must eliminate all rivals. Thus the whole world is not large enough for both Caesar and Antony, as Octavia feared and Enobarbus foresaw (3.4.30–32, 3.5.13–15). The larger Rome became, the less room it had for more than one man.

41. "sovereign": supremely efficacious or potent (medical terminology, as in "a sovereign remedy").

42. "competitor": (1) partner, (2) rival.

43. "In top . . . design": in the loftiest of all enterprises.

44. "front": front line, face.

46. "his": its.

45–46. "the heart . . . kindle": Antony's heart inflamed my thoughts of courage.

47–48. "should divide . . . to this": should have torn apart our equal partnership to this extent (namely, to Antony's death).

35–48. Caesar begins the speech by justifying Antony's death as a political necessity, but ends it by blaming the stars for dividing them. Not their ambitions, but their stars, were irreconcilable. Evidently thinking about his reputation in history, Caesar seeks not only to avoid moral blame but to elevate himself above political exigencies. As he presents himself, always moderate and just, he was in no way responsible for the grievous wars or their lamentable outcome; see, further, lines 76–77n. On the difficulty of writing history under the Caesars, see Tacitus, *Histories*, 1.1; Dio, 53.19.

49. "meeter season": more appropriate time.

The business of this man looks out of him. **50**
We'll hear him what he says.—Whence are you?

Egyptian: A poor Egyptian yet, the Queen my mistress,
Confined in all she has, her monument,
Of thy intents desires instruction,
That she preparedly may frame herself **55**
To th' way she's forced to.

Caesar: Bid her have good heart.
She soon shall know of us, by some of ours,
How honorable and how kindly we
Determine for her. For Caesar cannot live
To be ungentle.

Egyptian: So the gods preserve thee! ***Exit.*** **60**

Caesar: Come hither, Proculeius. Go and say
We purpose her no shame. Give her what comforts
The quality of her passion shall require,
Lest, in her greatness, by some mortal stroke
She do defeat us, for her life in Rome **65**
Would be eternal in our triumph. Go,

---

50. "The business . . . of him": the urgency of his business shows itself in his eyes and expression.

52. "A poor Egyptian yet": The Folio's comma after "yet" allows the phrase to refer to Cleopatra, though it may refer to the Egyptian himself. Some editors substitute a period for the comma, excluding the possible reference to Cleopatra.

53. "her": which is her.

55. "preparedly . . . herself": may prepare to adapt her course of action.

57. "ours": my people.

58. "honorable": honorably.

59. "live": The Folio reads "leave," which might mean "stop being himself so as to become ungentle."

60. "So": thus may.

61. Proculeius (Gaius Proculeius) is an intimate friend of Caesar, who at one time considered making him his son-in-law. He is also Maecenas' brother-in-law. He fought for Caesar against Sextus Pompey in Sicily and against Antony in Egypt (Tacitus, *Annals*, 4.40.6; Dio, 54.5).

63. "quality of her passion": nature of her passionate grief.

65–66. "her life . . . our triumph": to exhibit Cleopatra alive in Rome in my triumphal procession would give my triumph eternal fame (Plutarch, *Antony*, 78.3).

And with your speediest bring us what she says
And how you find of her.

Proculeius: Caesar, I shall.

Caesar: Gallus, go you along.   *Exeunt Proculeius [and Gallus].*
                              Where's Dolabella,
To second Proculeius?

All but Caesar: Dolabella!   70

Caesar: Let him alone, for I remember now
How he's employed. He shall in time be ready.
Go with me to my tent, where you shall see
How hardly I was drawn into this war,
How calm and gentle I proceeded still   75
In all my writings. Go with me and see
What I can show in this.   *Exeunt.*

67."with your speediest": as speedily as you can.

68."how you find of her": what you find out about her.

69. Gallus (Cornelius Gallus [c. 70–27/26]) is a soldier and distinguished poet.
He is a friend of Caesar, Virgil, and Pollio. Commonly regarded as love elegy's
founder, he is ranked by Quintilian, along with Ovid, Propertius, and Tibullus,
as one of Rome's four great elegiac poets (Quintilian, 10.93). Virgil dedicates his
Eclogue 10 to him, and Ovid praises him highly (Ovid, *Tristia*, 2.445, 4.10.53). After
Gallus distinguished himself in the war against Antony, Caesar appointed him the
first governor of Egypt. Gallus, however, angered Caesar at his insolent display of
pride by setting up statues of himself throughout Egypt and inscribing a list of his
achievements on the pyramids. Convicted by the senate, he killed himself (Dio,
53.23.5–7).

74."hardly": reluctantly.

75."calm and gentle": moderately.

75."still": always.

76."writings": letters to Antony.

76–77."see . . . show in this": Directing posterity how and what to think of him,
Caesar offers evidence that he was, even under the pressures of war, always temper-
ate and restrained, as eminent Roman poets and historians—those "with serious
gravity and . . . the best" (Suetonius, *Augustus*, 89.3; Holland, 1:155)—will soon
record and exaltedly praise. "The best of emperors teaches his citizens to do right
by doing it, and though he is greatest among us in authority, he is still greater in
the example which he sets" (Velleius Paterculus, 2.126.5; see also Augustus, *The
Deeds of the Divine Augustus*, 8; and 4.14.99n).

ACT FIVE, SCENE TWO

[Alexandria. The monument.]

Enter Cleopatra, Charmian, and Iras.

Cleopatra: My desolation does begin to make
A better life. 'Tis paltry to be Caesar;
Not being Fortune, he's but Fortune's knave,
A minister of her will. And it is great
To do that thing that ends all other deeds,   5
Which shackles accidents and bolts up change,
Which sleeps and never palates more the dung,
The beggar's nurse, and Caesar's.

---

1. "desolation": (1) ruin, devastation, (2) having been forsaken.

2. "A better life": a life which despises the greatest political glory (lines 2–4) and sees death as defeating Fortune's rule over mortal life (lines 4–8).

3. "knave": servant.

4. "minister": mere agent.

2–4. "'Tis paltry ... her will": Caesar's accomplishment is paltry because it depends not on him but on Fortune. As Plutarch points out, Caesar owes his success to the good fortune of having had friends and enemies alike who originally raised him up but were then themselves thrown down, leaving him to rule alone. "[I]t was for [Caesar's] sake that Cicero gave counsel, Lepidus led an army, Pansa vanquished the enemy, Hirtius lost his life in the field, and Antony lived riotously in drunkenness, gluttony and lechery." Caesar himself, when sending his grandson to war, will pray that he might prove "as valiant as Scipio, and as well beloved as Pompey, and as fortunate as himself, ascribing the making of himself as great as he was unto Fortune" (Plutarch, *Fortune of the Romans*, 7 [319e–f]; Holland, 632). For Pansa and Hirtius, see 1.4.58–59. Cleopatra, however, does not limit her indictment to Caesar. One might have expected her to say, "Not being virtuous, he's but Fortune's knave." But Cleopatra dismisses the distinction. With heroic virtue now gone from the world, Fortune, she says, rules human affairs, and so, unless someone is Fortune herself, he is simply her servant. Whatever anyone accomplishes merely carries out Fortune's wishes.

5. "do that thing": commit suicide.

6. "shackles ... change": chains up every chance event and locks up every change (preventing both).

7–8. "sleeps ... Caesar's": is a sleep in which I never again have to taste the dung which nourishes beggars and Caesar alike.

Enter Proculeius.

Proculeius: Caesar sends greeting to the Queen of Egypt,
    And bids thee study on what fair demands   **10**
    Thou mean'st to have him grant thee.

Cleopatra: What's thy name?

Proculeius: My name is Proculeius.

Cleopatra: Antony
    Did tell me of you, bade me trust you, but
    I do not greatly care to be deceived
    That have no use for trusting. If your master   **15**
    Would have a queen his beggar, you must tell him
    That majesty, to keep decorum, must
    No less beg than a kingdom. If he please
    To give me conquered Egypt for my son,
    He gives me so much of mine own as I   **20**
    Will kneel to him with thanks.

Proculeius: Be of good cheer.
    You're fall'n into a princely hand; fear nothing.
    Make your full reference freely to my lord,
    Who is so full of grace that it flows over
    On all that need. Let me report to him   **25**
    Your sweet dependency, and you shall find
    A conqueror that will pray in aid for kindness
    Where he for grace is kneeled to.

Cleopatra: Pray you tell him
    I am his fortune's vassal and I send him

---

10. "study on": consider.
10. "fair demands": requests for favorable terms.
14. "to be deceived": whether or not I am deceived.
15. "That have no use": since I have no need.
17. "majesty, to keep decorum": to do what is fitting for majesty.
18. "No less beg": beg no less.
20. "as": that.
23. "Make . . . my lord": put yourself entirely in Caesar's hands.
26. "sweet dependency": docile submission.
27. "pray in aid": beg your assistance (a legal term).
27. "for kindness": in thinking of kind acts to do for you.

The greatness he has got. I hourly learn 30
A doctrine of obedience, and would gladly
Look him i'th' face.

Proculeius: This I'll report, dear lady.
Have comfort, for I know your plight is pitied
Of him that caused it.

> [*Gallus and Soldiers enter and seize Cleopatra.*]

You see how easily she may be surprised. 35
Guard her till Caesar come.

Iras: Royal queen!

Charmian: O, Cleopatra, thou art taken, queen!

Cleopatra: Quick, quick, good hands!   [*Draws a dagger.*]

Proculeius: Hold, worthy lady, hold!
                         [*Disarms her.*]
Do not yourself such wrong, who are in this
Relieved, but not betrayed.

Cleopatra: What, of death, too, 40
That rids our dogs of languish?

Proculeius: Cleopatra,

29–30. "fortune's vassal . . . has got": I submit to Caesar's fortune and recognize the greatness he has won by conquering me.

31. "doctrine": lesson.

31–32. "gladly . . . i'th' face": Cleopatra invites the exchange with Caesar. See line 110n.

34. "Of": by.

35. "surprised": captured.

35–36. Some editors give these lines to Gallus. The Folio assigns them to Proculeius. In Plutarch, Gallus engages Cleopatra in conversation, while Proculeius seizes her from behind (Plutarch, *Antony*, 79.1–2).

40. "Relieved": rescued (from death).

40. "What, of death too": Cleopatra understands Proculeius' "relieved" to mean "deprived of."

41. "That rids . . . languish": death relieves even suffering dogs of their misery, caused by disease or injury.

41. "Cleopatra": Proculeius fails to address Cleopatra by any title or term of respect. Previously, she was "Queen of Egypt," "dear lady," and "worthy lady" (lines

Do not abuse my master's bounty by
Th'undoing of yourself. Let the world see
His nobleness well acted, which your death
Will never let come forth.

Cleopatra: Where art thou, Death?   **45**
Come hither, come! Come, come, and take a queen
Worth many babes and beggars.

Proculeius: O, temperance, lady!

Cleopatra: Sir, I will eat no meat; I'll not drink, sir.
If idle talk will once be necessary,
I'll not sleep neither. This mortal house I'll ruin,   **50**
Do Caesar what he can. Know, sir, that I
Will not wait pinioned at your master's court,
Nor once be chastised with the sober eye
Of dull Octavia. Shall they hoist me up
And show me to the shouting varletry   **55**

9, 32, 38), although initially he addressed her (thrice) with familiar pronouns (lines 10–11).

42. "abuse": cheat (by preventing Caesar from using it).

43. "undoing": destruction.

44. "well acted": (1) generously accomplished, or (2) theatrically simulated.

45. "come forth": show itself.

47. "babes and beggars": people who die in large numbers.

47. "temperance": calm yourself.

48. "meat": food.

49. "once": at any time, ever.

49–50. "necessary . . . sleep neither": necessary to keep herself awake (and deny herself life-sustaining sleep).

50. "mortal house": her body.

52. "wait": attend (as a slave or servant).

52. "pinioned": with clipped wings, shackled, unable to fly.

53–54. "sober eye . . . Octavia": For Cleopatra's fear of Octavia's moral judgment, see 4.15.28–29n.

55. "varletry": rabble, mob (literally, "servants," "menials").

Of censuring Rome? Rather a ditch in Egypt
Be gentle grave unto me; rather on Nilus' mud
Lay me stark naked, and let the water-flies
Blow me into abhorring; rather make
My country's high pyramides my gibbet   **60**
And hang me up in chains!

Proculeius: You do extend
These thoughts of horror further than you shall
Find cause in Caesar.

                    Enter Dolabella.

Dolabella: Proculeius,
What thou hast done thy master Caesar knows,
And he hath sent for thee. For the Queen,   **65**
I'll take her to my guard.

Proculeius: So, Dolabella,
It shall content me best. Be gentle to her.
[*to Cleopatra.*] To Caesar I will speak what you shall please,
If you'll employ me to him.

---

56. "censuring": judging, condemning.

54–56. On the treatment of captives, particularly monarchs, in a Roman triumph, see lines 207–20n.

57. "gentle": a grimly ironic pun: (1) noble, (2) maggot, the larva of the flesh-fly or bluebottle (*OED*, s.v. "gentle," sb 3).

59. "Blow me into abhorring": lay eggs in me until I am bloated and abhorrent to see.

60. "pyramides": pyramids. Cleopatra may have in mind the pyramids in Egypt shaped like obelisks, with tapering, four-sided columns of stone and pyramidal peaks, from which a hanging would be possible (see Pliny, 36.64–74).

60. "gibbet": a post from which executed bodies were hung for exhibition.

56–61. On Cleopatra's imagining herself dying in Egypt, see 4.9.9–26n.

61. "extend": magnify.

65. "For": as for.

66. "to": under.

67. "content": please.

68. "what": whatever.

69. "employ me": use me as your messenger,

Cleopatra: Say I would die.

Exit Proculeius [with Gallus and Soldiers].

Dolabella: Most noble empress, you have heard of me.   70

Cleopatra: I cannot tell.

Dolabella: Assuredly you know me.

Cleopatra: No matter, sir, what I have heard or known.
     You laugh when boys or women tell their dreams;
     Is't not your trick?

Dolabella: I understand not, madam.

Cleopatra: I dreamt there was an emperor Antony.   75
     O, such another sleep, that I might see
     But such another man!

Dolabella: If it might please you—

Cleopatra: His face was as the heavens, and therein stuck
     A sun and moon, which kept their course and lighted
     The little O, the earth.

Dolabella: Most sovereign creature—   80

---

69. "would": wish to.

70. "Most noble empress": The title seems to disregard Octavia and recognize Cleopatra as Antony's widow. Only Iras has called her by the title before (3.11.33; 4.15.75).

71. "Assuredly . . . me": Plutarch describes Dolabella as a young companion of Caesar who was charmed by Cleopatra (Plutarch, *Antony*, 84.1). He is probably the son of a man of the same name who was an ally of Julius Caesar, fought for him at Pharsalus, was Antony's co-consul after Caesar's assassination, killed Caesar's assassin Trebonius in Smyrna, and was helped by Cleopatra when he sought to avenge Caesar's death by fighting against Cassius in Syria (Plutarch, *Antony*, 9–11; Appian, 2,122, 3.7–8, 26, 4.58, 61, 5.8). Little is known of the younger Dolabella after this episode.

74. "trick": customary way (typical of a Roman officer).

75–77. "I dreamt . . . another man": Cleopatra remembers Antony as he wished her to do (see 4.15.54–57). Her description of her dream uses hyperbolic, heroic likenesses throughout.

78. "stuck": were placed.

78–80. "His face . . . the earth": Antony's face stood as the heavens to the earth, his eyes lighting the earth with their sight.

Cleopatra: His legs bestrid the ocean, his reared arm
    Crested the world. His voice was propertied
    As all the tuned spheres, and that to friends;
    But when he meant to quail and shake the orb,
    He was as rattling thunder. For his bounty,   **85**
    There was no winter in't; an Antony 'twas
    That grew the more by reaping. His delights
    Were dolphin-like; they showed his back above
    The element they lived in. In his livery
    Walked crowns and crownets; realms and islands were   **90**
    As plates dropped from his pocket.

Dolabella: Cleopatra—

81–82. "His legs . . . the world": Alluding to the Colossus of Rhodes, one of the Seven Wonders of the World, Cleopatra likens Antony to the gigantic statue of the sun god, Helios, straddling the entrance to the harbor at Rhodes, its raised arm reaching toward Olympus (Pliny, 34.41).

82. "propertied": as harmonious.

82–83. "His voice . . . to friends": to friends, Antony's voice was like "the music of the spheres." It resembled the divine harmony of the motions of the heavenly planets, which, revolving in concentric spheres around the earth, produce a beautiful sound too sublime to be heard by human ears (Cicero, *Republic*, 6.18; Pliny, 2.84).

84. "quail": cause to quail, terrify.

84. "orb": globe.

84–85. "But when . . . thunder": when he intended to frighten and shake the earth, his voice was like the divine thunder of a punishing god.

86. "an Antony": Nearly all editors, following Lewis Theobald (1733), emend the Folio to read "an autumn." However, Cleopatra, identifying Antony's boundless bounty as "an Anthony," puns on his name. *Anthos*, in Greek, means "flower," hence "the height or the pick of something," for example, "Flower of warriors" (*Cor.*, 1.6.33). If Caesar's name is the highest political title (see 3.2.13n), Antony's marks the richest munificence. In giving, Antony fully lived up to his superlative name.

87. "That grew . . . reaping": his generosity became more abundant the more he gave.

87–89. "His delights . . . lived in": as the dolphin shows its back above the water, Antony always rose above, was never dragged down by, the (coarse) pleasures in which he lived.

89–90. "In his livery . . . crownets": kings and princes were his servants (kings wear crowns, prince wear coronets ["crownets"]).

91. "plates": silver coins.

Cleopatra: Think you there was, or might be, such a man
    As this I dreamt of?

Dolabella: Gentle madam, no.

Cleopatra: You lie up to the hearing of the gods!
    But if there be nor ever were one such,   **95**
    It's past the size of dreaming. Nature wants stuff
    To vie strange forms with fancy, yet t'imagine
    An Antony were nature's piece 'gainst fancy,
    Condemning shadows quite.

Dolabella: Hear me, good madam.
    Your loss is as yourself, great; and you bear it   **100**
    As answering to the weight. Would I might never
    O'ertake pursued success but I do feel,

---

92. "might": could.

94. "up to . . . the gods": so loudly even the gods would hear it.

95. "nor ever": or never.

96. "size" capacity.

95–96. "But if . . . of dreaming": but supposing you are right and no such man exists or ever existed, I could not have imagined him, for he exceeds the bounds of imagination.

96–97. "Nature wants . . . fancy": natures lacks the material to compete with imagination in producing wondrous forms.

97–99. "yet t'imagine . . . shadows quite": if one could imagine such a man as my Antony, he would be nature's triumphant masterpiece, discrediting anything that imagination could create. Enobarbus described Cleopatra, dressed like Venus, as surpassing a picture of Venus in which the artist's imagination surpassed nature itself. She was superior to art, which is superior to nature (2.2.208–11). Cleopatra speaks differently. Always an actress, she has often elevated the imaginary over the natural or the real. But now that Antony is dead, she reverses the terms, for it is of the greatest importance to her that the Antony she loves was real, not merely a dream or imaginary. She both poeticizes Antony and insists that her idealized depiction is true. Reflecting the twin (if conflicting) tendencies of spiritedness to idealize or poeticize—to elevate, beautify, simplify, surpass, and suppress—and to insist that its exaggerated or distorted description is true, she is never more concerned with what is actual than when she is most poetic.

101. "As answering . . . weight": in proportion to its gravity.

101–2. "Would I . . . feel": may I never achieve the success I desire if I do not feel (a conditional self-curse).

By the rebound of yours, a grief that smites
My very heart at root.

Cleopatra: I thank you, sir.
Know you what Caesar means to do with me?   **105**

Dolabella: I am loath to tell you what I would you knew.

Cleopatra: Nay, pray you, sir.

Dolabella: Though he be honorable—

Cleopatra: He'll lead me, then, in triumph.

Dolabella: Madam, he will. I know't.

> ***Flourish. Enter Caesar, Proculeius, Gallus, Maecenas,
> and others of his train.***

All: Make way there! Caesar!   **110**

Caesar: Which is the Queen of Egypt?

Dolabella: It is the Emperor, madam.   ***Cleopatra kneels.***

Caesar: Arise. You shall not kneel.
I pray you, rise. Rise, Egypt.

Cleopatra: Sir, the gods
Will have it thus. My master and my lord   **115**

---

103. "rebound": reflection.

103. "smites": strikes a heavy blow to.

110. This is the only time Caesar and Cleopatra are together. Each will try to deceive the other. Caesar, with a mixture of assurances and threats, will try to keep Cleopatra from killing herself, so he can exhibit her in Rome. Cleopatra, fearing captivity and public shame in Rome, will try to throw him off his guard by indicating that she wants to live, so she will be able to kill herself. Each attempts to lull the other—he, by appearing gracious and kind; she, by appearing covetous and compliant.

111. "Which . . . Queen of Egypt": Caesar's question is less likely a deliberate insult of Cleopatra than an indication of just how much her grief and self-inflicted wounds have altered her appearance (Plutarch, *Antony*, 82.1). When Dolabella returns, he, too, will have difficulty recognizing her (line 196).

113. "shall": must.

114. "Sir": lord, master.

115. "My master and my lord": Cleopatra's final words to Caesar will repeat these words (line 189).

I must obey.   **[*She stands.*]**

Caesar: Take to you no hard thoughts.
The record of what injuries you did us,
Though written in our flesh, we shall remember
As things but done by chance.

Cleopatra: Sole sir o'th' world,
I cannot project mine own cause so well   **120**
To make it clear, but do confess I have
Been laden with like frailties which before
Have often shamed our sex.

Caesar: Cleopatra, know
We will extenuate rather than enforce.
If you apply yourself to our intents,   **125**
Which towards you are most gentle, you shall find
A benefit in this change; but if you seek
To lay on me a cruelty by taking
Antony's course, you shall bereave yourself
Of my good purposes, and put your children   **130**
To that destruction which I'll guard them from
If thereon you rely. I'll take my leave.

Cleopatra: And may through all the world. 'Tis yours, and we,

---

116. "hard thoughts": harsh thought (of me).

120. "project": set forth, explain.

120. "cause": case.

121. "clear": blameless, innocent.

121–23. "I have . . . our sex": Cleopatra plays to Caesar's view of women as weak (3.12.29–31); see line 188n.

124. "extenuate . . . enforce": make light of rather than stress (legalistic language).

125. "apply . . . our intents": submit yourself to my purposes.

128. "lay on me a cruelty": make me look cruel.

129. "bereave": rob.

130–32. "put your children . . . rely": Caesar tacitly threatens Cleopatra's children, whom she has stressed in asking him for concessions (3.12.16–19; line 19).

133. "And may . . . the world": Cleopatra puns on Caesar's conventional farewell. A secondary meaning of "leave" is the permission or liberty to do something: Caesar may do whatever he pleases anywhere in the world.

Your scutcheons and your signs of conquest, shall
Hang in what place you please. Here, my good lord.   **135**

[Hands him a paper.]

Caesar: You shall advise me in all for Cleopatra.

Cleopatra: This is the brief of money, plate, and jewels
I am possessed of. 'Tis exactly valued,
Not petty things admitted. Where's Seleucus?

[Enter Seleucus.]

Seleucus: Here, madam.   **140**

Cleopatra: This is my treasurer. Let him speak, my lord,
Upon his peril, that I have reserved
To myself nothing. Speak the truth, Seleucus.

Seleucus: Madam,
I had rather seel my lips than to my peril   **145**
Speak that which is not.

Cleopatra: What have I kept back?

Seleucus: Enough to purchase what you have made known.

Caesar: Nay, blush not, Cleopatra. I approve

---

134. "scutcheons": the shields (with coats of arms) of defeated enemies, hung up as trophies.

135. "Here, my good lord": Cleopatra does not let Caesar leave before handing him an inventory of her possessions. He has not asked for one and would have left without it.

136. "in all for Cleopatra": regarding everything concerning you.

137. "brief": concise list, inventory.

139. "Not petty things admitted": not including trivial items.

142. "reserved": kept.

143. "truth": This is Cleopatra's only mention of "truth," which she demands here as part of her strategy to deceive Caesar; see 4.14.128n.

145. "seel": sew shut; see 3.13.117n.

147. "Enough . . . made known": Cleopatra seems intent on encouraging Caesar to believe that she has tried unsuccessfully to trick him because she desires to live. Her real deception of him is to feign a failed deception of him.

Your wisdom in the deed.

Cleopatra: See, Caesar, O, behold
How pomp is followed! Mine will now be yours,   **150**
And should we shift estates, yours would be mine.
The ingratitude of this Seleucus does
Even make me wild. O slave, of no more trust
Than love that's hired! What, goest thou back? Thou shalt
Go back, I warrant thee! But I'll catch thine eyes   **155**
Though they had wings. Slave, soulless villain, dog!
O rarely base!

Caesar: Good queen, let us entreat you.

Cleopatra: O Caesar, what a wounding shame is this,
That thou vouchsafing here to visit me,
Doing the honor of thy lordliness   **160**
To one so meek, that mine own servant should
Parcel the sum of my disgraces by
Addition of his envy! Say, good Caesar,
That I some lady trifles have reserved,

148–49. "I approve . . . the deed": A man given to guarding his own revenue and expenses (for example, 3.6.30–31, 4.1.16–17), Caesar may well consider such an action wise. This is his sole mention of "wisdom" or of a "deed."

150. "How pomp is followed": how (faithlessly) majesty is served.

150. "Mine": my servants.

151. "shift estates": exchange places and conditions.

153. "Even": fully, quite (adds emphasis).

154. "love that's hired": a prostitute's love.

154. "goest thou back": Seleucus is retreating as Cleopatra advances to attack him.

155. "Go back": get the worst of it.

155. "catch": attack (scratch).

157. "rarely": exceptionally.

159. "vouchsafing": condescending, deigning.

159–60. "That thou . . . thy lordliness": Cleopatra employs an ingratiating combination of obsequious deference and familiar pronouns. This is the only time she uses the familiar pronoun in speaking to Caesar.

162. "Parcel": (1) specify, enumerate, (2) add to, increase.

163. "envy": malice.

Immoment toys, things of such dignity   165
As we greet modern friends withal, and say
Some nobler token I have kept apart
For Livia and Octavia, to induce
Their mediation, must I be unfolded
With one that I have bred? The gods! It smites me   170
Beneath the fall I have. [*to Seleucus*] Prithee, go hence,
Or I shall show the cinders of my spirits
Through th'ashes of my chance. Wert thou a man,
Thou wouldst have mercy on me.

Caesar: Forbear, Seleucus. [*Exit Seleucus.*]

Cleopatra: Be it known that we, the greatest, are misthought   175
For things that others do; and when we fall,
We answer others' merits in our name,
Are therefore to be pitied.

---

165. "Immoment toys": trinkets of no moment or value.

165. "dignity": worth.

166. "modern": ordinary.

166. "withal": with.

168. "Livia": Caesar's wife.

169. "mediation": intercession (in her behalf). Cleopatra's confession, seemingly showing a broken spirit (Plutarch, *Antony*, 83.4; Dio, 51.13.3), ostensibly acknowledges that she expects to go to Rome.

169–70. "unfolded With": exposed, betrayed by.

170. "have bred": brought up as a member of my household.

171. "Beneath": lower than.

172. "cinders": embers.

173. "chance": (fallen) fortunes (her ruin does not prevent her revenge).

173. "Wert thou a man": not a eunuch.

174. "have": have had.

173–74. "Wert thou ... mercy on me": your bitter unmanliness makes you unmerciful.

174. "Forbear": leave us.

175. "misthought": misjudged.

177. "merits": deserts (whether good or bad).

177. "answer ... our name": answer (are held responsible) for the deeds of others.

178. "Are": and are.

Caesar: Cleopatra,
Not what you have reserved nor what acknowledged
Put we i'th' roll of conquest. Still be't yours;   **180**
Bestow it at your pleasure, and believe
Caesar's no merchant to make prize with you
Of things that merchants sold. Therefore be cheered.
Make not your thoughts your prisons. No, dear queen,
For we intend so to dispose you as   **185**
Yourself shall give us counsel. Feed and sleep.
Our care and pity is so much upon you
That we remain your friend. And so adieu.

Cleopatra: My master and my lord!

Caesar: Not so. Adieu.

[*Flourish. Exeunt Caesar and his train.*]

Cleopatra: He words me, girls, he words me, that I should not **190**
Be noble to myself. But hark thee, Charmian.

---

180. "roll of conquest": inventory of the spoils of victory.

180. "Still": let it still.

181. "Bestow": make use of.

182. "make prize": haggle. Caesar converts a military term, meaning to confiscate, seize, or capture, into a commercial term.

184. "Make not . . . your prisons": do not imagine yourself a prisoner.

185. "dispose you": make arrangements for you.

188. Caesar, evidently pleased with the way the meeting has gone, thinks he has fooled Cleopatra. But she dissembles, and he is deceived. "I'll seem the fool I am not" (1.1.43). Turning against him his usual strength of taking advantage of other people's weaknesses, she presents herself in accordance with his view that women are no stronger than their fortunes. Deceiving him by pretending to fail to deceive him, she lets him see through her pretense so that, seeing what he thinks is true of all women, he complacently concludes that that is all there is to be seen. He does not see the pretending within or behind her pretending, the deeper level of play-acting which conceals even while revealing her playacting. "And so he took his leave of her, supposing he had deceived her. And indeed he was deceived himself" (Plutarch, *Antony*, 83.5; Spencer, 289). Cleopatra's deception, which allows Caesar to leave her unattended, is his only major defeat in the play.

190. "words me": tries to beguile me with mere words.

191. "Be noble to myself": take the noble action (by killing myself). Although the word is used in a sharply diminished sense throughout the play, once Antony, the "[n]oblest of men" (4.15.61), dies, "noble" (and its variants) all but once in eleven

[*Whispers to Charmian.*]

Iras: Finish, good lady. The bright day is done,
     And we are for the dark.

Cleopatra: Hie thee again.
     I have spoke already, and it is provided.
     Go put it to the haste.

Charmian: Madam, I will.   **195**

Enter Dolabella.

Dolabella: Where's the Queen?

Charmian: Behold, sir.   **[*Exit.*]**

Cleopatra: Dolabella.

Dolabella: Madam, as thereto sworn by your command,
     Which my love makes religion to obey,
     I tell you this; Caesar through Syria

---

mentions concerns women. The sole exceptions refers to Antony's sword stained with "his most noble blood" (5.1.26). See, further, Introduction, xvi–xviii and n20, and line 343n.

193. "are": are headed.

193. "Hie thee again": hurry back.

194. "spoke": given orders.

194. "it is provided": Cleopatra has made provisions for the asp.

195. "Go . . . haste": do it quickly.

197–99. "as thereto sworn . . . you this": Nothing we have seen showed Cleopatra commanding Dolabella or Dolabella swearing to obey. Cleopatra entreated him to say what he knew, and Dolabella, cursing himself conditionally if he did not feel deeply for her, confirmed Caesar's plans (lines 101–9). Now, however, his heartfelt grief having turned into love, and love having the power to command, Dolabella says that he tells her because his love makes a religion to obey her command. A harbinger of Christianity, Dolabella obeys a new religion whose commandment is love: "Jesus said to him, 'Thou shalt love the Lord thy God with all thine heart, with all thy soul, and with all thy mind. This is the first and the great commandment. And the second is like unto this: Thou shalt love thy neighbor as thyself'" (Matt. 22:37–39); "A new commandment give I unto you, that ye love one another; as I have loved you, that ye also love one another" (John 13:34–35). Dolabella, a Roman officer, personifies the transformation of Rome's principle of war, which teaches men to love their fellow citizens and hate their country's enemies. By following the principle, Rome conquered the world. But Rome's universal conquests have turned the principle of war into the commandment of

Intends his journey, and within three days   200
You with your children will he send before.
Make your best use of this. I have performed
Your pleasure and my promise.

Cleopatra: Dolabella,
I shall remain your debtor.

Dolabella: I your servant.
Adieu, good queen. I must attend on Caesar.   205

Cleopatra: Farewell, and thanks.   *Exit [Dolabella].*
                    Now, Iras, what think'st thou?
Thou an Egyptian puppet shall be shown
In Rome as well as I. Mechanic slaves
With greasy aprons, rules, and hammers shall
Uplift us to the view. In their thick breaths,   210
Rank of gross diet, shall we be enclouded
And forced to drink their vapor.

Iras: The gods forbid!

Cleopatra: Nay, 'tis most certain, Iras. Saucy lictors
Will catch at us like strumpets, and scald rhymers

---

love. For Rome's former enemies are now Romans, and, with no enemies left to
hate, all of mankind are now fellow citizens or fellow subjects. Mirroring the general tendency of spiritedness itself, the principle of war destroys itself by fulfilling
itself and turns itself into its opposite.

207. "puppet": someone who can be easily manipulated and controlled.

208. "Mechanic slaves": workmen.

209. "greasy aprons": aprons worn by workmen.

209. "rules": measuring sticks.

210. "Uplift us": lift us up.

210. "thick": foul.

211. "of": because of.

212. "drink": drink in, inhale.

213. "Saucy": insolent and lascivious (a strong term).

213. "lictors" minor public officials, usually of low birth, who arrest and punish
offenders. A public office dating back to Romulus (Livy, 1.8), lictors accompanied
Rome's chief magistrates, each bearing a bundle of rods and single-headed axe
(*fasces*) before him to use for punishment, at the magistrate's command.

214. "catch at": grab at.

214. "scald": paltry, contemptible.

Ballad us out o'tune. The quick comedians   **215**
Extemporally will stage us and present
Our Alexandrian revels. Antony
Shall be brought drunken forth, and I shall see
Some squeaking Cleopatra boy my greatness
I'th' posture of a whore.

Iras: O the good gods!   **220**

Cleopatra: Nay, that's certain.

Iras: I'll never see't, for I am sure mine nails
Are stronger than mine eyes!

Cleopatra: Why, that's the way
To fool their preparation and to conquer
Their most absurd intents.

                    Enter Charmian.

                        Now, Charmian!   **225**
Show me, my women, like a queen. Go fetch

---

215. "Ballad us": sing ballads about us.

215. "quick comedians": quick-witted actors.

218. "shall see": The dishonor will be compounded by her having to witness the spectacle herself.

219. "Some . . . my greatness": some boy with a shrill voice parodying my majesty.

220. "posture": demeanor, attitude (a sexual allusion as well as a theatrical term).

207–20. Roman triumphs traditionally displayed the captives, particularly their leaders, publicly mocked them with pictures, puppets, songs, and skits, publicly abused them in innumerable ways, and led them to slavery and their leaders usually to death. Every part of the triumph was an extraordinary spectacle displaying Rome's majesty. "It is impossible adequately to describe the multitude of those spectacles and their magnificence under every conceivable aspect, . . . [which] by their collective exhibition . . . displayed the majesty of the Roman empire" (Josephus, *Jewish War*, 7.132). Especially wondrous was the moveable pageant (Josephus, 7.138–47). In Caesar's forthcoming triumph, "Among other features, an effigy of the dead Cleopatra lying upon a couch was carried by, so that in a sense she, too, together with the live captives, who included her children, Alexander, named the Sun, and Cleopatra, named the Moon, formed a part of the spectacle and a trophy in the procession" (Dio, 51.21.8).

224. "fool": frustrate.

My best attires. I am again for Cydnus
To meet Mark Antony. Sirrah Iras, go.
Now, noble Charmian, we'll dispatch indeed,
And when thou hast done this chare, I'll give thee leave   **230**
To play till doomsday. Bring our crown and all.   **[*Exit Iras.*]**

                                           A noise within.

Wherefore's this noise?

                         Enter a Guardsman.

Guardsman: Here is a rural fellow
      That will not be denied your Highness' presence.
      He brings you figs.

Cleopatra: Let him come in.   *Exit Guardsman.*
                          What poor an instrument   **235**
      May do a noble deed! He brings me liberty.
      My resolution's placed, and I have nothing
      Of woman in me. Now from head to foot
      I am marble-constant. Now the fleeting moon

---

227. "for": ready for.

227. "Cydnus": the river on which Cleopatra "pursed up" Antony's heart; see 2.2.196–236.

226–28. "Show . . . Mark Antony": Rather than be staged by Caesar as a captive in Rome, Cleopatra will stage her own royal death in Egypt. Her death, a repeated stage play, will be another grand theatrical performance. As magnificent as her most magnificent moment in life, it will exhibit the splendor of the Egyptian monarchy. It is to be a royal performance, presented in full costume.

228. "Sirrah": a familiar term of address to servants, both male and female.

229. "dispatch": (1) act quickly, (2) make an end.

229. "Now . . . indeed": The Folio places this line in parentheses, suggesting that the next two may be addressed to Iras rather than to Charmian, as usually supposed. But cp. line 318n.

230. "chare": chore, task.

232. "Wherefore's": what is.

235. "What": how.

236. "brings me liberty": Death is liberty from servitude and disgrace (see *JC*, 1.3.89–100).

237. "placed": set, fixed.

237–38. "I have . . . in me": On Cleopatra's facing death "without womanly fear," see Velleius Paterculus, 2.87.1; also Horace, *Odes*, 1.37.22–23.

No planet is of mine.

Enter Guardsman and Clown, [with a basket].

Guardsman: This is the man.   **240**

Cleopatra: Avoid, and leave him.   *Exit Guardsman*
Hast thou the pretty worm of Nilus there
That kills and pains not?

Clown: Truly I have him, but I would not be the
party that should desire you to touch him, for his   **245**
biting is immortal. Those that do die of it do seldom
or never recover.

Cleopatra: Remember'st thou any that have died on't?

237–40. "I have nothing . . . of mine": Cleopatra unsexes herself. Women, like the moon, she suggests, are ever-changing, never constant (cp. 2.2.245–50). They lack the constancy and resolution that she now claims to have. Cleopatra at the same time undeifies herself. The Egyptians identify her with Isis (3.6.16–18n) and Isis with the moon (3.13.158n). In claiming to be "marble-constant," Cleopatra denies her identification with Isis. Her unsexing and undeifying herself go together. Isis is "the female part of nature, apt to receive all generation. . . . [C]apable of all, she receives all forms and shapes" (Plutarch, *Isis and Osiris*, 53 [372e]; Holland, 1309). This may explain why Cleopatra appears to ignore Caesar's threat to kill her children (lines 128–32). Unlike earlier, her children now seem very far from her mind.

S.D. 240. "*Clown*": A clown is a rustic or countryman. By extension, the word, like "clod" from which it is derived, means both a small piece of earth and someone who is crude and stupid. "The wise, the fool: the country clown: the learned and the lout" (Ovid, *Metamorphosis*; Golding, To the Reader, 194).

241. "Avoid": withdraw.

242. "worm": serpent.

242. "the pretty worm of Nilus": cp. 1.5.26. The serpent, in Greek an "asp," is most likely a hooded cobra (*Naja haje*), the Egyptian royal symbol and protector. Its distinctive emblem appears on royal crowns threatening enemies of the king or queen. The serpent was closely associated with Isis. "[I]n her left hand [Isis] bare a cup of gold, out of the mouth whereof the serpent Aspis lifted up his head, with a swelling throat" (Apuleius, *The Golden Ass*, 11.4, trans. William Adlington [1566], London: John Lehmann, 1945, 223).

244. "him": it.

246. "immortal": mortal. The Clown is disposed to malapropisms. This one, however, promises the immortality that Cleopatra longs for (see line 279–80).

248. "died": In his reply, the Clown, while punning on "worm" as penis, will take "die" in its sexual sense of experiencing an orgasm.

248. "on't": of it.

Clown: Very many, men and women too. I heard of
one of them no longer than yesterday—a very honest   **250**
woman, but something given to lie, as a woman
should not do but in the way of honesty—how she
died of the biting of it, what pain she felt. Truly, she
makes a very good report o'th' worm; but he that
will believe all that they say shall never be saved by   **255**
half that they do. But this is most falliable, the
worm's an odd worm.

Cleopatra: Get thee hence. Farewell.

Clown: I wish you all joy of the worm.

[Sets down his basket.]

Cleopatra: Farewell.   **260**

Clown: You must think this, look you, that the worm
will do his kind.

---

249. "of": from.

250. "honest": (1) truthful, (2) chaste.

251. "something given": somewhat inclined.

251. "lie": (1) tell lies, (2) lie with men.

252. "but": except.

254–56. "but he . . . most fallible": The Clown, in his fashion, refers to man's Fall in the Garden of Eden. In addition to his malaprop pun on Fall ("fallible"), he alludes to Adam and Eve. While death results from the man's belief in what the woman said of the serpent ("th' worm"), the man who believed what she said, but could not be saved by what she had done, is Adam (Genesis 3:1–19). (Note the guard's mention of "fig leaves" in connection with the outcome of the serpent's work [line 350]). The Clown at the same time alludes to the Protestant doctrine of Salvation by Faith, not Works (cp. Martin Luther, *The Freedom of a Christian*, in Harold J. Grimm, ed., *Luther's Works*, 55 vols. [Philadelphia: Muhlenberg, 1957], 31:348). Thus, while pointing on the one hand to the biblical account of the origin of death, the Clown points on the other to the Christian account of what comes with death. The new heaven of Christianity offers a new understanding of death. As sin brings death into the world, men can share eternal life with God after death: "Jesus said unto her, 'I am the resurrection and the life. He that believeth in me, though he were dead, yet shall he live. And whosoever liveth, and believeth in me, shall never die'" (John 11:25–26). If sin brings worldly death, death can bring eternal life through salvation. "For as in Adam all die, even so in Christ shall all be made alive" (1 Cor. 15:22). No longer distinguishing man from the gods, death now comes to link man to God.

262. "do his kind": act according to its nature, specifically its sexual instincts.

Cleopatra: Ay, ay, farewell.

Clown: Look you, the worm is not to be trusted but
in the keeping of wise people, for indeed there is 265
no goodness in the worm.

Cleopatra: Take thou no care; it shall be heeded.

Clown: Very good. Give it nothing, I pray you, for it
is not worth the feeding.

Cleopatra: Will it eat me? 270

Clown: You must not think I am so simple but I know
the devil himself will not eat a woman. I know that
a woman is a dish for the gods if the devil dress her
not. But truly these same whoreson devils do the
gods great harm in their women, for in every ten that 275
they make, the devils mar five.

Cleopatra: Well, get thee gone. Farewell.

Clown: Yes, forsooth. I wish you joy o'th' worm. *Exit.*

[**Enter Iras bearing Cleopatra's royal regalia.**]

Cleopatra: Give me my robe. Put on my crown. I have
Immortal longings in me. Now no more 280

---

272. "eat": Cleopatra meant bite. The Clown means sexually enjoy.

273. "dish": sexually attractive.

273–74. "dress her not": (1) not season or cook (the dish), (2) leave her undressed.

274. "whoreson": bastard (a coarse slang expression of contempt).

275. "their women": women in general (ethical dative).

276. "make" create.

276. "mar": lead into temptation.

278. "forsooth": truly. For the Clown's emphasis on his speaking truly, see also lines 244 (his first word), 253.

280. "Immortal longings": longings for immortality.

The juice of Egypt's grape shall moist this lip.

[*The women dress her.*]

Yare, yare, good Iras, quick. Methinks I hear
Antony call. I see him rouse himself
To praise my noble act. I hear him mock
The luck of Caesar, which the gods give men   285
To excuse their after wrath. Husband, I come!
Now to that name my courage prove my title.
I am fire and air; my other elements
I give to baser life. So, have you done?
Come then, and take the last warmth of my lips.   290
Farewell, kind Charmian. Iras, long farewell.

[*Kisses them. Iras falls and dies.*]

Have I the aspic in my lips? Dost fall?
If thou and nature can so gently part,

---

281. "moist": moisten.

280–81. Cleopatra echoes Jesus at the Last Supper: "I will not drink hence forth of this fruit of the vine until that day when I shall drink it new with you in my Father's kingdom" (Matt. 26:29).

282. "Yare": quickly.

282. "Methinks": it seems to me that.

285–86. "The luck . . . wrath": The gods' wrath is their jealousy in disguise. Unlike Antony, who deserved to rival the gods (4.15.79–82), Caesar owes everything to his good fortune, which the gods have given him only to excuse their punishment afterwards.

286–87. "Husband, . . . my title": Only her courage in killing herself can entitle her to be Antony's wife. For both her and Antony, only a noble death can earn the other's undying love (see 4.14.98–102).

288. "other elements": the heavier elements, earth and water; see 4.10.3–4n.

288–89. "I am fire . . . baser life": Claiming to be composed only of the higher elements (fire and air), Cleopatra repudiates her bodily elements. Formerly the incarnation of bodily pleasure, she now sees herself as the decarnation of bodily life. Desiring and finding meaning in death, she, like Antony, unknowingly alludes to the vision of the new Jerusalem—he as the groom, she as the bride or as the holy city itself (see Introduction, xxi–xxii, and 4.14.100–102n). Death is not only a release or even a refuge, but a reward for them.

292. "the aspic": the asp (or the poison of the asp).

292. "Have I . . . Dost fall": Neither Shakespeare nor any of his ancient sources explains Iras' death. What we see, however, strongly suggests that she dies from the grief of taking her mistress' leave, and not from the venom of the asp, as some

The stroke of death is as a lover's pinch,
Which hurts and is desired. Dost thou lie still?   295
If thus thou vanishest, thou tell'st the world
It is not worth leave-taking.

Charmian: Dissolve, thick cloud, and rain, that I may say
The gods themselves do weep!

Cleopatra: This proves me base.
If she first meet the curled Antony,   300
He'll make demand of her, and spend that kiss
Which is my heaven to have.
                              Come, thou mortal wretch,

[*She applies an asp.*]

With thy sharp teeth this knot intrinsicate
Of life at once untie. Poor venomous fool,
Be angry and dispatch. O, couldst thou speak,   305
That I might hear thee call great Caesar ass
Unpolicied!

Charmian: O eastern star!

---

editors suggest. From the start, Cleopatra has been surrounded by a female court, and, in the end, her serving women are her most—and virtually only—loyal friends.

297. "leave-taking": saying farewell.

299. "This": that Iras died first.

300. "curled": with curled hair (note 2.2.234).

301. "make demand of": question.

300–302. "If she first . . . have": If Antony meets Iras first, he will ask her about Cleopatra and then fall in love with Iras for being nobler. Cleopatra's jealous fear carries beyond the grave (cp. 1.1.42n).

302. "mortal": deadly.

303. "knot intrinsicate": an intricate and intrinsic union (of body and soul). Death untangles the soul from its mortal combination with the body.

304. "fool": term of endearment (often for children).

305. "Be angry and dispatch": "[S]he did prick and thrust it with a spindle of gold, so that the Aspic, being angered withal, leapt out with great fury, and bit her in the arm" (Plutarch, *Antony*, 86.2; Spencer, 292–93).

307. "Unpolicied": lacking statecraft, outsmarted.

307. "eastern star": Venus, the morning star. The eastern star captures the sensuality and the spirituality of the East. While Venus is associated with the East and the East with voluptuous excesses (2.2.210, 2.3.39, 2.6.50; see also 1.5.48), the eastern

Cleopatra: Peace, peace!
   Dost thou not see my baby at my breast,
   That sucks the nurse asleep?

Charmian: O, break! O, break!

Cleopatra: As sweet as balm, as soft as air, as gentle—   **310**
   O Antony!—Nay, I will take thee too.

               [*She applies another asp.*]

   What should I stay—   ***Dies***

Charmian: In this vile world? So, fare thee well.
   Now boast thee, Death, in thy possession lies
   A lass unparalleled. Downy windows, close,   **315**

---

star also signifies the birth of Jesus (see Introduction, xxi, 1.2.29–31n). The eastern star's double nature also reflects Christianity's double treatment of the body. Christianity incarnates God as a man ("And the word was made flesh" [John 1:14]) and at the same time decarnalizes man's body. While the son of God not only lives but dies, man is promised an eternal life in death ("[T]he gift of God is eternal life" [Rom. 6:23]). While Jesus accepts all the sufferings of death in the flesh, man's life becomes wholly spiritualized.

308. "my baby": cp. lines 237–40n.

308–9. "at my breast . . . asleep": Cleopatra's application of the asp to her breast is Shakespeare's invention. None of his ancient sources says that.

309–10. "that sucks . . . as gentle": "The biting of an Aspic, the which only causeth a heaviness of the head, without swounding or complaining, and bringeth a great desire also to sleep, . . . and so by little and little taketh away the senses and vital powers, no living creature perceiving that the patients feel any pain" (Plutarch, *Antony*, 71.5; Spencer, 267); see, further, lines 344–45n.

312. "What": why. "What" has the sense of "why" when the expected answer has the force of a negative (Schmidt, s.v. "what," 1.b.).

312. "What . . . stay": Cleopatra's final words are an unfinished rhetorical question which answers itself (see previous note). The irony of her dying words is akin to that of Antony's. While he had a passion for "more," which ended only when he was "no more" (see 4.15.61n), she ends her life of constant change with the word "stay," while implicitly denying there is reason to. Her last words, like his, speaking against themselves, at once epitomize and contradict her life.

313. "vile": The Folio reads "wild," meaning savage, uninhabitable. Both words express contempt for the world.

313. "In this vile world": Charmian completes Cleopatra's question.

315. "Downy windows": eyelids.

And golden Phoebus, never be beheld
Of eyes again so royal. Your crown's awry;
I'll mend it, and then play—

    Enter the Guard rustling in.

1 Guard: Where's the Queen?

Charmian: Speak softly. Wake her not.

1 Guard: Caesar hath sent—

Charmian: Too slow a messenger.   **320**

    [Applies an asp.]

O, come apace, dispatch! I partly feel thee.

1 Guard: Approach, ho! All's not well. Caesar's beguiled.

2 Guard: There's Dolabella sent from Caesar. Call him.

    [Exit a Guardsman.]

What work is here, Charmian? Is this well done?

Charmian: It is well done, and fitting for a princess   **325**
Descended of so many royal kings.
Ah, soldier!   *Charmian dies.*

---

316. "Phoebus": a name for Apollo, the Roman sun god, from the Greek word for bright, shining, radiant.

317. "Of": by.

318. "mend": straighten.

318. "play": While echoing Cleopatra's verb allowing—or encouraging—her to "play till doomsday" (line 231), Charmian also rhymes Cleopatra's last word "stay." She seems to mean "to play my part," that is, to die. Like Cleopatra's final line, Charmian's line is broken off. The Folio places a (rare) long dash after "play."

S.D. 318. "*rustling*": rushing noisily.

320. "Caesar . . . a messenger": Despite Caesar's usual quickness, Cleopatra outpaced him. "[S]he hath . . . celerity in dying" (1.2.151).

321. "partly": to some degree, already.

322. "beguiled": tricked, cheated.

326. "of": from.

325–26. Cleopatra, dressed in her royal robes, her crown on her head, and her face composed, dies a dignified regal death (Plutarch, *Antony*, 85.3–4). It marks the end not only of a queen or even of the three centuries of Ptolemaic royal line, but of three millennia of Egyptian pharaohs. Egypt now becomes a Roman province.

298–327. The Soothsayer's prophecies have come true, but not as Charmian and Iras understood them. Charmian has proved "far fairer"—more noble—than she

Enter Dolabella.

Dolabella: How goes it here?

2 Guard: All dead.

Dolabella: Caesar, thy thoughts
    Touch their effects in this. Thyself art coming
    To see performed the dreaded act which thou   **330**
    So sought'st to hinder.

Enter Caesar and all his train, marching.

All but Caesar: A way there, a way for Caesar!

Dolabella: O sir, you are too sure an augurer:
    That you did fear is done.

Caesar: Bravest at the last,
    She leveled at our purposes and, being royal,   **335**
    Took her own way. The manner of their deaths?
    I do not see them bleed.

Dolabella: Who was last with them?

1 Guard: A simple countryman that brought her figs.
    This was his basket.

Caesar: Poisoned, then.

1 Guard: O Caesar,
    This Charmian lived but now; she stood and spake.   **340**

---

was (1.2.18) and "more beloving than beloved" (1.2.24). She has "outlive[d] the lady whom [she] serve[d]," though only by a few moments (1.2.32). She had then seen "a fairer former fortune" than that which was to come (1.2.35–36). And, dying with and for Cleopatra, hers and Iras' "fortunes are alike" (1.2.57).

329. "Touch their effects": are fulfilled.

330. "performed": accomplished.

333. "augurer": augur, prophet, seer.

334. "That": what.

334. "Bravest": most splendid, most courageous.

335. "leveled at": guessed at, realized.

335–36. "being royal . . . own way": having royal dignity, took her own life in a show of triumph.

338. "simple": humble.

340. "lived": was alive.

I found her trimming up the diadem
On her dead mistress; tremblingly she stood,
And on the sudden dropped.

Caesar: O, noble weakness!
If they had swallowed poison, 'twould appear
By external swelling; but she looks like sleep,   **345**
As she would catch another Antony
In her strong toil of grace.

Dolabella: Here on her breast
There is a vent of blood, and something blown.
The like is on her arm.

1 Guard: This is an aspic's trail, and these fig leaves   **350·**
Have slime upon them, such as th'aspic leaves
Upon the caves of Nile.

Caesar: Most probable
That so she died, for her physician tells me
She hath pursued conclusions infinite
Of easy ways to die. Take up her bed,   **355**
And bear her women from the monument.

---

341. "trimming up": straightening.

343. "noble weakness": a Roman oxymoron; see line 191n.

344–45. "If they . . . swelling": On the absence of swelling and the painless, slumberous death of an asp's bite, see Nicander, *Theriaca*, 187–89; Philumenus, *On Poisonous Animals*, 16.3.

345. "like sleep": as if asleep.

346. "As": as if.

347. "toil": net, snare (a hunting image).

347. "grace": beauty, charm.

348. "vent": discharge, emission.

348. "blown": Some editors gloss this as "swollen," but Caesar has just denied any swelling. The Guard's next speech identifies it as the trail of the asp, that is, of the eggs it deposited.

354. "conclusions": experiments.

354–55. "She hath pursued . . . die": On her experiments and selection of an asp, see Plutarch, *Antony*, 71.4–5.

355. "her bed": "But when they had opened the doors, they found Cleopatra stark dead, laid upon a bed of gold, attired and arrayed in her royal robes" (Plutarch, *Antony*, 85.3; Spencer, 291–92).

She shall be buried by her Antony.
No grave upon the earth shall clip in it
A pair so famous. High events as these
Strike those that make them; and their story is   **360**
No less in pity than his glory which
Brought them to be lamented. Our army shall
In solemn show attend this funeral,
And then to Rome. Come, Dolabella, see
High order in this great solemnity.   **365**

        Exeunt omnes [*, the guards bearing the dead bodies*].

---

357. "buried by her Antony": Caesar, like Dolabella (line 70), speaks as though Cleopatra, not Octavia, had been Antony's wife. Yet, however gracious it may seem, burying Antony with Cleopatra in Egypt underscores Caesar's principal political claim that Antony was a traitor who fought against Rome in behalf of an Egyptian queen; see 3.7.5n.

358. "clip": enclose, embrace.

358–59. "No grave . . . so famous": Burying Antony with Cleopatra as lovers gives them the distinction which Antony had sought (1.1.37–41, 4.14.52–55).

360. "Strike . . . make them": shock, afflict those who make them happen (Caesar, in this instance).

360–62. "their story . . . lamented": the story of Antony and Cleopatra is no less pitiable than the glory of the one (namely, Caesar) who caused them to be lamented.

362–65. "Our army . . . great solemnity": Caesar's final words stress formal dignity, gravity and stateliness. They anticipate his return to Rome, where his title or designation as "Augustus," identifying him as an object of reverence or worship, will rest largely on his preeminent dignity and authority. "Afterwards, he assumed the surname . . . of Augustus . . . , because religious and holy places, wherein also anything [that] is consecrated . . . , [are] called Augusta" (Suetonius, *Augustus*, 7.2; Holland, 1:85). With the new surname, he will assume a name that ranks with Jove: "With Jove himself Augustus name doth share" (Ovid, *Fasti*, 1.608; Gower, 18).

SELECTED BIBLIOGRAPHY

Shakespeare's Other Roman Works

Coriolanus, Arden Shakespeare, edited by Peter Holland. London: Bloomsbury, 2013.

Julius Caesar, Focus Books, edited by Jan H. Blits. Indianapolis: Hackett Publishing, 2018.

"The Rape of Lucrece," in *The Poems*, New Cambridge Shakespeare, edited by John Roe. Cambridge: Cambridge University Press, 2006.

Selected Ancient Sources

Apollodorus. *Library*, translated by Keith Aldrich. Lawrence: Coronado, 1975.

Appian. *An Ancient History and Exquisite Chronicle of the Roman Wars, Both Civil and Foreign*, translated by W. B.[aker]. London: Raulfe Newberrie and Henrie [B]ynniman, 1578.

_____. *The Civil Wars*, in *Appian's Roman History*, 3 vols., Loeb Classical Library, translated by Horace White. Cambridge: Harvard University Press, 1972.

Apuleius, Lucius. *The Golden Ass*, translated by William Adlington (1566). London: John Lehmann, 1946.

Aristotle. *Nicomachean Ethics*, Focus Philosophical Library, translated by Joe Sachs. Indianapolis: Hackett Publishing, 2002.

_____. *On Rhetoric*, translated by George A. Kennedy. New York: Oxford University Press, 1991.

_____. *On the Heavens*, Loeb Classical Library, translated by W. K. C .Guthrie. Cambridge: Harvard University Press, 1971.

_____. *Physics,* The New Hackett Aristotle, translated by C. D. C. Reeve. Indianapolis: Hackett Publishing, 2018.

_____. *Rhetorica ad Alexandrum* (cited as *Rhetoric to Alexander*), Loeb Classical Library, translated by H. Rackham. Cambridge: Harvard University Press, 1957.

Augustine. *The City of God*, translated by Marcus Dods. New York: Modern Library, 2000.

Caesar, *The Gallic War*, Loeb Classical Library, translated by H. J. Edwards. Cambridge: Harvard University Press, 1971.

Cicero. *Brutus* and *Orator*, Loeb Classical Library, translated by G. L. Henrickson and H. M. Hubbell. Cambridge: Harvard University Press, 2001.

_____. *De Inventione* (cited as *On Invention*), Loeb Classical Library, translated by H. M. Hubbell. Cambridge: Harvard University Press, 1960.

_____. *Marcus Tullius Cicero's Three Books of Duties*, translated by Nicholas Grimald (1556). Washington: Folger Books, 1990.

_____. *Pro Murena* (cited as *For Murena*), Loeb Classical Library, translated by C. Macdonald. Cambridge: Harvard University Press, 1976.

————. *De Officiis* (cited as *On Duties*), Loeb Classical Library, translated by Walter Miller. Cambridge: Harvard University Press, 1975.

————. *De Partitone Oratoria* (cited as *Of the Classification of Rhetoric*), Loeb Classical Library, translated by H. Rackham. Cambridge: Harvard University Press, 1968.

————. *Philippics*, Loeb Classical Library, translated by Walter C. A. Ker. Cambridge: Harvard University Press, 1969.

————. *Pro Sestio* (cited as *For Sestius*), Loeb Classical Library, translated by R. Gardner. Cambridge: Harvard University Press, 1966.

————. *Tully's Offices*, translated by Sir Roger L'Estrange, 5th edn. London: Tonson, Knaplock and Hindmarsh, 1699.

————. *Tusculan Disputations*, Loeb Classical Library, translated by J. E. King. Cambridge: Harvard University Press, 1971.

Dio Cassius. *Dio's Roman History*, Loeb Classical Library, 9 vols., translated by Earnest Cary. Cambridge: Harvard University Press, 1968-80.

Diodorus Siculus. *The Bibliotheca Historica of Diodorus Siculus*, translated by John Skelton (c. 1489). London: Early English Text Society, 1956.

————. *Library of History*, Loeb Classical Library, 12 vols., translated by C. H. Oldfather. Cambridge: Harvard University Press, 1962–77.

Dionysius of Halicarnassus. *Roman Antiquities*, Loeb Classical Library, 7 vols., translated by Earnest Cary. Cambridge: Harvard University Press, 1961–78.

Epicurus. *The Extant Remains*, edited by Cyril Bailey. New York: Georg Olms Verlag, 1975.

Eusebius. *The Theophania*, translated by Samuel Lee. Cambridge: Cambridge University Press, 1843.

Gellius. *Attic Nights*, Loeb Classical Library, 3 vols., translated by John C. Rolfe. Cambridge: Harvard University Press, 1967–70.

Herodotus. *The Histories*, Penguin Classics, translated by Aubrey de Sélincourt. London: Penguin Books, 2003.

Hesiod. *Theogony*, in *The Homeric Hymns and Homerica*, Loeb Classical Library, translated by Hugh G. Evelyn-White. Cambridge: Harvard University Press, 1977.

Hippocrates. *Hippocratic Writings*, Penguin Classics, translated by J. Chadwick and W. N. Mann. Harmondsworth: Penguin Books, 1983.

Homer. *Iliad*, Hackett Classics, translated by Stanley Lombardo. Indianapolis: Hackett Publishing, 1997.

Horace. *The Complete Odes and Epodes*, Oxford World's Classics, translated by David West. Oxford: Oxford University Press, 2008.

Josephus. *The Jewish War*, Penguin Classics, translated by G. A. Williamson. New York: Penguin, 1981.

Leo Africanus, Joannes. *A Geographical Description of Africa*, translated by John Pory. London: Impensis Georg. Biship, 1600, reprint Amsterdam: De Capo Press, 1969.

Livy. *Ab urbe condita libri* (cited as *History*), Loeb Classical Library, 14 vols., translated by B. O. Foster, F. G. Moore, Alfred C. Schlesinger, and Evan T. Sage. Cambridge: Harvard University Press, 1965–79.

_____. *The Roman History*, translated by Philemon Holland (1600). London: Gabriel Bedell, 1659.

Origen. *On First Principles*, translated by G. W. Butterworth. New York: Harper and Row, 1966.

Ovid. *Fasti*, Loeb Classical Library, translated by Sir James George Frazer. Cambridge: Harvard University Press, 1976.

_____. *Heroides*, translated by George Turberville. London: Henry Denham, 1567.

_____. *Metamorphoses*, Loeb Classical Library, 2 vols., translated by Frank Justus Miller. Cambridge: Harvard University Press, 1960-64.

_____. *Ovid's Festivals or Roman Calendar*, translated by John Gower. London: University of Cambridge, 1640.

_____. *Shakespeare's Ovid*, translated by Arthur Golding. London: Willyam Seres, 1567, reprint New York: Norton, 1961.

Pliny. *Natural History*, translated by Philemon Holland. London: Adam Islip, 1601.

_____. *Natural History*, Loeb Classical Library, 10 vols., translated by H. Rackham. Cambridge: Harvard University Press, 1967–80.

Plutarch. *Lives of Noble Greeks and Romans*, Loeb Classical Library, 11 vols., translated by Bernadotte Perrin. Cambridge: Harvard University Press, 1967–75.

_____. *Moralia*, Loeb Classical Library, 14 vols., translated by F. C. Babbitt. Cambridge: Harvard University Press, 1957–76.

_____. *The Philosophy, commonly called, the Morals*, translated by Philemon Holland. London: A. Hatfield, 1603.

_____. *Plutarch's Lives*, 6 vols. translated by Sir Thomas North, 1579. The Tudor Translations. London: David Nutt, 1896.

_____. *Shakespeare's Plutarch*, translated by Sir Thomas North, 1579, edited by T. J. B. Spencer. Harmondsworth, Middlesex: Penguin Books, 1964.

Polybius. *The Histories*, Loeb Classical Library, 6 vols., translated by W. R. Paton. Cambridge: Harvard University Press, 1960–70.

_____. *History of Polybius*, translated by Edward Grimeston. London: Simon Waterson, 1634.

Quintilian. *Institutio Oratoria* (cited as *Institutes*), Loeb Classical Library, 4 vols., translated by H. E. Butler. Cambridge: Harvard University Press, 1966–80.

Sallust. *Catiline's War, The Jugurthine War, Histories*, translated by A. J. Woodman. New York: Penguin, 2007.

Seneca. *Ad Lucilium Epistalae Morales* (cited as *Letters*), Loeb Classical Library, 3 vols., translated by Richard M. Gummere. Cambridge: Harvard University Press, 1961–71.

Strabo. *Geography*, Loeb Classical Library, 8 vols., translated by Horace Leonard Jones. Cambridge: Harvard University Press, 1966–70.

Suetonius. *De Grammaticis et Rhetoribus* (cited as *On Teachers of Grammar and Rhetoric*), translated by Robert A. Kaster. Oxford: Clarendon Press, 1995.

_____. *History of Twelve Caesars*, 2 vols., translated by Philemon Holland (1606). London: David Nutt, 1899.

————. *Lives of the Caesars*, Loeb Classical Library, 2 vols., translated by J. C. Rolfe. Cambridge: Harvard University Press, 1979.

Tacitus. *The Annals*, Loeb Classical Library, 3 vols., translated by John Jackson. Cambridge: Harvard University Press, 1969–70.

————. *Dialogue on Oratory*, Loeb Classical Library, translated by Sir William Peterson. London: William Heinemann, 1980.

Tertullian. *The Apology*, Loeb Classical Library, translated by T. R. Glover and Gerald H. Rendall. Cambridge: Harvard University Press, 1977.

Tibullus. *Elegies*, Oxford World Classics, translated by A. M. Juster. Oxford: Oxford University Press, 2012.

Valerius Maximus. *Memorable Deeds and Sayings*, Loeb Classical Library, 2 vols., translated by D. R. Shackleton Bailey. Cambridge: Harvard University Press, 2000.

Velleius Paterculus. *The Roman History*, translated by J. C. Yardley and Anthony A. Barrett. Indianapolis: Hackett Publishing, 2011.

Virgil. *Aeneid*, Hackett Classics, translated by Stanley Lombardo. Indianapolis: Hackett Publishing, 2005.

Other Sources

Burton, Robert. *The Anatomy of Melancholy*, 6 vols., edited by Thomas C. Faulkner. Oxford: Clarendon Press, 1989.

Craig, A. R. *The Book of the Hand*. London: Sampson, Low, Son, and Marston, 1867.

The Geneva Bible. Geneva: Rovland Hall, 1560, reprint Madison: University of Wisconsin Press, 1969.

Gibbon, Edmund. *The Decline and Fall of the Roman Empire*, 3 vols. New York: Modern Library, n.d.

Harrison, William. *Description of England*, in Raphael Holinshed's *Chronicles* (1586), 6 vols. Reprint New York: AMS Press, 1976.

Montesquieu, Charles Secondat. *Considerations on the Causes of the Greatness of the Romans and their Decline Romans*, translated by David Lowenthal. New York: Free Press, 1965.

Noble, Richmond. *Shakespeare's Use of Song with the Texts of the Principal Songs*. London: Oxford University Press, 1923.

Scot, Reginald, *Discoverie of Witchcraft* (1584). New York: Dover Publications, 2013.

Wagenvoort, H. *Roman Dynamism*. Oxford: Basil Blackwell, 1947.

Reference Works

Abbott, E. A. *Shakespearean Grammar*, 1870. Reprint, New York: Dover Publications, 1966.

Schmidt, Alexander. *Shakespeare Lexicon and Quotation Dictionary*, 2 vols., 1902. Reprint, New York: Dover Publications, 1971.

Further Reading

Alulis, Joseph. "'TheVery Heart of Loss': Love and Politics in 'Antony and Cleopatra,'" in *Shakespeare and the Body Politic*, Bernard J. Dobski and Dustin Gish, eds. Lanham: Lexington Books, 2013.

Alvis, John. "The Religion of Eros: A Re-interpretation of *Antony and Cleopatra*." *Renascence: Essays on Value in Literature* 30 (1978).

Bevington, David, ed. *Antony and Cleopatra*, New Cambridge Shakespeare. Cambridge: Cambridge University Press, 2005.

Blits, Jan H. *The Heart of Rome: Ancient Rome's Political Culture*. Lanham: Lexington Books, 2014.

————. *New Heaven, New Earth: Shakespeare's "Antony and Cleopatra."* Lanham: Lexington Books, 2009.

————. *Rome and the Spirit of Caesar: Shakespeare's "Julius Caesar."* Lanham: Lexington Books, 2015.

————. *Spirit, Soul and City: Shakespeare's "Coriolanus."* Lanham: Lexington Books, 2006.

————. *Telling, Turning Moments in the Classical Political World*. Lanham: Lexington Books, 2011.

Bloom, Allan. "Antony and Cleopatra," in *Love and Friendship*. New York: Simon and Schuster, 1993.

Burrow, Colin. *Shakespeare and Classical Antiquity*. Oxford: Oxford University Press, 2013.

Cantor, Paul A. *Shakespeare's Rome: Republic and Empire*. Ithaca: Cornell University Press, 1976.

————. *Shakespeare's Trilogy: The Twilight of the Ancient World*. Chicago: University of Chicago Press, 2017.

Eliot, T. S. Introduction to G. W. Knight's *Wheel of Fire*. London: Methuen, 1930.

Fraser, P. M. *Ptolemaic Alexandria*, 3 vols. Oxford: Clarendon Press, 1972.

Kahn, Coppélia. *Roman Shakespeare: Warriors, Wounds and Women*. London: Routledge, 1997.

Kujawinska-Courtney, Krystyna. *"Th' Interpretation of the Time": The Dramatury of Shakespeare's Roman Plays*. Victoria: English Literary Studies, 1993.

Miles, Geoffrey. *Shakespeare and the Constant Romans*. Oxford: Clarendon Press, 1996.

Miola, Robert A. *Shakespeare's Rome*. Cambridge: Cambridge University Press, 1983.

Pelling, C. B. R. *Plutarch: Life of Antony*. Cambridge: Cambridge University Press, 1988.

Seaton, Ethel. "*Antony and Cleopatra* and the *Book of Revelation*," *Review of English Studies* 22 (1946).

Thomas, Vivian. *Shakespeare's Roman Worlds*. London: Routledge, 1989.

Wells, Charles. *The Wide Arch: Roman Values in Shakespeare*. New York: St. Martin's Press, 1972.

INDEX

References are to line numbers of the notes and to pages of the Preface and the Introduction.